The Conscious Parent

Shefali Tsabary, PhD

THE CONSCIOUS PARENT

SHEFALI TSABARY

yellow
kite

First published in Great Britain in 2014 by Yellow Kite
An imprint of Hodder & Stoughton
An Hachette UK company

First published in the US in 2010 by Waterside Press

1

A CIP catalogue record for this title
is available from the British Library

Trade Paperback ISBN 978 1 473 61938 8
eBook ISBN 978 1 473 61939 5

Printed and bound by Clays Ltd, St Ives plc

Hodder & Stoughton policy is to use papers that are natural, renewable
and recyclable products and made from wood grown in sustainable forests.
The logging and manufacturing processes are expected to conform to the
environmental regulations of the country of origin.

Hodder & Stoughton Ltd
338 Euston Road
London NW1 3BH

www.hodder.co.uk

Advance Acclaim for

THE CONSCIOUS PARENT

Shefali Tsabary's invaluable book shows how the challenges of parenting can become a great opportunity for spiritual awakening. Becoming a fully conscious parent is the greatest gift you can give your child.

> — **Eckhart Tolle**, author of the *The Power of NOW*
> and *A New Earth*

The Conscious Parent is a wonderful contribution to a deeper inquiry into what it means to parent well. Bringing body, mind and spirit together in a new parental paradigm is essential, and *The Conscious Parent* help us get there.

> — **Marianne Williamson**, author *A Return to Love* and
> *Age of Miracles*

The Conscious Parent shows how children can lead us to the discovery of our own true being. A beautiful and practical guide for raising children to live an authentic, aware, and fulfilled life.

> — **Marci Shimoff**, NY Times bestselling author, *Happy for
> No Reason* and *Chicken Soup for the Woman's Soul*

The Conscious Parent is a spiritual vision of how to care for a child's body and soul. This book is practical and full of love and hope for both parents and children.

> — **Michael Gurian,** New York Times bestselling author of
> *The Wonder of Boys* and *The Wonder of Girls*

Dr. Tsabary's gentle, thoughtful, and beautifully written book embraces the lovely idea of a mutually respectful and loving parent-child dyad. Readers are sure to profit enormously from its essential message—that of the profound importance of treating one's children with great openness, respect, and empathy. As Dr. Tsabary writes and as Joni Mitchell once sang, there is so much said in listening. There are great lessons here for parents and parents-to-be.

> — **Barry Farber,** Ph.D. Professor of Psychology and
> Education, Director of Clinical Training, Teachers
> College, Columbia University

Move over Dr. Spock! This is the book every parent must have to raise well-adjusted, responsible children. The surprise may be that to accomplish that, the true work at hand will be your own. Face every truth in this wonderful book and enjoy your parenting ride.

> — **Laura Berman Fortgang,** author of *The Little Book on*
> *Meaning* and *The Prosperity Plan*

The *Conscious Parent* will introduce the reader to a set of principles that, if followed—and, perhaps most importantly, used in the spirit it recommends—will help parents and children form relationships that focus on shared responsibility and deep communication.

> — **Eva Leveton,** Author of *Adolescent Crisis*

DEDICATION

To my husband Oz. My wizard.

Acknowledgments

Constance Kellough — for having a vision for this book and birthing it with such love, unwavering conviction, and unconditional support. My deepest appreciation.

David Robert Ord — for your genius. You are an editor like no other. There are no words to express my gratitude.

The many clients I have worked with through the years — for allowing me to enter your lives.

My friends and family — for always being there. You know who you are and what you mean to me: the world.

My husband Oz and my daughter Maia — words will never capture the feeling. Nothing I do or am exists separate from your presence.

Thank You.

THE DALAI LAMA

PREFACE

In this book Dr Shefali Tsabary describes the importance of compassion in simple, secular terms, discussing how we can learn to develop it from our relationship with our children.

Although I am 75 years old, I still remember my mother's spontaneous love and unselfish affection. Thinking about it today still gives me a sense of peace and inner calm. In our modern world one of the challenges we face is how to retain an appreciation of that kind of unselfish giving throughout our lives. When we grow up, our misguided intelligence tends to make us short-sighted, giving rise to fear, aggression, jealously, anger and frustration, which diminish our potential.

When we are born we may not have a clear idea, 'This is my mother.' but we have a spontaneous connection based on our basic biological needs. From our mother's side there is also a tremendous drive to look after her child's physical needs, to comfort and feeding him or her. This has nothing to do with abstract values, but arises naturally because of biology.

In my own limited experience, the basic source of all happiness is love and compassion, a sense of kindness and warm-heartedness towards others. If we can be friendly and trusting towards others, we become more calm and relaxed. We lose the sense of fear and suspicion that we often feel about other people, either because we don't know them well or because we feel they are threatening or competing with us in some way. When we are calm and relaxed we can make proper use of our mind's ability to think clearly, so whatever we do, whether we are studying or working, we will be able to do it better.

Everyone responds positively to kindness. This is evident to anyone who has been a parent. One of the causes of the close bond between children and parents is the natural kindness that exists between them. From the moment of conception in our mother's womb until we are able to look after ourselves we receive great kindness from many different people, without which we would not survive. Reflecting on this and how we are all just human beings, whether we are rich or poor, educated or uneducated, and whether we belong to one nation, religion, culture or another, may inspire us to repay the kindness we have received by being kind to others ourselves.

July 7, 2010

NOTE TO PARENTS

To parent perfectly is a mirage. There is no ideal parent and no ideal child.

The Conscious Parent underscores the challenges that are a natural part of raising a child, fully understanding that, as parents, each of us tries the best we can with the resources we have.

The objective of this book is to illumine how we might identify and capitalize on the *emotional and spiritual lessons* inherent in the parenting process, so that we can use them for our *own development*, which in turn will result in the ability to parent more effectively. As part of this approach, we are asked to open ourselves up to the possibility that our imperfections may actually be our most valuable tools for change.

There may be times during the reading of these pages when the material stirs uncomfortable feelings. I invite anyone who experiences such feelings simply to take note of this energy. Pause in your reading and sit with the feelings that are coming up. As you do so, you may find you spontaneously metabolize these feelings. Suddenly what's being said starts to make greater sense.

The Conscious Parent is written for anyone involved with a child of any age. Whether you are a single parent, a young adult who is planning to have a family or has recently started one, a parent with children in their teens, or a grandparent or child-care provider, making a commitment to the overall principles outlined in the book can bring transformation to both yourself and the child.

If you are struggling to raise a child on your own with little help,

The Conscious Parent may lighten your burden. If you are a mother or father who is a full-time child-care provider, *The Conscious Parent* can enrich your experience. In the case of those who are able to employ help with raising their children, you may find it helpful to seek out someone who is committed to the principles set forth in this book, especially if your child is under six years of age.

I remain continually humbled by the enormous opportunity raising a child offers us to shed our old skin, let go of stale patterns, engage new ways of being, and evolve into a more conscious parent.

Namaste,
Shefali

TABLE OF CONTENTS

CHAPTER 1

A Real Person Like Myself

One morning, my daughter shook me from sleep with great excitement. "The fairy has left you an amazing present," she whispered. "See what the tooth fairy left you!"

I reached under the pillow and found a one dollar note, torn down the middle in exactly half. Said my daughter, "The fairy left half a dollar for you, and the other half is under daddy's pillow."

I was speechless.

Simultaneously I found myself in a dilemma. All of those messages about "money doesn't grow on trees" and how important it was for my daughter to learn the value of currency came flooding into my mind. Should I use this opportunity to teach her about not wasting money, explaining to her that a dollar note torn in half is worthless?

I realized that this was a moment in which how I responded could make or break my child's spirit. Thankfully I chose to shelve the lesson and tell her how proud I was of her willingness to be so generous with her one and only dollar. As I thanked the fairy for her big-heartedness and her acute sense of fairness in giving both daddy and myself an equal share, my daughter's eyes responded with a sparkle bright enough to illumine the bedroom.

YOU ARE RAISING A SPIRIT
THROBBING WITH ITS OWN SIGNATURE

Parenthood affords many occasions in which we find ourselves in a battle between our mind and our heart, which makes raising a child akin to walking a tightrope. A single misplaced response can shrivel a child's spirit, whereas the right comment can encourage them to soar. In each moment, we can choose to make or break, foster or cause to freeze up.

When our children are just being themselves, they are unconcerned about the things we parents so often obsess over. How things look to other people, achievement, getting ahead—none of these issues that preoccupy adults are a child's agenda. Instead of engaging the world in an anxious mental state, children tend to plunge head first into the experience of life, willing to risk all.

The morning the fairy visited my bedroom, my daughter wasn't thinking about either the value of money or the egoic issue of whether I would be impressed she had shared her dollar. Neither was she worried she might be waking me too early. She was simply being her wonderfully creative self, joyously expressing her generosity and delighting in her parents' discovery that the fairy had visited us for a change.

As a parent, I repeatedly find myself presented with opportunities to respond to my daughter as if she were a real person like myself, with the full range of feelings I experience—the same longing, hope, excitement, imagination, ingenuity, sense of wonder, and capacity for delight. Yet like many parents, I tend to become so caught up in my own agenda that I often miss the opportunity afforded by these moments. I find myself so conditioned to sermonize, so oriented to teaching, that I am often insensitive to the wondrous ways in which my child reveals her uniqueness, showing us she's a being unlike any other who has ever walked this planet.

When you parent, it's crucial you realize you aren't raising a "mini me," but a spirit throbbing with its own signature. For this reason, it's important to separate who you are from who each of your children is. Children aren't ours to possess or own in any way. When we know this in the depths of our soul, we tailor our raising of them to *their* needs, rather than molding them to fit *our* needs.

Instead of meeting the individual needs of our children, we tend to project our own ideas and expectations onto them. Even when we have the best intentions of encouraging our children to be true to themselves, most of us unwittingly fall into the trap of imposing our agenda on them. Consequently the parent-child relationship frequently deadens a child's spirit instead of enlivening it. This is a key reason so many of our children grow up troubled and in many cases plagued by dysfunction.

We each enter the parenting journey with visions of what it will be. For the most part these visions are fantasies. We hold beliefs, values, and assumptions we have never examined. Many of us don't even see a reason to question our ideas because we believe we are "right" and have nothing to rethink. Based on our unexamined worldview, we unknowingly lay down rigid expectations of how our children ought to express themselves. We don't realize that through our imposition of our ways on our offspring, we constrain their spirit.

For instance, if we are super-successful at what we do, we are likely to expect our children to be super-successful also. If we are artistic, we may seek to push our children to be artistic. If we were an academic wizard in school, we tend to carry a torch for our children to be brilliant. If we didn't do well academically and have struggled in life as a result, we perhaps live in fear that our children will turn out like us, which causes us to do everything in our power to ward off such a possibility.

We want what we consider to be "best" for our children, but in seeking to bring this about, we can easily forget that the most important issue is their right to be their *own* person and lead their own life in accord with their unique spirit.

Children inhabit a world of "it is," not a world of "it isn't." They come to us with their being brimming with potential. Each of our children has their own particular destiny to live out—their own *karma*, if you like. Because children carry a blueprint within them, they are often already in touch with who they are and what they want to be in the world. We are chosen as their parents to help them *actualize* this. The trouble is that if we don't pay close attention to them, we rob them of their right to live out their destiny. We end up imposing on them our own vision for them, rewriting their spiritual purpose according to our whims.

It's no surprise we fail to tune into our children's essence. How can we listen to them, when so many of us barely listen to ourselves? How can we feel their spirit and hear the beat of their heart if we can't do this in our own life? When we as parents have lost our inner compass, is it any wonder so many children grow up directionless, disconnected, and discouraged? By losing contact with our inner world, we cripple our ability to parent from our essential being in the way conscious parenting requires.

Having said this, I want in this book to throw a life preserver to parents who are just trying to survive—especially those with teens. I am convinced from my experience with many teens that if you have a teenager with whom you have been struggling to stay connected, it's not too late. Of course, if you have younger children, the earlier you begin building a strong connection, the better.

Parenting Unconsciously Is Where We All Begin

One of the more challenging tasks any of us takes on is to bring another human being into the world and raise this individual. Yet most of us approach this task in a way we would never approach our business life. For example, were we to head up a billion-dollar organization, we would craft a carefully considered mission. We would know our objective and how to achieve it. In seeking to realize our mission, we would be familiar with our personnel and how to draw out their potential. As part of our strategy, we would identify our own strengths and figure out how to capitalize on them, as well as identify our weaknesses so we minimize their impact. The success of the organization would be the result of *strategizing* for success.

It's helpful to ask ourselves, "What is my parenting mission, my parenting philosophy? How do I manifest this in my everyday inter-action with my child? Have I mapped out a thoughtful, mindful mission, as I would were I running a major organization?"

Whether you are a couple, separated, or a single parent, it would be beneficial to think through your approach to parenting in the light of research about what works and what doesn't. Many of us don't consider how the way we parent affects our children, which might cause us to change our approach. Does our method especially include listening to our child's spirit? Would we be willing to change the way we interact with our child if it became clear that what we are doing isn't working?

Each of us imagines we are being the best parent we can be, and most of us are indeed good people who feel great love for our chil-dren. It certainly isn't out of a lack of love that we impose our will on our children. Rather, it stems from a lack of *consciousness*. The real-ity is that many of us are unaware of the dynamics that exist in the relationship we have with our children.

None of us likes to think of ourselves as unconscious. On the contrary, it's a concept we tend to balk at. So defensive are many of us that, let someone say a word about our parenting style, and we are instantly triggered. However, when we begin to be aware, we redesign the dynamic we share with our children.

Our children pay a heavy price when we lack consciousness. Overindulged, over-medicated, and over-labeled, many of them are unhappy. This is because, coming from unconsciousness ourselves, we bequeath to them our own unresolved needs, unmet expectations, and frustrated dreams. Despite our best intentions, we enslave them to the emotional inheritance we received from our parents, binding them to the debilitating legacy of ancestors past. The nature of unconsciousness is such that, until it's metabolized, it will seep through generation after generation. Only through awareness can the cycle of pain that swirls in families end.

To Connect with Your Children, First Connect with *Yourself*

Until we understand exactly *how* we have been operating in an unconscious mode, we tend to resist opening ourselves to an approach to parenting that rests on entirely different ideals from those we may have relied on until now.

Traditionally parenthood has been exercised in a manner that's hierarchical. The parent governs from the top down. After all, isn't the child our "lesser," to be transformed by us as the more-knowledgeable party? Because children are smaller and don't know as much as we do, we presume we are entitled to control them. Indeed, we are so used to the kind of family in which the parent exercises control, it perhaps doesn't even occur to us that this arrangement might not be good for either our children *or* ourselves.

On the parent's side of the equation, the problem with the traditional approach to parenting is that it rigidifies the ego with its delusions of power. Since our children are so innocent and ready to be influenced by us, they tend to offer little resistance when we impose our ego on them— a situation that holds the potential for our ego to become stronger.

If you want to enter into a state of pure connection with your child, you can achieve this by setting aside any sense of superiority. By not hiding behind an egoic *image*, you will be able to engage your child as a *real person* like yourself.

I use the word "image" in connection with the ego intentionally, so I want to make clear exactly what I mean by "ego" and its associated term "egoic." In my experience, people tend to think of the ego as their "self," in the sense of who they are as a *person*. The word egoic would then refer to an inflated sense of ourselves such as we associate with vanity.

Crucial to an understanding of this book is the fact that I am using these terms in a quite different way.

I want to propose that what we regard as our "ego" isn't our *true* self at all. I see the ego as more like a *picture* of ourselves we carry around in our head—a picture we hold of ourselves that may be far from who we are in our essential being. All of us grow up with such an image of ourselves. This self-image begins to form when we are young, based largely on our interactions with others.

"Ego" as I'm using the term is an *artificial* sense of ourselves. It's an *idea* we have about ourselves based mostly on other people's opinions. It's the person we have come to *believe* we are and *think of ourselves* as. This self-image is layered over who we truly are in our essence. Once our self-image has formed in childhood, we tend to hold onto it for dear life.

Although this idea of who we are is narrow and limited, our core self—our fundamental being, or essence—is limitless. Existing in complete freedom, it has no expectations of others, no fear, and no feelings of guilt. While to live in such a state may *sound* strangely detached, this state actually empowers us to connect with others in a truly meaningful way because it's an *authentic* state. Once we have detached from our expectations of how another person "should" behave and we encounter them as they really are, the acceptance we inevitably demonstrate toward them naturally induces connection. This is because authenticity automatically resonates with authenticity.

Because we are so close to our ego, to the point we imagine it's who we really are, it can be difficult to spot. In fact, other than the more obvious displays of ego such as boastfulness and grandiosity, the ego tends to be mostly disguised, which is how it tricks us into believing it's our genuine self.

As an example of how the ego masquerades as our true self, many of us are unaware that *a lot of our emotions are ego in disguise.* For instance, when we say, "I'm angry," we imagine it's our core being that's angry. The reality may be quite different. It's quite possible that at some level, we are actually resisting a situation that has arisen, preferring to attach ourselves to how we *think* things *ought* to be. If we then unleash our anger on others, it becomes a full-blown manifestation of ego.

As we all know from personal experience, our attachment to

anger or other emotions such as jealousy, disappointment, guilt, or sadness ultimately causes a feeling of separation between ourselves and others. This happens because, not recognizing our anger as an egoic reaction, we believe it's part of who we essentially *are*. Masquerading as our true self, egoic attachments obscure our ability to stay in a state of joy and oneness with all.

At times our ego gets channeled through our profession, interests, or national identity. We tell ourselves, "I'm a tennis player," "I'm religious," or, "I'm American." None of these are who we are within. Rather, they are roles to which we attach ourselves, often without even realizing we are attached to them, so that they soon create a sense of "I." If someone questions one of our roles, we feel threatened, imagining *we* are being attacked. When this happens, instead of releasing our egoic attachment to our sense of "I," we tend to hold onto it more tightly. This attachment to ego is at the root of many a conflict, divorce, and war.

I don't wish to imply that the ego is "bad" and shouldn't exist. On the contrary, the ego *in and of itself* is neither good nor bad: it just *is*. It's a stage in our development that serves a purpose much like the eggshell in which a chick forms until it hatches. The eggshell has a role to play during the chick's formation. However, were the shell to stay in place beyond the period when it serves a protective purpose, instead of being broken apart and discarded, it would stifle the development of the chick. Similarly, the ego needs to be progressively shed in favor of the re-emergence of our true self from the mists of childhood.

Although we might not become entirely free of ego, to parent consciously requires us to become increasingly *aware* of the influence of our ego. Awareness is transformative and is the essence of becoming a conscious parent. The more aware we become, the more we recognize all the ways in which we have been living in the grip of unexamined conditioning from our own upbringing, then imparting this to our children. In the course of this book, we will see a variety of examples of the different ways in which this happens from the lives of people to whom I will introduce you.

Becoming aware of the fact that your ego isn't who you really are, and of how it operates to trick you into believing it is, requires observing those moments when a little space opens up and you catch yourself thinking, experiencing emotions, or behaving in ways that aren't entirely true to yourself. As you begin to notice these moments, you'll find yourself spontaneously distancing yourself from your ego.

You Can Build a Feeling of Kinship in Your Family

Conscious parenting embodies our longing to experience the *oneness* inherent in the parent-child relationship, which is a partnership and quite different in character from the dominance parents generally exercise.

In seeking to restore an experience of oneness between your children and yourself, the path leads by way of the discovery of communion with *your own forgotten self.* This is the case because establishing a meaningful partnership with your children will inevitably cause you to attend to the development of your own authentic being. As your growing awareness disintegrates the parent-child hierarchy, it will spontaneously equalize the playing field in your family. Moving away from egoic behavior—surrendering your opinions of how situations *ought* to be, and how people *should* act—will allow you to step off your pedestal of dominance.

Because our children are so moldable, we often ignore the invitation to mold *ourselves* into our children's spiritual partner. However, by paying attention to the one who is, for all apparent purposes, *in our control*, we have an opportunity to release ourselves from *all need to be in control.* By providing us with a way to shed the eggshell of our ego and step into the freedom that living in our truer state of *being* allows, our children facilitate our evolution. We find ourselves exposed to the truly transformative potential of the parenting journey.

With the myth that the relationship between parent and child should be unidirectional shattered, the circular potential of this journey comes into view, as we discover that our children contribute to our growth in ways that are perhaps more profound than we can ever contribute to theirs. Although a child appears in a "lesser than" form, susceptible to the whims and dictates of a more powerful parent, it's precisely the child's seemingly less-powerful status that has the potential to call forth the greatest transformation in a parent.

Viewing parenthood as a process of spiritual metamorphosis allows us to create the psychic space to invite the lessons of this journey in. As a parent, to the degree you are able to recognize that your children are in your life to foster a renewed sense of who *you* are, you will discover their potential to lead you to the discovery of your own true being.

In other words, while you may believe your most important challenge is to raise your children well, there's an even more essential task you need to attend to, which is the foundation of effective parenting. This task is to raise *yourself* into the most awakened and present individual you can be. The reason this is central to good parenting is that children don't need our ideas and expectations, or our dominance and control, only for us to be attuned to them with our engaged *presence*.

How Consciousness Changes How We Parent

Consciousness isn't a magical quality bestowed on the few who are lucky. Rather than being dropped out of the sky, it's a state that emerges as part of a process.

To engage this process, it helps to be aware that consciousness isn't a sudden and total absence of unconsciousness. On the contrary, consciousness emerges progressively from unconsciousness. Those who walk the path of consciousness are no different from anyone else, except that they have learned to mine their unconsciousness for its potential for heightened awareness. This means that consciousness is accessible to *all* of us. Indeed the magical thing about the parent-child relationship is that it constantly presents us with opportunities to raise ourselves to a state of intensified consciousness.

While we believe we hold the power to raise our children, the reality is that our children hold the power to raise *us* into the parents they need us to become. For this reason, the parenting experience isn't one of parent *versus* child but of parent *with* child. The road to wholeness sits in our children's lap, and all we need do is take a seat. As our children show us our way back to our own essence, they become our greatest awakeners. If we fail to hold their hand and follow their lead as they usher us through the gateway of increased consciousness, we lose the chance to walk toward our own enlightenment.

When I speak of our children transforming us as parents, don't for a moment imagine I'm advocating relinquishing our influence on our children and becoming their minions. As much as conscious parenting is about listening to our children, honoring their essence, and being fully present with them, it's also about boundaries and discipline. As parents, we are required to provide our children not only with the basics of shelter, food, and education, but also to teach them the value of structure, appropriate containment of their emotions, and such skills as reality testing. In other words, conscious parenting encompasses *all* aspects of bringing up a child to be a well-rounded, balanced member of the human race. Hence there's nothing "permissive" about parenting consciously, and throughout this book we will see examples of parents learning to truly *be* parental in a constructive manner that empowers their children to become emotionally and behaviorally mature.

This being the case, I think it's important for me to explain why I have reserved the *specific* information I wish to impart concerning discipline for the final chapter. The conscious approach to discipline is grounded in our ability to *exercise real presence* with our children. It's crucial parents realize that this approach is only effective once they have learned through the parent-child dynamic *how to be present* with their children, which is something that will unfold chapter by chapter as we proceed on this journey together.

Parental metamorphosis is the key to a leap in human consciousness. However, when parents come to see me, they aren't usually looking for a way to grow personally. Rather, they are eager to find answers to their children's behavior. They hope I have a magic wand that will transform their children into youngsters with a resolute and healthy psyche. I point out that conscious parenting is more than applying clever strategies. It's an entire life philosophy involving a process that has the power to transform both parent and child on an elemental level. The only meaningful way for parent and child to relate is as spiritual partners in *mutual spiritual advancement*. For this reason, conscious parenting goes beyond techniques aimed at fixing a specific behavior, speaking instead to the deeper aspects of the relationship between parent and child.

The beauty of the conscious approach to bringing up a child is that, rather than trying to apply a technique and hoping it's the right one for the particular situation, consciousness informs us moment-by-moment how best to go about the task of parenting. For instance, when my daughter tore a dollar bill in half, was a reprimand required or praise? I allowed my inner being to guide me, which in our oneness resonated with her inner being. Even when we are called upon to discipline, consciousness shows us how to do so in a manner that bolsters our child's spirit rather than diminishing it.

As you muster the courage to abandon the control inherent in a hierarchical approach and step into the spiritual potential of a circular parent-child dynamic, you will find yourself increasingly free of conflict and power struggles. The parent-child dynamic then becomes a transcendent experience, replete with soulful exchanges worthy of beings who recognize the privilege of finding a spiritual partner. By surrendering to the oneness of a conscious parent-child relationship, we elevate parenting out of the purely physical and into the realm of the sacred.

CHAPTER 2

THE SPIRITUAL REASON
WE BIRTH OUR CHILDREN

Despite all the evidence before our eyes that many of our parenting strategies don't work and frequently even backfire, most of us stick to the unconscious approach that originally triggered the difficulties we are experiencing with our children.

To shift to a more effective way of relating to our children, we must be willing to face and resolve issues in ourselves that stem from the way *we* were parented. Unless we invite such transformation, we will likely parent with a certain irreverence, unheeding of the cry of our children's spirit and blind to their wisdom. Only to the degree we as parents are attuned to our own being will we know how to help our children attune themselves to their unique essence.

For this reason, to parent consciously requires us to undergo personal transformation. In fact, it's my experience that the relationship between parent and child exists for the primary purpose of the *parent's* transformation and only secondarily for the raising of the child.

When I point out to parents the ways in which they need to undergo transformation, I frequently meet with resistance. "Why *us*?" they retort, puzzled that I would suggest *they* need to change. When I explain that the only way their children will alter their behavior is if they as parents become more conscious, they tend to be disappointed, unable to accept that the focus needs to be on changing their own mindset rather than on their children. I find that many parents are afraid of opening themselves to the unknown in the way that shifting from unconsciousness to consciousness requires.

This path isn't for the faint-hearted, but for those courageous souls who wish to experience kinship with their children. Our children come to us so we may recognize our psychic wounds and call up the courage to transcend the limitations these wounds place on us. As we uncover the ways in which our past drives us, we gradually become capable of parenting consciously. Until then, try as we may to bring awareness to the way we parent, unconsciousness seeps into our interactions with our children at the least provocation.

I want to stress that there's no point wishing your unconsciousness didn't exist. Rather, understanding the ramifications of unconsciousness and becoming aware of its consequences can motivate a person to embark on the penetrating self-examination that's required to become an effective parent.

In this your children are your allies, as they repeatedly mirror aspects of your unconsciousness, affording you opportunity after opportunity to awaken from slumber. Because children deserve parents who are conscious, don't we owe it to them to allow ourselves to be transformed by them at least as much as we seek to transform them?

While the precise details of the transformation we must each undergo are unique to us as individuals, the nature of this transformation is in many ways universal. Hence a conscious approach to parenting urges parents to address issues that are the hallmarks of consciousness, such as:

> Am I allowing myself to be led toward greater spiritual
> awakening through my relationship with my children?

> How can I parent my children with an awareness of
> what they truly need from me, and thus become the
> parent they deserve to have?

How can I rise above my own fear of change and
   transform myself to meet the requirements of
   my child's spirit?

Dare I go against the stream and parent from a
   place where the inner life is valued far more
   than the external?

Do I recognize every aspect of my parenting as a call
   to my higher evolution?

Am I able to perceive my relationship with my
   children as a sacred relationship?

HOW CAN A *CHILD* AWAKEN AN *ADULT*?

A certain child enters our life with its individual troubles, difficulties, stubbornness, and temperamental challenges in order to help us
become aware of how much we have yet to grow. The reason this
works is that our children are able to take us into the remnants of our
emotional past and evoke deeply unconscious feelings. Consequently, to understand where our internal landscape needs to
develop, we need look no further than our children's gaze.

Whether we unconsciously generate situations in which we feel the
way we did when we were children, or we desperately struggle to avoid
doing this, in some shape or form we inevitably experience the identi-
cal emotions we felt when we were young. This is because, unless we
consciously integrate the unintegrated aspects of our childhood, they
never leave us but repeatedly reincarnate themselves in our present,
then show up all over again in our children. Hence by offering us a
reflection of our unconsciousness, our children bestow on us an ines-
timable gift. As they provide us with opportunities to recognize our

unconsciousness as it manifests in the here and now, we have a chance to break free of the clutches of our past so that we are no longer ruled by our early conditioning. Our children also reflect back our success or failure in this venture, thereby showing us in which direction to proceed.

Because we interact with our children based on how we were raised, before we know it—and despite our best intentions—we find ourselves recreating the dynamics of our own childhood. Let me illustrate how this happens by telling you about a mother and daughter I was privileged to help. Jessica was a good student and the ideal daughter until her fourteenth year. However, during the next two years, she turned into her mother's worst nightmare. Lying, stealing, clubbing, and smoking her way through life, she became rude, defiant, and even violent. Being around her daughter, whose moods fluctuated by the minute, made Anya anxious. Too deeply triggered by Jessica to contain her emotions, she unleashed her fury on her daughter, yelling, screaming, and calling her names a child should never be subjected to.

Anya knew that Jessica's behavior didn't warrant these extreme explosions of anger, but she could neither control her rage nor understand where it was coming from. Feeling incompetent, thinking herself a failure as a parent, she was unable to provide Jessica with the connection she needed.

In due course, Jessica confided in a school counselor that she had begun cutting herself.

When Anya learned how much pain Jessica was in, she contacted me for help. "It's as if I were six again," she shared. "When my daughter yells at me, I feel the way I did when my mother yelled at me. When she slams the door on me and shuts me out of her world, I feel as though I'm being punished, like I did something wrong. The difference is that whereas with my parents I could never protest, yell, or scream, now I can't stop. Every time my daughter makes me feel like my parents made me feel, it's as if my world crashes around me and I lose my sanity."

The only way we could unlock the unconsciousness that Anya's daughter triggered in her was by revisiting her past, in particular her family of origin. Anya's father was emotionally cold, which meant she felt starved for affection. Her mother "was just never there," Anya explained. "Even when she was there physically, it was like she was never there. I was seven or eight when I began to know loneliness."

So great was the pain of Anya's isolation and the lack of acceptance by her parents that she resolved to create a new personality. "I decided I would start acting just like mom, then dad would begin to love me as much as he loved her." Anya's mother was always well put together, beautifully dressed, on top of things. "I changed from a girl into a grown-up woman overnight," Anya recalls. "I began to exercise like crazy and did brilliantly at school."

Unfortunately, no matter how responsible Anya became, she was never good enough for her extremely strict father. One incident in particular led to a turning point. As Anya tells it: "I remember one day my father was annoyed with me because I wasn't sitting still to do my homework. Not a man of many words, he took me to the corner of the room and raised my arms in the air. He then folded my knees and sent me to the floor. I knelt on the floor for the next two hours with my arms raised in the air. He didn't say a word the entire time. My mother didn't dare say anything either. No one looked me in the eye. I think that what hurt me more than the punishment was the lack of acknowledgment. I cried and begged for forgiveness, but no one seemed to hear me. After two hours, my father told me to get up and start studying. From that day on, I swore I would never get myself into trouble again. I swallowed my anger and hid beneath layers of resentment."

In the same way Anya had learned to be the "perfect" child, she had trained her daughter Jessica to be her little automaton, devoid of emotional expression, super-responsible, perfectly controlled and manicured. However, being a different spirit, Jessica could only take her mother's rigidity for her childhood years. The minute she was able to break free, she did. Not having any sense of a center, her emotional pendulum now swung to the other extreme. The more Jessica rebelled, the more controlling and dominant Anya became. Finally, Jessica snapped. So it was that the cutting began.

Through all her daughter's behavior, Anya only saw her own wounds, caused by her own parents' anger, rejection, and betrayal of her. Instead of seeing Jessica's rebellion as a cry for help, she interpreted it as undermining her role as a parent. This served as a reminder of how powerless and worthless her parents made her feel as a child. Only now, instead of becoming the "perfect daughter" as she had all those years ago in her parents' home, as a parent herself she fought back. The tragedy was that she was fighting with *the wrong person.*

Anya had no awareness that her daughter was behaving quite normally given the circumstances of her rigid upbringing. She couldn't see that Jessica was saying, "Enough of the charade. Wake up and notice that I'm a unique individual with different needs from you. I can't be yours to control any longer."

Jessica was in effect screaming for the release Anya could never claim for herself. She was the flag bearer of her mother's unfought war. Though she appeared "bad" in the eyes of the public, she was in truth being a dutiful daughter, enacting her mother's unlived past for her. Through her antisocial behavior, she was facilitating her mother in finally expressing all that had been trapped inside her for decades.

In terms of the journey of becoming a conscious parent, Jessica's "badness" was a service to her mother, the opportunity for Anya to revisit her childhood resentment and heartache. Thus Anya was finally allowing herself to scream, letting out her emotional toxicity. Our children are generous in this way, willingly becoming receptacles for our misplaced emotions so we can ultimately set ourselves free. It's our unwillingness to walk toward this freedom that creates the illusion our children are "bad" and must be doing things maliciously.

If you understand that the inappropriate behavior of your children is a call to increased consciousness on *your* part, you are able to view the opportunities they afford you to grow differently. Instead of reacting to them, you look within yourself and ask *why* you react. In the asking, you open a space for consciousness to arise.

It was only when Anya was able to revisit her childhood and uncover her anger toward her parents that she could release her daughter from the trap of "perfection" she herself had lived in all her life. As she embarked on the process of freeing herself, she began losing the layers of pretense she had cloaked herself in, slowly emerging as a vibrant, fun, easygoing person who was full of joy. Her apology to her daughter for all the burdens she had insensitively placed on her allowed Jessica to heal her own wounds. Mother and daughter were helping each other emerge into the authentic beings they had really been all along.

The ways in which our past influences our present are indelible, yet paradoxically obstructed from plain view. This is why it takes someone close to us to mirror for us the wounds from our past, which is the reason our children are able to help us become free. Unfortunately, we parents don't often allow them to fulfill their spiritual purpose in our life. Instead, we seek to make them fulfill *our* egoic plans and fantasies.

How can we guide, protect, and provide for our children in the physical world, yet rigorously relinquish all sense of domination of their spirit, unless we have nurtured a free spirit within *ourselves*? If your spirit was squelched by parents who were divorced from their own emotional freedom, there is a risk you will squelch your own children. You might unconsciously engender in them the same pain you endured in your childhood, passing on the pain that has been handed down for generations. This is why it's so important to consciously free ourselves from our unconscious state and move toward an enlightened way of being.

How Conscious Parenting Is Learned

A conscious parent doesn't look outside the parenting relationship for answers, but is confident the answers can be found for both parent and child within the parent-child dynamic. For this reason, conscious parenting is learned through the actual *experience* of relating to our children, not through reading books that offer quick fixes or taking classes that specialize in techniques. The conscious approach embodies values that emanate from the relationship. Of course, to parent this way requires the full and willing participation of the parent, for only through interaction with the parent's own developing consciousness can change take place within a child.

This approach takes the relationship between parent and child *as it is,* then introduces the element of awareness. In other words, conscious parenting uses ordinary, moment-by-moment engagement with our children to foster authentic connection. Because this approach is highly relational, it can't be packaged like a prescription. Rather, as stated earlier, it's a life philosophy, which means that each lesson is intrinsically connected to every other lesson, so that nothing stands apart, isolated from the fabric of the family unit.

Using the present moment as a living laboratory, everyday interactions have the potential to teach invaluable lessons. The most ordinary of moments provide us with opportunities to nurture self-definition, resilience, tolerance, and connectedness, all of which spring from presence. There's no need for grand interventions or staged strategies. We use what we have before us to introduce a shift in perspective in both ourselves and our children. In this way, the humblest of situations become inspiring portals for transformation. Again and again, you will see this in action in the lives of individuals I will talk about as we proceed.

Because as parents we desperately want our children's behavior to be "fixed" right now, without having to go through the difficult process of having to change ourselves first, it needs to be emphasized that the conscious approach to parenting won't change a family overnight. This book isn't a "how to" manual because such manuals miss the point of the *present moment nature* of conscious parenting. What I want to make clear is that the *how to* is built into each situation as it arises, not found in a set of instructions. This book is about how to use the parenting relationship to *become* conscious, so that we can spot what's required in our children's lives *in the moment an issue arises.* Through the accumulation of many a conscious moment over time, an aware family dynamic emerges, which radically alters the playing field from what happens in many families. For this aware dynamic to become a reality requires patience.

Neither is the goal to change a *particular* behavior. Our concern isn't with "how to put my child to sleep" or "how to get my child to eat." The principal task is to put spiritual foundations under both our child's life and our own. This triggers a shift in the elemental way in which we relate to our children, with the result that their behavior *automatically* falls in line as they become aware of, and true to, who they really are. Behavioral changes are an outgrowth of a shift in the relationship.

Once our parenting is in alignment with consciousness, the precise manner in which things get implemented becomes a non-issue. If the underlying foundation is strong, the life built on that foundation is going to be a constructive life. Again, it's for this reason I placed the chapter on discipline last—not to minimize its importance, but to stress that unless discipline arises in a field of consciousness, it will be ineffective in the long term.

To walk the path of parenting consciously, it's unhelpful to adopt an all-or-nothing approach. Instead, the savvy parent picks up a piece here and a piece there, aware that even a tiny shift in the vibes in a family has the power to alter the consciousness of the entire family. So keep in mind as you read that the conscious way of parenting I'm depicting is something we inch our way into.

I repeat: it all begins in *this* moment now, and in the most ordinary situations.

A Conscious Parent Doesn't Emerge Overnight

Because parenting isn't an intellectual exercise but a molecular, energetic, moment-by-moment exchange in which our psyche interacts with that of our children, unless we are conscious of how we are influencing our children at any given moment, we will raise them without heed to their true needs. For this reason, the ability to see—*really* see—our children separate from who we are is our greatest gift to them. Conversely, our greatest weakness as parents is our inability to honor a child's path as it emerges.

To parent consciously, we have to become astute observers of our own behavior when we are with our children. In this way we can begin to be aware of our unconscious scripts and emotional imprints as they arise in the moment.

As we seek to be conscious in the way we interact with our children, we may feel we repeat the same patterns of behavior despite our best intentions. When this happens again and again, we wonder whether our unconsciousness will ever end. It can be discouraging.

The fact is that a conscious parent doesn't emerge overnight. To raise children consciously is both a daily and lifelong practice of becoming vigilant witnesses of our own unconsciousness. Each time we become aware of an element of unconscious behavior, however small it may be, an energetic shift occurs. As we catch ourselves in an unconscious moment and are able to detach from it, we expand our consciousness.

Clarity of mind and spirit don't come without a price. We all have generations of unconscious material to integrate. Unconsciousness by its nature will not—indeed, *cannot*—be stifled. No matter what our consciousness wills, our *un*consciousness has its own rhythm. It will leak into our habits, thoughts, emotions, and presence without our even realizing. Only by witnessing our unconsciousness as our children reflect it back to us are we able to integrate it.

In concluding this chapter, I want to be sure that it's clear in our minds that consciousness and unconsciousness aren't polarities, aren't at two ends of a spectrum. Unconsciousness isn't our enemy. On the contrary, it provides the platform on which consciousness arises if we are willing to allow it to do so.

Consciousness isn't a state to arrive at, a destination. After we become conscious, it doesn't mean we experience no more moments of unconsciousness. Rather, living consciously is an ongoing process.

Nobody is fully conscious, and we can be conscious in one aspect of our life and not in another—conscious in the way we act one moment but unconscious the next moment. To become conscious is to *witness* our unconsciousness, which progressively makes it conscious. For this reason, there's no need to treat our unconsciousness as if it were the boogey man. It's nothing to be frightened of, but is the portal to our development into whole human beings.

CHAPTER 3

RELEASE YOUR CHILDREN FROM THE NEED FOR YOUR APPROVAL

Without our realizing it, we bind our children to us by tying them to our approval, making them slaves to our judgments of them. Either we constantly starve them of our approval, or we cause them to become dependent on it.

Can you imagine how it must feel for a child to be starved of our approval and fearful of our disapproval? How different this must be from knowing they are unconditionally accepted and honored.

Every child realizes that their behavior sometimes gets them into a pickle, but this isn't at all the same as not being accepted and respected for who they fundamentally are. This is why it's so crucial that, as parents, we free ourselves of the illusion that it's our place to approve of who are children are. Who are we to judge them? They need to know that by simply being on this Earth, they have a right to approval of who they intrinsically are. *We* don't confer this right on them. Just by the fact they draw breath, they have the right to speak their mind, express their feelings, and embody their spirit. Such rights are bestowed with the birth certificate.

It may come as a surprise to hear that both disapproval *and* approval are tentacles of control. While we can certainly praise our children and celebrate their successes, it's so easy to introduce the taint of approval or disapproval, which quickly affects how our children feel about their basic being.

Whether our children are artistic, academicians, risk takers, into sports, musical, dreamers, or introverts, it need have no bearing on how we regard them. On a grander scale, it isn't our place to approve or disapprove of whether our children are religious, gay, the marrying kind, ambitious, or manifest any number of other traits. While a child's behavior is subject to modification that brings the child more closely in line with its essential being, their core must be unconditionally celebrated.

When our children choose a religion other than ours, a different profession than we dreamed of for them, are homosexual in orientation, or marry someone out of their race, how we respond is a barometer of how conscious we are. Are we able to respond to them with the realization that they have the right to manifest their inner being in their unique way?

Our children need to grow up with the awareness that who they are is worthy of celebration. Of course, parents will say they do celebrate their children. After all, don't they celebrate their children's birthdays, take them to the movies, buy them gifts, spend fortunes at the toy store? If this isn't celebrating a child's being, then what is?

Without our realizing, we so often endorse our children for their actions, rather than for just being. Celebrating our children's being means allowing them to exist without the snares of our expectations. It's to revel in their existence without them having to do a single thing, prove anything, or accomplish any kind of goal.

No matter how it manifests, our children's essence is pure and loving. When we honor this essence, they trust we understand that their internal world is good and worthy, regardless of what manifests externally. Our ability to stay connected to their essence, holding steady through those periods in which their external world may be falling apart, conveys the message that they are of immense value.

Allow me to suggest some of the ways in which you can let your children know they are accepted simply for themselves, quite apart from anything they do:

> They are resting, and you tell them how appreciated they are.

> They are sitting, and you tell them how happy you are to sit with them.

> They are walking in the house, and you stop them to say, "Thank you for being in my life."

> They hold your hand, and you tell them how much you love to hold theirs.

> They wake up in the morning, and you write them a letter saying how blessed you are to get to see them first thing in the day.

> You pick them up from school and tell them how much you missed them.

> They smile, and you tell them your heart is warmed.

> They kiss you, and you tell them you love being in their presence.

Whether you have an infant or a teen, your children need to feel that just because they exist, they delight you. They need to know they don't have to do anything to earn your undivided attention. They deserve to feel as if just by being born, they have earned the right to be adored.

Children who grow up with an intrinsic sense of "rightness" become adults who forever carry the imprint of inner connection and, consequently, emotional sturdiness. They learn early that it's their spirit that means the most in a relationship, and it's this they will call upon to navigate their adult experiences. Operating from this intrinsic connectivity, they don't need to seek validation externally, don't thirst for accolades, but celebrate who they are out of their own sense of validity.

ACCEPTANCE IS KEY

Accepting our children in their as-is state requires us to surrender our ideas of who they "should" be—a surrender that's akin to a psychic death—and enter into a state of pure communion with them so that we can respond to them as they need us to.

As we die to ourselves as we have known ourselves, we have the opportunity to be birthed all over again along with our children's budding spirit. For this to happen, all we need do is yield to the ever-shifting adventure of parenthood. Our children will lead the way. This is why parenting a young child is our greatest opportunity for change. If we are open to it, our child acts as our guru.

How this works can be seen from Anthony and Tina, who had been struggling with their son's learning disabilities for years. A high-achieving couple, they were unable to come to terms with their son's academic limitations. Sean's learning disabilities weren't limited to academics, but also encompassed his ability to socialize and handle life in general. Indeed, he couldn't have been more different from the fantasies his parents had of him had he tried. Although Anthony, his father, was a star tennis player and a bicycling enthusiast, Sean hated the outdoors, was terrified of insects, and preferred to play video games or read in his room.

Exasperated by his son's idiosyncratic personality, Anthony belittled him daily. Tina, his mother, a high powered attorney, believed that men should be strong and dominant, which meant she was irritated by her son's tentative ways. Trying to "man him up," she wanted him to work out at the gym, wear cooler clothes, and talk to girls even though he was terrified of them.

Homework and examination times were peak periods of stress and strife. Sean couldn't cope with the demands of mainstream education—a fact his parents wouldn't accept. Though each of his parents had a different approach to handling their son, both were abusive, calling him names and yelling at him, ridiculing his inability to learn basic math, and not allowing him to eat until he had mastered a concept. When I talked with them, they kept emphasizing, "Our son isn't retarded. He doesn't belong with 'those' people in special education."

Fights were a daily occurrence in this household. If it wasn't Sean and his father fighting, it was Sean and his mother. Anthony and Tina reached such a state of despair in trying to parent their son, they stopped acting as a team, slowly coming to resent each other and inevitably drifting apart. When they announced they had decided to get a divorce, it was no surprise to me, and neither was the reason they gave: "We can't take Sean's behavior. He's driving a wedge between us. We can't deal with him anymore. He makes us crazy."

When Anthony and Tina told Sean that it was because of him they were separating, they imagined this would jolt him out of his "bad" behavior. Having found a target for their misery in their son, they actually believed that were it not for Sean, they would be happy together. Though they took his behavior as a personal affront, it was in truth a painful reminder of their own failings as a couple. Sean, for his part, had grown so accustomed to being the vessel of his parents' anguish that he played the part of the demon to the hilt.

It was only when Anthony and Tina were willing to see how their negativity stemmed from their basic inability to accept their son that they embarked on the process of transformation, a process that required them to confront their anxiety about Sean's differentness. As they became aware of their unconscious patterns, they began noting how they dumped these onto Sean, who then acted out these patterns, thereby causing them more problems.

As Anthony and Tina realized how they had been inflicting their own agenda on their son, they began addressing the real issue, their relationship as a couple. After many painful months of working on the rift in their marriage, they were able to release Sean from the burden of carrying their pain.

While we may not endorse a particular behavior, we must always unequivocally and wholeheartedly endorse our children's right to be who they are in their core state. Accepting our children enables us to raise them without judgment, dealing with them from a neutral state. Responding to them as they need to be responded to, instead of in a manner reflective of our own past conditioning, requires unequivocal surrender to the wisdom of who they are, who they are yet to become, and what they can teach us about ourselves in the process.

THERE'S NOTHING *PASSIVE* ABOUT ACCEPTANCE

Acceptance is often considered a passive matter. This is a gross misunderstanding. Acceptance can't just be an intellectual decision, but must involve our entire heart and mind. I want to emphasize that acceptance is anything but passive. It's a highly active, intensely alive process.

To illustrate what acceptance looks like in practice, let me share with you how John and Alexis responded to their son Jake, who was growing up in ways that weren't typically boyish. Not into sports or loud games, Jake was quiet and artistic, preferring the arts and dance. As a consequence, even when he was a small boy, his parents had to endure seeing him come under fire from his peers. It occurred to them that he might be gay, though they didn't want to typecast him just because he evinced more typically feminine than masculine traits. Although at times they struggled with wanting him to be like most other boys, they held their concerns at bay, nurturing his love of music and dance. As they watched and waited, he began to blossom into the kind and sensitive male he was destined to be.

If Jake was to be gay, John and Alexis wanted him to enter into his sexual orientation for himself. Who he was in this aspect of his

life was immaterial to them because they saw his sexuality as one of
the many magnificent manifestations of his essence. When Jake
received hurtful treatment from his peers, his parents sought not to
take away his pain, but to help him sit with it.

As Jake grew older, John and Alexis purposefully created a
community of friends that included both gay and straight. They
wanted him to know that, if and when he was ready to disclose his
gayness, there would be a circle of accepting individuals around him.
Accordingly, when he was well into his teens, the day came when he
revealed his sexuality to them. Without saying a word, they opened
their arms wide. Because they had accepted their son in his *as is*
form right from the start, he had been able to nurture his authentic
self without condition, judgment, or guilt. The entire family celebrated his life for what it was.

Here was a family who didn't need their son to enact their
fantasies or fulfill their dreams. They didn't use their son to heal their
own unresolved wounds or to bolster their ego. Who he was in his
essence was clearly different from them. The ability to create
spaciousness between ourselves and our children helps foster the
greatest togetherness.

DON'T PARENT WITH A COOKIE-CUTTER APPROACH

When you are able to respect the unfolding of your child's particular
journey, you teach them to nurture their own inner voice and simultaneously honor the voice of others. This fosters their ability to engage
in relationships in a manner that reflects a healthy interdependence.
Because each individual's path emerges in its own unique way, no
longer is there a toxic dependence on the other. This equips your children for their adult years, in which a healthy interdependence is the
hallmark of successful intimate relationships.

To accept children requires disengaging from toxic life-scripts and
engaging each child on a cellular level. When you attune yourself to a

child's uniqueness, you realize it's futile to try to parent with a cookie-cutter approach. Instead, each child requires something different from you. Some children need a parent to be soft and gentle, whereas others need the parent to be more assertive—even "in their face." Once you accept your children's basic nature, you can contour your style to meet their temperament. To do so means letting go of your fantasies of yourself as a certain kind of parent and instead evolving into the parent you need to be for the particular child in front of you.

Before I became a parent, I had a vision of who my child would be. When I learned I was having a girl, I had countless expectations of her. Surely, I thought, she would have all my positive attributes. She would be gentle, soft, and artistically inclined. She would be innocent and infinitely malleable.

When my daughter's spirit began to develop, I realized she was anything but what I had anticipated. She is gentle, yes, but in a vigorous and assertive way. She has a take-charge approach and can be boisterous and stubborn. She is also anything but an artist. Her mind isn't dreamy like mine, but highly mechanical and logical. In temperament, rather than being "innocent" or even gullible, she is street smart and clever. More than anything, she isn't a "pleaser," a role I never dared step out of when I was a child. Instead, she is who she is, unapologetically.

It was a challenge to accept the reality of the daughter who had come into my world. I had to recalibrate my expectations, letting go of my fantasies. So caught up was I in who I thought she *should* be that, for a long time, I couldn't believe she was who she was. To embrace the fact that *this* is the daughter I have been blessed with has proved more difficult than actually dealing with her. Isn't this so for most of us as parents? Often it's the adjustment of our expectations, rather than reality itself, that's the hurdle we have to leap.

When we accept our children for who they are, we mistakenly believe this is to passively allow them to continue with behavior that may be destructive. Passivity isn't at all what I have in mind. I'm speaking of accepting our children's *being*, the *as is* state of their nature. Accepting is foundational. Adjusting their behavior to be more in line with their essential being comes later.

If our children are behaving in a manner we deem to be "bad" out of a sense of defiance, the appropriate response is firmness. If they are being "bad" because they are having trouble handling painful emotions, we need to be understanding. If they are needy and clingy, we may need to be cuddly and attentive, or—if we have been overly attentive and haven't fostered independence in them—we may need to help them learn to be content in themselves and comfortable being alone. If they are feeling private and quiet, we need to give them space and respect their desire for disengagement. If they are boisterous and playful at an appropriate time, we need to allow them to bask in their joy without interference. If they are boisterous and playful when it's time to do homework, we need to contain them and bring them to a state of attention and focus.

Acceptance of our children can take the form of any of the following:

I accept my child is different

I accept my child is quiet

I accept my child can be stubborn

I accept my child takes time to warm up to things
    or people

I accept my child is friendly

I accept my child gets upset quickly

I accept my child likes to please people

I accept my child resists change

I accept my child is fearful of new people

I accept my child can misbehave

I accept my child is moody

I accept my child is gentle

I accept my child is timid

I accept my child is shy

I accept my child is bossy

I accept my child is defiant

I accept my child is a follower

I accept my child is temperamental

I accept my child is below the curve in academics

I accept my child isn't as driven or motivated as most

I accept my child often lies when under pressure

I accept my child can be too dramatic

I accept my child finds it hard to sit still

I accept my child has their own way of being in
the world

I accept my child is their own unique person

I accept that to thrive, my child needs firm boundaries.

You Will Only Accept Your Child to the Degree You Accept Yourself

Accepting our children for who they are brings with it another component: accepting the kind of parent we need to be for a particular child.

When I accepted that my daughter was way more street smart than I had given her credit for, I was able to change my approach toward her. It was time to treat her as the clever girl she was, instead of as the little Miss Innocent I had hoped she was going to be. Instead of always being two steps behind her, which led to my resenting her ability to render me helpless, I learned to think two steps ahead of her. She had always been able to outsmart me, and beginning to think two steps ahead of her because I at last embraced how smart she was enabled me to avert her cleverness showing up as manipulation. How thankful I am that I let go of my desire to be the parent of my fantasy and instead became the parent my daughter needed me to be.

Our ability to accept our children is directly linked to our ability to accept ourselves—both as we are presently, and for what we have the potential to become. After all, how can we hope to raise our children to be freethinkers and free-spirited if we aren't these things ourselves? How can we raise independent, autonomous children if we ourselves aren't independent and autonomous? How can we raise another human being, another spirit, if our own being has been largely dismissed, our spirit systematically squelched?

It may be helpful for me to share with you some of the areas in which I am learning to accept myself:

I accept I am a human being before I am a parent

I accept I have limitations and many shortcomings,
   and this is okay

I accept I don't always know the right way

I accept I am often ashamed to admit my own failings

I accept I frequently lose my center worse than my
   child ever does

I accept I can be selfish and unthinking in my dealings
   with my child

I accept I sometimes fumble and stumble as a parent

I accept I don't always know how to respond to my child

I accept that at times I say and do the wrong thing
   with my child

I accept that at times I'm too tired to be sane

I accept that at times I'm too preoccupied to be
   present for my child

I accept I am trying my best, and that this is good
   enough

I accept my imperfections and my imperfect life

I accept my desire for power and control

I accept my ego

I accept my yearning for consciousness (even though
I often sabotage myself when I am about to enter
this state).

When we are unable to accept our children, it's because they open up old wounds in us, threatening some ego-attachment we are still holding onto. Unless we address why we can't embrace our children for precisely who they are, we will forever either seek to mold, control, and dominate them—or we will allow ourselves to be dominated by them.

It's essential to realize that any barrier we experience when it comes to fully accepting our children originates in our own past conditioning. A parent who is unable to accept their own being in all its glory will never be able to accept their children. Acceptance of our children goes hand-in-hand with an acceptance of ourselves. Only to the degree that we honor ourselves will we honor our children.

If we ourselves have somewhat of a victim mentality, we are likely to tell ourselves, "I accept my child is, and will always be, defiant." This isn't acceptance but resignation. Conversely, to have a victor mentality and tell ourselves, "I accept my child is a genius," isn't acceptance but grandiosity.

When we mold our children to meet our expectations, we resist who they are, which is to sow the seeds of dysfunction. In contrast, to accept our children for who they are at any given moment brings a feeling of release and inner spaciousness. No longer defining ourselves by our need for control, we enter into kinship. Beginning from where our children are, not from a place in our imagination, we are positioned to *help them shape themselves* in line with who they find themselves to be in their essence.

When I speak of who our children "find themselves to be," it's important to recognize that this is a fluid state. We forget that our children aren't fixed entities, but ever-evolving beings who are constantly transforming themselves. If we are attached to our own sense of ourselves in a rigid way and fail to recognize ourselves as ever-evolving beings, we inevitably do the same with our children. We determine who they are, ego to ego, and respond to them in this stuck fashion. This is why we keep on making mistake after mistake. Most of us don't even know who our children are *right now*, let alone allow their moment-by-moment newness to emerge.

To break free of stereotyping, you would have to truly enter the present and respond to your children with complete openness. You would need to ask yourself, "Do I really know who my child is? Can I create the space within myself to know my child each new day, one day to the next?" To do this would require becoming silent in your children's presence, freeing yourself of all distractions, and attuning yourself to them in a state of curiosity and delight.

CHAPTER 4

A Blow to Our Ego

To give your children the total acceptance they deserve will expose you to the diamond of the spiritual tradition: the chance to *lose your ego*.

As parents, it's hard not to be egoic. By the very fact we say, "This is *my* child," we enter into ego. Indeed, we are rarely *not* in ego when it comes to our children, for there is nothing we take more personally than how they fare in school, how they look, who they marry, where they live, and what they do for a living. Few parents can allow their children to exist without seeing them as an extension of their own ego.

I asked a group of parents why they had children. Their answers included, "I wanted to experience what it was like," "I love children," "I wanted to become a mother," "I wanted a family," and, "I wanted to prove to everyone I could be a good mother." In each case, the reason for wanting children was infused with *ego*. This is doubtless the case with many of us.

Parenting is a journey that tends to begin with a high level of egoic narcissism, an energy we take into our relationship with our child. The consequence is that we can easily, though in many cases inadvertently, fall into the trap of *using* our children to fill some need in ourselves, all the while under the illusion that we are loving, giving of ourselves, and nurturing. We use them to try to heal our broken self, use them by thrusting them into roles in the family that aren't theirs by right, use them to provide ourselves with a sense of worth, and use them to magnify our illusion of our influence in the world.

We find it hard to believe that many of us became a parent, at least in part, *to fulfill our own longing*. Unless we realize how strongly our ego drives us and gradually free ourselves from our identification with it, we will parent our children from this false state, which will render us unable to connect with their core self.

How Does Ego Function?

We have seen that our ego is a blind attachment to the *image* we have of ourselves, the picture of ourselves we carry around in our head. Our entire way of thinking, emoting, and acting is rooted in this self-image.

To gain a better understanding of the ego, recall how I noted earlier that when I suggest to parents *they* must change if their children's behavior is to improve, they insist I'm mistaken. They then present various explanations for why their relationship with their children is as it is.

We find it difficult to sit with the knowledge there may be a piece of us that contributed to whatever negativity we are experiencing in our life, preferring to place responsibility for our situation on factors in the world around us. When all we know ourselves to be is the image we have of ourselves, the idea of having to change threatens our identity, which is why we vigorously defend ourselves and vainly hope that the others in our life will be the ones to change.

Ego is in operation anytime we find ourselves attached to a thought pattern or belief system. We often don't even recognize we are attached until we are triggered on an emotional level. However, whenever anger, control, domination, sadness, anxiety, or even a positive emotion such as happiness takes over and our sense of our "rightness" reigns supreme, we are in ego. When we operate from this rigid place of "rightness," we bring to our reality an already-formulated assumption, ideal, or judgment. If a situation or individual doesn't conform to our will, we react to control the situation or the individual, bringing them under our domination.

Living in an egoic state, we fail to see others for who they are in their true being, their essence. A classic example is that of Stuart, whose son Samuel was an energetic, vibrant young man who was good at everything he undertook. Samuel particularly excelled at acting, desiring more than anything to go to drama school. Stuart opposed this. A first-generation immigrant, all his life he had worked in unstable, low-paying blue collar jobs, which caused him to want more than anything for his son to enjoy the security of a steady job, not an acting career with its uncertainty and instability.

When the time to apply to college arrived, Samuel wanted to select schools with fine drama programs, whereas his father insisted he attend business school. The two fought daily. Finally, Stuart threatened Samuel that if he applied for acting school, he wouldn't help with his tuition and would cut him out of his life forever. When Samuel saw it meant so much to his father, he caved in. Being the bright young man he was, he was accepted at Columbia's Business School and went on to have a prosperous career.

Even though Samuel owns his decision to let go of his acting career, he still resents his father for negating his passion. The lifestyle afforded by his corporate career doesn't begin to compensate for the joy of spirit and sense of purpose he felt when onstage. For him, acting was his true calling—an expression of his essence, his very being. Now, mired in mortgages and student loans, he feels little freedom to change course.

Samuel's father parented his son from a place of pure projection. At the root of his anxiety over his son's choice of career was an emotional script he carried within himself that said "uncertainty is bad." Consumed by the anxiety he had suffered as a first-generation immigrant, he sought to control his son's destiny.

As long as the pillars of your ego remain intact, as they were in the case of Samuel's father, you will struggle to live authentically;

and if you are inauthentic, you will have difficulty allowing your children to be authentic. To parent children from ego is to live with the unconscious mandate that your way is the right way. Consequently, you urge your children—as happened to Samuel—to enter *your* world and *miss the opportunity to enter theirs*. Sadly, it's likely you feel the most competent when your children are under your domination, willing to follow your word as gospel.

Our ego-attachments are a mask for our fears, the greatest of which is surrendering to the mysterious nature of life itself. When we come from ego rather than from pure being, we don't connect with our children's essential being. As a result, they grow up disconnected from their own essence, and thus learn to distrust their connection to all that exists. Approaching life from fear stifles the emergence of their genuine, uninhibited, unaffected being. Our ego therefore needs to crumble to allow our authenticity to emerge, which in turn frees our children to grow up true to themselves.

If we free ourselves from our ego and simply observe our children's development as life spontaneously teases it out of them, they become *our* teachers. In other words, living authentically allows us to cease looking at our children as blank canvases on which we can project our image of who they should be, seeing them instead as fellow travelers on the journey, *changing us as much as we are changing them*.

The question is, are you willing to give up thinking you "know," step down from your egoic pedestal of authority, and allow yourself to learn from these creatures who are most able to live in a state of egoless consciousness?

To live authentically instead of in ego is to embrace continuous evolution, realizing we are always in flux, always a work in progress. Authenticity requires us to access that deep, silent aspect of our being that is nevertheless audible beneath the whirring din of whatever may be happening in our life. While supported and guided by the external environment, this authentic state of being doesn't *need* the external environment in order to survive. Rather, it requires a synchronicity with our mind and a moment-by-moment connection with our body.

When we live authentically, we may still have the relationship, house, car, and other luxuries that ego is drawn to (the things Samuel's father so wanted him to have), but the purpose for which these things exist is completely different. If our relationship, house, job, car, and other externals are what we rely on to make us happy, we are enslaved to ego. If they exist so we may serve others through fulfilling our purpose, they further our commitment to our essential being.

Although the manner in which ego manifests is different in each person, there are common patterns the ego follows on its path toward self-entrapment—several universal ego styles. It's helpful to have a clear picture of how each of these functions.

THE EGO OF IMAGE

When a young mother received a phone call from the principal's office informing her that her nine-year-old son was in a fight with another boy, she was devastated. Unable to believe her precious son had become one of "those" children, she felt ashamed and flustered. What to do? How to respond?

Becoming defensive, this mother found herself blaming anyone and everyone. She argued with the principal, the teachers, the parents of the other boy, insisting that her son had been wrongly accused. She wrote letters to the district superintendent about how her son had been blamed unjustly.

Without her realizing, this mother's ego made this incident *all about her*, as if it were *her* competence that was in question. Unable to separate herself from her son's behavior enough to see it for what it was, she blew things out of proportion. It was as if *she* had been personally attacked—as if *she* were the one being called into the principal's office and reprimanded for not being a good parent. The upshot was that instead of this nine-year-old experiencing the natural consequences of his actions, from which he might have learned, he felt guilt and embarrassment over the way his mother acted.

Many of us fall into the trap of allowing our sense of worth to become entangled with our children's behavior. When they behave in a manner that's out of the norm, we feel personally responsible. Unable to detach our ego from the situation, we blow their behavior out of proportion.

None of us likes to be perceived as an incompetent parent. Our ego needs us to be seen as a superlative parent. Anytime we feel less perfect than what we wish to be, we experience anxiety because we believe we have "fallen" in the eyes of others. Then we react in an emotional manner.

THE EGO OF PERFECTION

Most of us harbor fantasies of perfection, but it's our attachment to such fantasies that keeps us from flowing with how our life really is.

For instance, when a mother planned her son's bar mitzvah, she spent over $30,000 on the arrangements, perfecting each detail. Despite the fact she had fussed for months, she was nevertheless extremely anxious when the day arrived.

As it turned out, the occasion was punctuated by what this mother saw as disaster after disaster. The day began with an unexpected thunderstorm. Thankfully, she had planned for such a possibility and had a tent backup. Then the DJ was caught in heavy traffic, which meant he arrived an hour late. Shortly thereafter, the boy's mother noticed that her son had become somewhat tipsy and was being rowdy in front of her relatives and high society friends.

Feeling utter embarrassment, the mother was devastated—and livid. Though she managed to maintain her image of the perfect mother as long as her guests were present, she unleashed her fury on everyone around her when they departed, ruining her son's revelry and shaming him in front of his buddies, who were spending the night at the house. On the heels of her explosion, she got into a fight with her husband, then created a scene with the DJ.

Because the occasion hadn't lived up to her expectations, she made everyone miserable.

When our life doesn't go according to plan and we respond with resistance and emotional velocity, it's because we feel threatened. As our fantasy of how life "should" be falls apart, our egoic need to control things shows itself. Unable to accept that our loved ones and life itself aren't our automatons, here to bend to our will, we impose our manic desire to "look" a certain way on everyone and everything. What we can't see is that holding onto the fantasy that life is supposed to have a fairy-tale ending often comes at the price of our loved ones' wellbeing.

When we parent from the traditional approach, we encourage our children to look up to us because this is how we were raised. To be good parents, we feel we need to be all-knowing and all-powerful. Little do we realize that when we portray ourselves as so competent, we foster inhibition and fear in our children. They look at us and see an image so out of reach that it causes them to feel inordinately small. In this way, we imprint in them the idea that they are "less than" us, which discourages them from getting in touch with their own competence.

When our children experience us as always "in the know," always there with a perfect solution or a correct opinion, they grow up believing they need to be the same way. Uncomfortable with our imperfections and resistant to exposing our flaws, we teach them to disguise their imperfections and overcompensate for their weaknesses. What they *really* need to learn is that *perfection is an ideal of the foolish*.

The goal isn't to be flawlessly "perfect," as the mother tried to be with respect to her son's bar mitzvah, but to embrace our "perfectly flawed" self—and, in this mother's case, embrace the fact that her son is also flawed like her and may mess up at the most inappropriate moment. It's important to release our children from the illusion that we always "have it together"—something we can only do once we have released *ourselves* from the grip of being "perfect" parents.

When you are comfortable acknowledging your flaws and daily mistakes, not in a self-flagellating manner but in a matter-of-fact manner, you convey to your children that mistakes are inevitable. By laughing at your errors and readily admitting your insecurities, you remove yourself from the pedestal of wonder. Setting aside hierarchy, you encourage your children to relate to you as human-to-human, spirit-to-spirit.

How sad that the mother who organized the bar mitzvah couldn't laugh at all the things that went awry. Had she done so, she would have taught her son one of the most valuable lessons he could ever learn—that of total acceptance of *what is*, including his misplaced behavior.

All we need to do is model. When our children realize we are perfectly okay with our okayness, it encourages a feeling of competence within them. By delighting in our follies, we teach our children not to take themselves too seriously. By being willing to make a fool of ourselves as we try new things, we teach them to explore life with little care for how they "look" or perform.

I wonder whether the mother who planned the bar mitzvah so perfectly ever purposely acted silly in front of her son, dancing and singing, or did something out of her element to demonstrate she is human and fallible. To do so encourages our children to step out of their comfort zone and enter unfamiliar territory. I wonder whether she played with her son and his friends at a child's level, not hesitating to bend on her knees and bray like a donkey or become the frog prince. When our children see us come down to their level, it equalizes the dynamic between us, allowing them to connect to us in a playful, non-threatening manner. I wonder, too, whether this mother ever allowed herself to trip, fall, break, bend, blotch, splotch, cry, and froth in front of her son, within measure, instead of trying to hide these aspects of her humanity. Did she ever demonstrate that she was okay with her house not perfectly clean, her nails not perfectly manicured, her makeup not perfectly in place? When we do so, we show our children that "good enough" is absolutely good enough.

We do ourselves and our children a favor when we accept our limitations and exude an "okayness" with being okay. In this way, our children are encouraged to become comfortable with who they are, able to see the humor and lightness in themselves, and thereby detach from the impossible rigidity of their ego.

The Ego of Status

Status is a huge issue for many parents. For instance, when a student wasn't accepted into any of the Ivy League schools to which he applied, instead being accepted at the local state school, his parents experienced a sense of overwhelming shame. In shock at the news, they had no idea how they would tell their relatives and friends that their son would be attending such a "substandard" school, especially since they were graduates of Yale and Columbia respectively.

When these parents made their immense disappointment known to their son, he knew he had let them down. In the parents' view, their son hadn't just failed them but had also squandered a much-treasured family legacy. Laden with a sense of shame, the young man entered pre-med, pushing himself harder than ever to prove to his parents that he was worthy of their validation, thus losing touch with his true self even more.

Many of us harbor rigid ideals of what it means to be successful. We have external yardsticks such as a high-paying job, a flashy car, a fancy house, the perfect neighborhood, classy friends, and so on. Then, when we fail at a task, lose our job, or are forced to realize our children aren't so achievement-oriented, we feel as if we have failed in some fundamental way. We imagine our core has been threatened, which causes us to lash out.

When we are attached to ideals, we impose these on our children, insistent that they preserve our carefully constructed persona of competence. We overlook the fact that each of our children is a being with its own calling, not realizing that only through the full acknowledgment of our child's unique and autonomous spirit can we seize the spiritual opportunities inherent in parenthood.

It's crucial to abandon all thought of why your children are the individuals they inherently are and to guard against any tendency to make them "wrong." The challenge to you as a parent is to allow your child's spirit to emerge without your domination. Can you let go of your relentless urge to have your children be extensions of yourself? Are you willing to foster the internal space in them that will enable them to flourish free of your need to project your will onto them?

If these things are to happen, you will need to create an inner space within *yourself* that's free of the tendency to possess and control. Only then can you meet your children as they truly are, not as you wish them to be, fully accepting them without attachment to whatever vision you may have for them.

When you relate to your children by honoring who they are at any given moment, you teach them to honor themselves. If, on the other hand, you seek to shift them from their present state, altering their behavior to meet your approval, you convey the message that their authentic being is inadequate. As a result, your children begin to adopt a *persona*, which takes them away from who they really are.

Letting go of your attachment to your vision of parenthood and your desire to write your children's future is the hardest psychic death to endure. It demands that you drop all prior agendas and enter a state of pure release and surrender. It asks that you forego your fantasies of who you thought your child would be and instead respond to the actual child in front of you.

THE EGO OF CONFORMITY

We humans like to think of ourselves as product-oriented creatures. We prefer to go from point A to point B. We want our interactions in life to be orderly, organized. Unfortunately, life doesn't come in a neat package. It doesn't provide us with easy solutions, ready-made answers. Instead of being orderly and organized, it's anything but—especially in the case of parenthood. This is why parents have the hardest time with a child who breaks out of the family's mold, choosing to be who they want to be, doing what they want to do, even if this means being a black sheep. If a child threatens our egoic attachment to conformity, we experience emotional turmoil.

I think of a teenage girl who was always different. Slower than her friends and difficult to handle, she experienced more emotional meltdowns than other girls, which tested her parents' patience to the limit. She was lazy, whereas her parents were just the opposite. She was a dreamer, whereas her parents were practical. She was unconcerned about her looks, whereas how her parents looked was of vital concern to them.

Though she didn't want to be, this teen knew she was an embarrassment to her parents. She was particularly irksome to her highly ambitious mother, who had taken great pains to carve her own place in society. The reality was that she didn't know how to become the child her parents wanted her to be. Although she tried, nothing she did was ever good enough.

When we resist our children's way of being, it's often because we secretly harbor the notion that we are somehow "above" what's happening, especially if what's happening is something we believe to be a mess. We tell ourselves that while what we consider undesirable aspects of life may befall others, they simply cannot and must not befall us. Engaging in the ordinary fallibility of life and exposing our own fallibility is simply too threatening. By refusing to accept life *as it is*, we become mired in our attachment to the idea we are superior to the common lot. A child who violates this image of ourselves then feels like our enemy.

Unlike the teen I have just described, I am reminded of a twenty-year-old who had been the perfect child, following her parent's lead on everything, excelling in everything, and generally being a delight. When she joined the Peace Corps and began to travel the world, her parents couldn't have been happier. Thrilled by their daughter's dedication to the underprivileged, it was as if she reflected their best qualities.

On her travels, this young woman fell in love with a young man from India. When they decided to marry, her parents disapproved, asserting she "could do better for herself." In an attempt to block the marriage, her father stopped engaging with her. Her mother, while not so drastic in her behavior, made no bones about how displeased she was with her daughter's selection, belittling her intended at every opportunity.

The young woman was tortured. Being the pleaser she was, in the end she broke up with this man, marrying within her own social class and race a few years later. To this day, this woman remembers that young Indian man as her soul mate and knows she will never love anyone in quite the same way. She also realizes she was too weak to choose love ahead of the wishes of her parents, a choice she will have to live with.

Many of us harbor the fantasy that, of all the people we have to deal with in life, at least our children will bend to our will. If they don't, daring instead to live their own life, marching to their own beat, we feel insulted. When our more discreet methods of gaining compliance fail, we become louder and more forceful, simply unable to bear the idea that our children are challenging our will. Of course, the alienation this results in is the reason our children lie to us, at times even cheating and stealing, and may go so far as to stop communicating with us.

To the degree we are able to let go of our need for conformity, we will be able to enter into mutually enhancing and reciprocal relationships with our children. Hierarchical ways of relating that focus on "authority" become a thing of the past.

THE EGO OF BEING "IN CONTROL"

When we are raised by parents who value emotional control over emotional expression, we learn early how to painstakingly monitor our emotional responses, weeding out those that evoke disapproval.

Because we believe an outburst of emotional expression is a weakness, suppressing our emotions becomes an automatic tactic.

Simultaneously, we develop rigid standards for those around us, as well as for life itself. We feel a need to exert our control over life by passing judgment on situations and expressing disapproval. The illusion of superiority gives us the feeling we are in charge of our emotions and somehow above the vagaries of life.

Wielding power over others through control, criticism, reprimand, guilt-tripping, judgment, or demonstrating our superior "knowledge" is an indicator not of a superior soul but of an impoverished soul. When a child never gets to witness its parents in a state of weakness or childishness, let alone as simply fumbling, bumbling humans, how can this child risk revealing its own weaknesses?

Growing up stifled in this way, we stop ourselves from exploring, taking risks, and thereby making mistakes. We fear the silent disapproval of our parents. Because we "just know" they will disapprove, we never embark on the true adventure of life, instead playing it safe, well within the box. Of course, because we are "in control," in school we are recognized by our teachers as little angels, a tag that comes at the cost of authenticity.

With this egoic imprint, our tendency is to view power and control as a means of security. Because we have bought into the belief that life is divided into those who wield power, often by virtue of their greater age or knowledge, and those who are powerless, we tell ourselves, "I must at all times be 'together' and in control of my emotions. I must always be logical, pragmatic, and 'in the know.'" Children who grow up with such a worldview become adults who are unable to access their inner empowerment. As parents, they are likely to unleash their need for control particularly on those who are disenfranchised, such as when parenting their own children or as teachers in school. They become adults who are unable to tolerate any disrespect for their status, using their role to foster inhibition in others.

Rarely have I witnessed a more contentious relationship than that of Christopher and his seventeen-year-old stepson Jaden. Jaden was distraught because of his parents' separation and quite naturally transferred his angst onto his new stepfather. Christopher interpreted Jaden's rejection of him on a deeply personal level. Christopher couldn't bear that he wasn't treated as the head of the household and demanded Jaden respect him, becoming enraged when he didn't receive the respect he asked for. Unable to find it within himself to step into Jaden's shoes and see things from his perspective, he couldn't handle Jaden's emotional rejection of him.

Preoccupied with his lack of power over his stepson, Christopher entered into conflict with Jaden on a daily basis, pushing him into corners that gave this teen no option but to retaliate. He also fought constantly with his new wife over Jaden, pushing her to take sides and threatening to leave her if she couldn't change her son.

Things became so bad that Jaden barely felt comfortable leaving his room when he was alone in the house with Christopher, often waiting to do so until his mother returned. In his desperation to numb his pain and anger, he began hanging out with the wrong crowd and consequently started to fail in school.

Christopher was insecure in his new roles as husband and step-father. Instead of becoming aware of his own inner conflict, he regarded Jaden as the cause of his distress. He couldn't recognize that, although we are each unique individuals with our own separate paths to walk in our own special way, there's no *fundamental* separation between "I" and "you," for we are all together on this journey. Had Christopher understood this, he would have seen how he was using Jaden as a cover for his own pain. He would have realized that by attacking Jaden, he was attempting to obliterate his own feelings of inadequacy. He would also have understood Jaden's lack of respect for him as a mirror of his own lack of respect for himself. No amount of control could change this.

As the egoic pattern of needing to be in control is passed from generation to generation, the children of these parents often grow up trying to be perfect in everything, to the point of being obsessively detail-oriented. Unable to express their emotions, they tend to store them in their body, becoming rigid. Because of their acute rigidity, which manifests intellectually as a black-and-whiteness concerning just about everything, these children are often snubbed by their peers. This is because, without realizing it, they come across as superior to the everyday behavior of their peers, which they view as "immature." Such children rarely let go, let alone let loose. You won't find them eating watermelons with their face dug deep into the fruit. These kids use a napkin, fork, and spoon.

Ironically, growing up with such a restricted worldview may produce a parent who allows their children to run amuck precisely because this is what they weren't allowed to do. Accustomed to being controlled, these parents allow their children to control *them*, duplicating the control they lived under when they themselves were young.

In contrast, if parents are unable to tolerate their own emotions when things don't go according to plan, their children soak up these emotions, which then form their emotional repertoire. Such individuals are triggered at every turn, apparently under the illusion that if they react strongly enough, life will bend to their will.

When a person with this egoic imprint experiences a downturn in some aspect of their life and becomes exasperated, their exasperation is an attempt to camouflage their insecurity. Unaccustomed to sitting with the painful feeling of helplessness in a situation, their ego converts their insecurity into indignation and rage. Anger is a powerful stimulant, seducing us to believe we are strong and in control. Paradoxically, when we are in the grip of anger, we are anything but in control. We are prisoners of ego.

YOU CAN TRANSITION OUT OF EGO

I have found that it helps parents to differentiate between essence and ego when I share with them examples of responses to their children that come from ego, in contrast to responses that come from essence. It's the difference between coming from thought, or from our heart—from the way we imagine things *ought* to be, or from acceptance of *what is*.

Examples of egoic reactions that emerge from fixation on the outcome of a situation, perfection, zip codes, bank balances, appearance, wealth, or success are:

Sermons: "If I were you…"

Opinions: "If you ask me…"

Judgments: "I like…," or, "I don't like…"

Orders: "Don't be sad," "Don't cry," "Don't be afraid"

Control: "If you do this, I will do that," or, "I won't accept you like that."

Examples of responses that flow from essence, which is our authentic *being*, include:

"I see you," embracing the individual as they are

"I understand you," accepting the person as they are

"I hear you," respecting the person as they are

"You are complete just as you are," honoring the wholeness within each of us

"This moment between us is perfect as it is," realizing the wholeness of life itself.

Our ego can be activated in a split-second, placing us in its clutches before we even realize what's happening. We are particularly susceptible to this whenever we discipline our children. If we are in a state of agitation, frustration, or fatigue, chances are we are going to botch the disciplining process. Many of our mistakes when setting boundaries with our children stem from our internal conflict, ambivalence, or tiredness—which is when ego often kicks in the most.

We are obligated *not* to displace our emotional state onto our children, no matter what the provocation. If we are aware of our tendency to come from ego, we will recognize that we are in a fragile state and that our judgment may be askew. Only when we are in a neutral state can we hope to respond to our children's behavior in the manner it warrants.

Whenever we respond to our child, it behooves us to realize that because the child imbibed its sense of identity from us in the first place, we are in fact responding to pieces of our own self that are reflected in the child. This is why we barely see our children for who they are, but imagine them as a "mini me," which of course solidifies our ego. We don't realize it, but most of the time when we think we are responding to our children, we are reacting to the pieces of *ourselves* that they have internalized. This is the reason we find ourselves overly-identified with our children, their feelings, and their problems. Unable to separate our emotions from theirs, and unable to be objective and rational, we are in reality identifying with something in our own past. In this rather complicated psychological process, we unintentionally squelch our children's ability to be who they are, binding them to our psyche in a way they don't need.

The undermining of ego that can be initiated by becoming a parent is a wonderful gift for both ourselves and our children. However, it involves passing through a precarious period. When the pillars of our ego begin to crumble, as they have to if we are to raise another spirit consciously, this crumbling takes place in a context in which the foundations of our own true being haven't yet been built on.

This transition phase, which usually takes place between our children's birth and their early school years, results in a sense of loss followed by confusion. As our children become more independent, we are confronted with the void in our own life—a void that was for so long inhabited by our children, who now seem to need us less and less. This process intensifies in the teen years and especially when our children leave home. As we seek to reinvent ourselves, we find ourselves fearful of who we are going to see in the mirror. For some of us, it has been so long since we thought of ourselves as separate from our children that we are terrified of the idea. Feelings of guilt, sadness, and apprehension well up as we contemplate moving back into the personalized space called "I." However, if we re-enter the "I" space with a sense of our regenerative potential, we begin to experience our own innate being and at last blossom into who we really are.

In all kinds of ways—if we are willing—our children take us into places in our heart we didn't know existed. In this way, they loosen the grip of our ego and help us expand our sense of our true self, allowing us to access our ability to love unconditionally, live fully in the present moment, and enter the experience of consciousness.

What a gift, then, to have our children in our lives so that we can journey together, benefitting each other through the continual exposure of our unconsciousness, coupled with countless opportunities to shift out of ego and into a more authentic way of being.

CHAPTER 5

IS YOUR CHILD GROWING YOU UP?

Being absorbent, our children soak in all our inanities and insanities. For this reason, we must become aware of the emotions we experience and unduly thrust upon them. We can only teach our children those insights we have inculcated in our own life. If our children see us constantly displacing our feelings onto others and witness how we blame others for the lack we experience in our life, this is how they will live too. If they observe how we invite opportunities for introspection and are readily able to admit our faults, they will learn to be fearless where their flaws are concerned and be able to transcend them.

Conscious parenting means that in our interactions with our children, we ask, "Am I dealing with my child in an aware manner or am I being triggered by my past?" The focus is always on us as parents, requiring us to look within and ask, "What am I bringing to this relationship in this moment that is mine to own and not my child's to receive?"

Especially in the early years, parents function as mirrors for their children. Consequently, if you are unable to access *your* joy, you will be unable to be a mirror of your children's joy. Thus they are barred from access to an essential aspect of their being. How sad for a child not to be able to enjoy their spontaneously joyous essence!

Our consciousness and unconsciousness are transmitted not only by our overt pain, but also in the energy we exude just by our presence, even when we say and do nothing. Thus our children pick up a great deal from how we embrace them each morning, how we react when they break our favorite vase, how we handle ourselves in a traffic accident, how we sit and talk to them, whether we really look at what they show us, and whether we take an interest in what they say. They notice when we intrude on their life with unwarranted questions and demands, and they feel it when we withdraw from them or utter reprimands. They are moved by how we praise their success, but wounded when we put them down for their failures. They are aware of how it feels to be in our presence when we sit in silence with them, and of the energy field of acceptance or rejection they experience around us. Each of these moment-by-moment exchanges transmits either consciousness or unconsciousness.

How can you give to your children unless you first allow yourself to be filled from your own well? Unless you are fulfilled, you will use your children to complete you. You will teach them how to live with your unacknowledged fears, your rejected emptiness, your forgotten lies—all the while unaware you are doing so. Such is the power of unacknowledged lostness.

FACE UP TO YOUR REACTIVITY

Through our children, we get orchestra seats to the complex theatrics of our immaturity, as they evoke powerful emotions in us that can cause us to feel as though we aren't in control—with all the frustration, insecurity, and angst that accompanies this sensation.

Of course, our children don't "make" us feel this way. They merely awaken our unresolved emotional issues from our childhood. Nevertheless, because our children are vulnerable and mostly powerless, we feel free to blame them for our reactivity. Only by facing up to the fact that it isn't our children who are the problem, but our own unconsciousness, can transformation come about.

How did we become so reactive? Not only do we inherit certain egoic scripts and roles from our family of origin, we also inherit an emotional signature. Beneath every role and script is a unique emotional imprint. This is the case because, as an infant, we are in a state of *being*, not ego, which means our defenses are unformed and we are susceptible to the emotional energy around us. We energetically interact with our parents' emotional state, absorbing their emotional imprint, until this energy becomes our own emotional stamp. Unless at some point in our life we become conscious of the emotional energy we have absorbed from our parents, we will inevitably transfer this imprint to our own children.

Because we weren't taught by either our parents or society to access our inner stillness and find the roots of our pain and pleasure within ourselves, we are reactive to external circumstances. Since we didn't learn to simply observe our emotions, honor them, sit with them, and grow from them, our response to external stimuli became increasingly emotionally toxic, which is the root of our cyclones of drama.

When we are raised to suppress our darker emotions, these emotions form a shadow from which we are cut off. When emotions are split from our consciousness, they lie dormant, ready to be activated at a moment's notice, which is why so many of us erupt out of the blue. Whenever these emotions are triggered by another's shadow, we find ourselves upset with the person who evoked these emotions in us. Again, let me emphasize that no one could evoke such emotions in us were they not already part of our shadow. Not realizing this, we seek to ease our discomfort at having to confront our shadow by projecting these emotions onto the other. We then see them as the villain in the situation. So afraid are we to face our suppressed emotions that whenever we recognize such emotions in another, we experience hatred, which leads to defiance, victimizing, and in some cases the killing of the individual.

Why do parents and children tend to clash once the teen years hit? Why do marriages fall apart? Why do people exhibit racism or commit hate crimes? These things occur when we are split off from our own shadow, our inner pain. For example, if we were bullied as a child, unless we have resolved our own pain, we will be unable to tolerate our children's pain when they are bullied. In such a situation, we are likely to foster in our children either an inability to handle their emotions, or a belief that under no circumstance must they ever portray themselves as vulnerable. Believing they must appear powerful and in control, they learn to be macho even if they don't feel strong. In countless subtle ways, our own issues around power and control are imposed on our children.

When people and circumstances press our buttons, we can easily begin to believe that life is against us. We adopt a life script of martyrdom, imagining that life "has it in for us" or is "cheating" us in some way, even though life is simply neutral. We may begin to believe that life *always* deals us a cruel hand.

The reality is that there is no enemy "out there." The person who triggers a reaction in us is just being a person, the situation just a situation. We regard them as an enemy only because of our inability to understand and master our internal shadow, which we project onto them.

The more helpful response to being triggered is to recognize your emotional charge as a signal that something is amiss within you. In other words, emotional reactivity is a reason to go inward, focusing on your own growth. Once you realize there are no enemies, only guides to inner growth, all who play a part in your life become mirrors of your forgotten self. Life's challenges then become emotionally regenerative opportunities. When you encounter a roadblock in your life, whether a person or a situation, instead of seeing it as an enemy to be reacted against, you pause and ask yourself, "What do I perceive I'm lacking?" You recognize that the lack you perceive in your environment arose because of an *internal* sense of lack.

This realization invites you to appreciate the person or situation for their kindness in serving as a mirror of your sense of lack. The split between yourself and the other is then no longer present because it's not so much about a separate "other," even though the person is a separate individual, but is a mirror of your internal state. You realize you brought this spiritual lesson into your life because your essential being desires change in your everyday behavior.

Since no other journey is able to evoke more emotional reactivity in us than parenting, to be a parent invites us to treat the reactions our children trigger in us as opportunities for spiritual growth. By bringing our emotional shadow into the spotlight as never before, parenting affords us a wonderful opportunity to tame our reactivity. Indeed, the parenting journey has the potential to be an especially regenerative experience for both parent and child, where every moment is a meeting of spirits, and both parent and child appreciate that each dances on a spiritual path that's unique, holding hands yet alone. Coming from this realization, we respond to each other creatively instead of reacting destructively.

DISCOVER YOUR EMOTIONAL INHERITANCE

Each of us is triggered on a daily basis by all kinds of things. As parents, we are especially susceptible to being triggered because our children are continually around us and in constant need of us.

However, the next time your children trigger a mood in you, instead of reacting out of frustration, sit with your reaction to see what the trigger is about. This willingness to look within, which doesn't require introspection into the *cause* of your mood, just the simple awareness that it comes from within your own self and not from the other person's actions, will enable you to suspend your thoughts long enough to shift out of reactivity and craft a response that's more grounded.

Most of us are able to identify our triggers on a superficial level, such as, "I get triggered when my child disrespects me," "I get triggered when my child doesn't do his homework," or "I get triggered when my child dyes her hair." These are the surface reasons we are triggered. But what in us is actually being triggered? What, on an elemental level, are we experiencing?

To be triggered is to be in resistance to whatever may be happening in our life. By reacting, we are saying, "I don't want this situation; I don't like the way things are." In other words, when we resist the way life manifests itself in our children, our intimate partner, or our friends, it's because we refuse to accept life's *as is* form. The reason for this is that the ideal view of ourselves to which we are attached—our *ego*—is being shaken, which is threatening to us. In this state, we bypass our ability to be resourceful and creative in our response, reacting instead. The manner in which this reaction manifests depends on our unique life scripts, roles, and emotional inheritance.

Consciousness means being awake, truly awake, to everything we are experiencing. It involves being able to respond to the reality in front of us *as it unfolds in the moment*. This reality may not be what we tell ourselves it ought to be, but *it is what it is*.

To be in a state of consciousness means we approach reality with the realization that life just *is*. We make a conscious choice to flow with the current, without any desire to control it or need for it to be any different from what it is. We chant the mantra, "It is what it is." This means we parent our children *as our children are*, not as we might wish them to be. It requires accepting our children in their *as is* form.

I mentioned earlier that when we refuse to accept our reality—be it our children for who they are, or our circumstances—we imagine that if we are angry enough, sad enough, happy enough, or domineering enough, things will somehow change. The opposite is the case. Our inability to embrace our reality in its *as is* form keeps us stuck. For this reason, not *resistance* but *acceptance* of our reality is the first step to changing it.

Relinquishing control allows us to engage life from the standpoint of seeking to learn. Indeed, to respond to life in its *as is* form is how our greatest lessons are learned. The key is to start with *what is*, not *what isn't*. We respond to our children where they are, rather than pushing them to where we want them to be.

Do you see the simplicity of embracing the *as is* of parenting? Even if your children are in pain, distress, or pitching a fit, can you accept this state as natural and therefore whole? Can you recognize the completeness of it, just as it is? Once you have accepted your children's *as is* state, even when this means their tantrums, with your acceptance there arises a pause. From this pause emerges an understanding of how to respond, rather than react.

Growing up with explosive, pouting, distancing, or otherwise emotionally manipulative parents, a child learns that life is to be dueled with. Situations are to be "managed," brought to heel by unleashing our emotions. Our watchwords become, "How dare you?" "How dare it?" and "How dare they?"

People who sport such an emotional style carry a heavy sense of entitlement, which causes them to repeatedly tell themselves such things as, "I deserve better." Believing that life owes them only pleasurable experiences, they attempt to avoid pain at all costs. When life doesn't comply, they are quick to blame someone else, declaring, "It's all their fault." They then assure themselves, "I have a right to be upset!"

When the children of parents with this imprint become parents, they are likely to react angrily to their own children. If a child deviates from the parents' plan for it, marching to its own rhythm instead of abiding by its parents' decrees, the parent may resort to outrage in order to control the child. Children brought up this way learn fear, not respect. They believe that the only way to effect change is through overpowering others, which leads to raising their own children to one day become dictators themselves, hostile in their reaction to the world, and perhaps even violent.

As mentioned earlier, there is of course always the possibility that a child who was totally overpowered by its parents' rage ends up with such a low sense of worth that, years later, this parent recreates in its own children shades of its abusive, raging parents. Feeling too insecure to claim respect, such a parent then allows its children to become narcissistic, which leads to the parent being overpowered by its own offspring.

How Can You Integrate Your Pain?

Children quite naturally feel all their emotions without blocking them. They spontaneously surrender to pure feeling, then release the emotion as it passes. In this way, their emotions ebb and flow in a wavelike fashion.

We adults are often afraid to surrender to our emotions. We find it difficult to tolerate feelings such as rejection, fear, anxiety, ambivalence, doubt, and sadness. So we run from our feelings either by burying them through avoidance, resisting them, or displacing them onto people and situations outside ourselves through emotional reactivity. Many of us resort to intellectualizing, plastic surgery, fatter bank accounts, or larger social networks as a way of avoiding having to feel. Or we deflect our pain by blaming, being resentful, and expressing anger toward the person we believe caused us pain.

A conscious person is able not just to tolerate their emotions, but to embrace them—and I do mean *all* of their emotions. When we don't know how to honor our own feelings, we don't honor our children's feelings. To the degree we live in a state of falsehood, our children learn to squelch their feelings and thereby also enter into falsehood. Were we to encourage our children to be real about what they feel in the way children naturally are until we shut them down, they would have no need to deny their emotions and would feel no desire to displace them onto others. For this reason, if we wish to teach our children how to live integrated lives in which they take full responsibility for their actions, we need to honor *all* their emotions, which means they don't have a need to generate a shadow. In this way they come to appreciate life as a seamless fabric in which every action and relationship is energetically connected.

Having said this, it's important to note that there's a difference between reacting emotionally and feeling our feelings. Many of us assume that when we are angry or sad, we are feeling our feelings. On the contrary, we are often merely *reacting*. Truly feeling an emotion means being able to *sit with* the incoherence we experience at such a time, neither venting it nor denying it, but simply containing it and being present with it.

Feeling our emotions without reacting to them can be terrifying. To sit with our emotions means we have to be in solitude, which is unbearable for many of us. We are too used to having a thought and being triggered by it, experiencing an emotion and reacting to it. For instance, if we feel anxious, we eat or self-medicate in some way. If we feel angry, we experience an urge to vent or even explode at someone. Sitting and watching our thoughts and feelings in stillness may seem pointless to us, but it's by doing precisely this that the core lessons of consciousness are learned. By silently witnessing our thoughts and feelings, we learn to accept them as they are, allowing them to rise and fall within us without resisting them or reacting to them.

As you learn to be with your emotions, they will no longer overwhelm you. In the full acceptance of surrender, which is of a quite different character from mere resignation, you come to see that pain is simply pain, nothing more and nothing less. Yes, pain is painful— it's meant to be. However, when you don't fuel your pain by either resisting or reacting, but sit with it, it transforms itself into wisdom. Your wisdom will increase in line with your capacity for embracing all of your feelings, whatever their nature. Along with increased wisdom comes a greater capacity for compassion.

When we learn to accept the whole of our experience—the fact that situations simply will not run to plan at times, but have their own will—we begin to dance with life. As our children observe us in the dance, they also learn that feeling all we are feeling is the way we grow. They learn to transcend their fear of emotions that are uncomfortable and even painful, so that no part of their being is squelched.

HOW TO HANDLE YOUR CHILD'S PAIN

When our children are hurt either physically or psychologically, it can be unbearable for parents. In the case of emotional hurt, we want to rescue them, which is partly driven by our own helplessness at not being able to assuage their pain. We call the principal, yell at the teacher, complain to the parent of the child who dared to hurt them, not realizing that this solidifies their pain. It also fosters an inability to tolerate pain, both their own and that of others.

If we want our children to master their emotions, we have to teach them to surrender to what they are experiencing. This isn't the same as getting sucked into our emotions or reacting. Surrender means we first accept whatever emotional state we are in. Thus we encourage our children to experience their feelings. We invite them to open a space up to allow the pain already present *in* them to have a presence *in the room*.

An example of what happens to a child when we don't allow our children's pain to have a presence is an eight-year-old, slightly overweight little girl with thick glasses, who was often teased or ostracized by her classmates. Acutely conscious of her looks, she tried hard to fit in by convincing her mother to buy her the latest clothes, bags, and shoes. Her mother, a fashionable young woman, was only too ready to indulge her. On those days this little girl came home and cried in her room for long periods, often refusing to eat or do her homework, her mother couldn't bear it. She felt shame herself for her daughter's physical appearance, which motivated her to buy her daughter a treadmill and hire a nutritionist, pushing her to exercise and eat fewer calories. She took her for regular hairdos and bought her contact lenses. Calling the school, she demanded a meeting with the teachers, asking that her daughter no longer be ostracized by her peers. Along with hiring a therapist to help them both cope, she started taking pills to calm her anxiety.

This mother's inability to handle her child's pain, let alone to help her child handle her own pain, denied this little girl the opportunity to feel her emotions. Instead of being allowed to feel hurt and disenfranchised, she was made to believe that if she changed her outer appearance enough, her peers would accept her. In this way, she was learning that painful emotions are too painful to deal with and need to be swept under the rug, or better still camouflaged by various forms of "doing," such as blaming others or fixing her outer appearance. Because all effort was directed to squelching her pain and disguising it, with no effort made to sit with it, the daughter was incorrectly coming to believe that her external persona was more valid than her inner world of feelings. Of course, she most desperately needed the tools to handle rejection.

When our children are permitted to feel their feelings, they are able to release them amazingly quickly. They come out of the pain understanding that pain is just another sensation. The anticipation of the pain is often more intolerable than the actual pain. When our children experience their pain *in its pure form,* without fueling it with resistance or coloring it with a reaction, the pain transforms itself into wisdom and perspective.

Once their emotions have been processed, children feel no need to hold onto them long after they have passed in the way adults tend to do. They intuitively know that, like the ebb and flow of the ocean, pain comes in waves—and just as it comes, it also leaves. The reason we adults feel like it stays forever is that our thoughts have become embroiled in it based on a vestige from the past. It's in the mind that the pain continues to exist, not in the actual situation. This is because we don't let go.

Part of our problem is that we are unused to handling pain alone. We would much rather project our pain onto others, roping them into our emotional drama through guilt, blame, or anger. Or we resort to an unhealthy habit, perhaps overindulging in food, alcohol, working out, drugs, or medication. In these and other ways, we seek to manage our pain by channeling it externally, which in the long run perpetuates it. The antidote is to *sit with* ourselves and become a witness to our pain, knowing well that the pain originates from our attachment to our ego.

Once our children learn to accept pain as a natural and inevitable part of life, they don't fear it so much, but simply acknowledge, "I'm in pain right now." Instead of intellectualizing about it, judging it, or resisting it, they sit with it. We teach them this by sitting with them when they are young. If they need to talk, they will talk, and all that's required from us is the acknowledgment of a nod, or a statement such as, "I see." There's no need for logic, cheerleading, or hurrying through the experience. Just allow it a space in the house.

Also, if pain stays a while, we make it a matter-of-fact experience, keeping all drama out of it. Perhaps we might talk about it in terms of "a thing," with colors, different appetites, and moods. Above all, we don't aspire that our child become "happy" despite their pain. Rather, we aspire that they be *authentic*.

Take One Step at a Time

Becoming nonreactive starts with awareness that what we have until now considered "just the way we are" is in fact not at all who we really are, but the product of unconsciousness. The process of losing our reactivity accelerates as our awareness deepens. Perhaps we don't stop yelling at our children right away, though now we yell for eight minutes rather than ten. This is because, part way through our yelling, we suddenly realize how unconsciously we are behaving and catch ourselves.

Maybe we still become anxious over something our child does, but instead of generating intense mental agitation that results in an entire day of emotional drama, we are able to calm ourselves after an hour or so, drop our reactivity, and sit in our anxiety simply watching it.

When a parent tells me they are upset that they lost control of their emotions in front of their child, they expect me to judge or guilt-trip them. Instead, I congratulate them. I say, "Now we know how your unconscious looks, which is an important step forward." It is indeed an important step forward, because most people in the world have no clue that their reactivity is a manifestation of unconsciousness. To realize this about ourselves is a huge breakthrough.

It's vital to accept unequivocally that we are going to unleash our unconsciousness from time to time. The conscious parent knows how to use the emergence of their unconsciousness in a manner that's ultimately healing. They know how to recognize a reaction, albeit after the fact. They aren't afraid to confront their unconsciousness. They live by the dictate, "I expect to be triggered, entangled, overwhelmed, and to engage in egoic parenting at times. However, I will use the lessons embedded in these occasions to evolve as a person and to help my children evolve as well."

As parents, we are often forced to react to our children with blinding speed, following our gut instincts, often not pausing for reflection before choosing our response. Before we know it, we have escalated a particular dynamic and within no time find ourselves caught in a negative equation with our children.

I once worked with a single father, Peter, who was having a particularly hard time with his fifteen-year-old son, Andrew. Their relationship was reaching a state of dysfunction. Andrew was manifesting the classic symptoms of a rebellious teenager—isolating himself from his father, only interested in hanging out with his friends, chatting via his computer until late at night, not doing his homework, failing his classes, and using marijuana.

Peter was enraged. They had shared a close relationship when Andrew was younger, but for the past few years their only engagements had been tense arguments. At one point, Andrew had asked to live with his grandparents in another state, which Peter didn't support because the grandparents were elderly. Day after day, father and son locked horns over household duties and homework, with Andrew saying he had already completed his homework even though he hadn't touched it.

During one particularly upsetting evening, Peter found himself so worked up that he threatened never to talk to his son again, then stormed out of the house. As he walked around his property in an agitated state, he called me to report, "I'm at my wits' end. This boy absolutely refuses to respect me or my ways. Here I am, setting everything aside to be with him, and all he does is be obnoxious and defiant. He puts forth no effort at all. I'm sick and tired of the way he treats me. If he doesn't want to be my son, so be it. I won't put out any effort either. I can be just as uncaring as he is. From today, I will no longer be loving or patient. I'm washing my hands of him."

Unable to see that he was in a highly reactive state of mind, Peter became even more volatile. Ending our phone conversation, he marched into his son's room, unplugged the computer, then threw it on the floor. When Andrew protested, Peter slapped him across his face and told him he regretted Andrew had ever been born.

Peter was going through what countless parents of teenagers endure. Although it appears that a parent may be justified in their reactions at such a time, we tend to forget that this dynamic was set in motion years ago. What started out as a battle of wills and a quest for control had escalated into a traumatic relationship for both.

Inextricably entangled in his own emotional drama, his own interpretation of his son's motivations, and his own feeling of a lack of power, Peter allowed himself to become so deeply triggered that he lost all control of himself. When we react out of our own need for power and control like this, we fail to ask, "What does my child need from me that I have been unable to give so far?" This father had long stopped listening for what his son truly needed from him.

It's possible Andrew reminded Peter of his own childhood, mirroring inadequacies he had worked hard to overcome over the years. Perhaps he was so wedded to the script of control that he couldn't bear his son to deviate from his expectations in the slightest way. Maybe he was so invested in the idea of perfection that he couldn't stand the fact Andrew was flawed. It's also likely that Peter saw his son as a reflection of the kind of parent he was, an issue doubtless laced with guilt for the fact he had divorced Andrew's mother years ago. Whatever the underlying motivation, it was clear that Peter had taken this personally, which had triggered an egoic reaction. Andrew, as all children do, picked up on the fact that his father had lost connection with his own authentic self.

Peter had created many negative interpretations around his son's acting out, all of which were personal. These interpretations involved such judgments as "my son doesn't care about my feelings," "my son is disrespectful of me," or, "my son is purposely being defiant." None of these interpretations served to improve either Peter's or Andrew's state of mind, yet this is how most of us react to situations we are uncomfortable with.

Whenever we make personalized interpretations of others' behavior, we risk plunging ourselves into cauldrons of roiling emotion. Were we to make depersonalized, neutral interpretations, we wouldn't suffer the consequences of negative emotions. Peter's interpretations evinced no neutrality, let alone curiosity about his son's behavior. None of his interpretations suggested "my son is in pain and needs help," "my son is crying out for help and doesn't know how to behave right now," or "my son has need of my patience as he passes through this difficult phase of identity-confusion." Instead, the interpretations Peter put on Andrew's behavior generated intense mental resistance to this behavior, rendering him incapable of responding in an *as is* manner. To respond *as is* engenders not just acceptance, but indeed reverence for the individual's unique path.

Interpretation happens in a split second, as we decide that something is either in tune with our ego attachments or isn't. As long as life mirrors our ego attachments, we are fine. The moment it dares to contradict our deeply held assumptions of how things are supposed to be, we lose our centeredness.

All dysfunction involves our deeply personalized interpretations of the events around us. The sad byproduct of this is that our children are left feeling they are the cause of our moods, which results in guilt and can lead to a sense of worthlessness. From this place, they then react back at us. It's crucial to recognize that the seeds of this equation lie in the initial judgment we make in response to their behavior.

Our children don't *intend* to trigger us; they are just being who they are. Being triggered is an inevitable part of any relationship, so there's no room for blaming ourselves or anyone else. However, we are responsible for examining our unconscious reactions so that we can curtail them. The reason we enter a state of blinding unconsciousness is that we have an unresolved emotional charge, which emerges in response to our children simply being children.

Being triggered is intimately connected to the life scripts we act out and the roles we play. For instance, perhaps we tell ourselves, "I deserve more respect." If we interpret our children's behavior as lacking respect, it's an indication we have a grandiose sense of entitlement. For someone to show us insufficient respect automatically triggers our narcissistic indignation. We tell ourselves, "I'm better than this. How dare this person behave like this toward me?"

If only we understood the power of our interpretations.

Just how distorted our view of things can be can be seen in the case of a beautiful young woman who was estranged from her family for over fifteen years. When the family finally decided to hold a reunion, the night before the reunion the young woman had a vivid dream in which she was watching her family engage in a duel, which naturally paralyzed her with fear. As the duel proceeded, she edged closer. Suddenly, she realized they weren't holding swords at all. "Oh," she thought, "they're not dueling—they're dancing!" When she awakened from her dream, she knew she had received a message from the part of her that longed for reconciliation. In that moment, she recognized she could choose how she interpreted her reality. The family reunion turned out to be a pivotal moment of healing that advanced her spiritual journey.

The first error on our path to ego activation is that of creating a deeply personalized interpretation of events. With our children, our immediate interpretation when they fail to follow "the plan" is that it's *they* who are wrong, and that they are doing what they are doing because they disregard our authority. We can't see that it's our *interpretation* that sets the stage for dysfunction. Neither can we see that the real issue is that we feel threatened in some way.

When we engage in this kind of drama, it's because we refuse to meet reality *as reality is*. We impose our past onto our present situation, which generates enormous anxiety in us, playing into our worst fears. Our manic state then causes us to rush to judgment, which gives us the feeling that at least we are *doing something,* as we make decisions that are detrimental to everyone concerned. So it is that we generate drama by confusing being *manic* with being "purposeful."

Let's return to Peter and his son Andrew for a moment. What if Peter had been able to meet his son's rebellion with an *as is* approach? Without imposing any sort of judgment or interpretation on his son's behavior, and—most critical of all, leaving *himself* out of the equation—he would diminish his rigidity, thereby freeing up much internal space and allowing him the flexibility to be creative in his response to his son. When we open up internal space, we discover new ways of encountering our children, which is refreshingly different from repeatedly engaging in the same battles. Coming from a need to "do" something divorces us from our flow of creativity. Life is then parent pitted against child, a battle for the supremacy of egos.

Only to the degree we live in a state of *being* are we able to approach circumstances in our life with openness and surrender. Freed from our stifling judgments, we are then able to interact with the actual situation before us in the manner each situation requires, rather than coming from unconscious projections. The more we hone this ability to meet life in a neutral state, without attributing "goodness" or "badness" to what we are encountering, but simply accepting its *as-is-ness,* the less our need to interpret every dynamic as if it were about *us.* Our children can then have their tantrums without triggering us, and we can correct their behavior without dumping on them our own residual resentment, guilt, fear, or distrust.

When the individuals in our life are allowed to possess their own emotions without everyone tripping over everyone else's emotional drama, we begin to fully accept all our emotions, knowing that they are *simply emotions.* Now we view life with its full spectrum of colors. We experience it without needing to narrow it into the limiting categories of "good" versus "bad," or "me" as opposed to "you." Life is too rich, too complex to be categorized. People are inherently unquantifiable.

What It Takes to Tame Your Anxiety

As we saw in Peter's case, he quickly reached a stage of anxiety and internal tension. He carried within his bones a tightness that his son naturally picked up on, gearing himself for battle as well.

Anxiety is our way of reacting to our mental judgments. Recognizing when we are anxious is one of the most important things we can do for ourselves in terms of the preservation of our relationships.

When we experience anxiety, something from deep within us has been triggered. If we are aware from moment to moment, we ask ourselves, "Why am I being triggered right now?" After asking this question, we remain in a state of openness, being careful not to project our anxiety onto others. The anxiety is coming from something unresolved within us and would continue to exist regardless of whether the triggering person or event was present. If one set of circumstances didn't trigger us, something else would.

Anxiety is a natural emotion there's no escaping. Rather than seeing it as something we need to control, we are asked to accept that it's natural and quietly witness it. Sitting in our anxiety, simply allowing it to exist, is a core practice of this journey. If we don't learn to just witness it, we are likely to become overwhelmed by our internal state and blindly react to it. We are then primed to engage others in a reactive, perhaps volatile manner—or, conversely, sink into depression. Either way, we inevitably leave a trail of unnecessary consequences. Only through awareness do we neither split off from our anxiety nor dump it on another.

Life happens, pure and simple. No matter how we try to manage it, it has a force beyond logic or coherence. When we swim in the ocean, we allow the water to move our body. We don't protest, "How dare this wave be so high? It should be low." We accept that we have no dominion over the ocean. Indeed, we find the unpredictability of the waves exhilarating. Why, then, when it comes to relationships or events in our life are we unable to simply go with them? Life isn't inherently good or bad, but like the waves of the ocean just *is*. The only way to live life is to enter into its *as-is-ness*. If we are able to sit with the *as-is-ness*, then our anxiety will wash over us. It's when we react that we turn it into a tsunami.

Peter's anxiety caused him to engage in daily confrontation with his son. Such confrontation escalated into fights, then into a truly regrettable and avoidable event. Had Peter engaged Andrew in a neutral state of mind, flowing with the *as is* nature of the situation, seeking an authentic connection with his son, Andrew would have responded differently. This would have placed him in a position to have a measure of influence, perhaps enabling him to mitigate some of his negative behavior. Instead, he left Andrew no choice but to become highly reactive.

No one wins when we come from our unconscious reactive state. Emotional drama can only lead to suffering. So much of our pain is self-created. Unless we learn to break free from our negative inter-pretations, we will forever be mired in one destructive emotional pattern after another.

The good news is that life is a wonderfully willing partner in our journey into a more conscious way of being. It assists us on every level, and all we have to do is open ourselves up and receive. A big plus is that our children are infinitely resilient. As we take this jour-ney, we can be assured that they will grow alongside our growth, even when the road to growth is full of pain. Knowing this allows us to commit ourselves to the journey without hesitation, holding nothing back, trusting that all things work for the wellbeing of both ourselves and our offspring.

CHAPTER 6

LIFE IS WISE

Since the way we parent mirrors who we are, to alter how we go about bringing up our children requires us to understand the way in which our everyday response to situations that arise embodies our worldview.

Ask yourself: How do I react when life doesn't turn out the way I want it to? Do I immediately scold myself, telling myself, "It must be my fault?" Do I take the opposite stance, declaring, "I deserve better; how dare this happen to me!" Do I tell myself, "I'm just unlucky; life is so unfair!" Such reactions reveal that your worldview is based on the belief that life happens *outside* of you—that it is this inexplicable "thing" unleashed by forces beyond your control.

When you think yourself "lucky" or "unlucky," it's because you aren't trained to view life as your spiritual partner on your journey into your authentic being. However, when you go within yourself in search of the emotional lessons life is asking you to learn, everything that happens to you becomes meaningful. Approaching each situation from this mindset, there is no "bad" or "good" luck. All of life's situations serve the purpose of your spiritual evolvement. Realizing this, you no longer resist those things you deem undesirable while craving those you consider agreeable. When you experience everything as a potential teacher, you embrace anything life sends your way. You cease either being at war with life when it presents you with a challenge, or being in love with it when it treats you kindly. Rather, you see both the dark and the light as opportunities for becoming a more conscious human being.

LIFE ITSELF TEACHES US

Whether we believe life is essentially good, or we spend our days waiting for the proverbial other shoe to drop because we see life as out to get us, depends on how we were raised. However, rarely are we raised with the understanding that life is essentially *wise*.

To understand that life is a wise teacher, willing to show us our higher self, revolutionizes how we live and how we parent. We approach everything with an attitude that our circumstances are here to help us come from our higher self. We see life as trustworthy, here to usher us into a deeper self-connection. We also know it's inherently good, a mirror of our own internal state of goodness. This approach recognizes that we are fundamentally interconnected to all that happens in our life, so that we are co-creators of the reality in which we live. Life doesn't happen *to* us, but happens *with* us.

Neither does our children's behavior happen in a void, but is a response to our energy. This means we have much opportunity to influence how our children turn out. While we are quick to teach them to impose negative evaluations on reality, few of us teach them how they can experience reality for what it is. The fact is, children learn how to relate to their experiences from how *we* relate to our own. When they see us constantly reacting to reality, manifesting ongoing anxiety, they learn to embody such a reactive, anxious mindset themselves. As they watch us judge and label every experience, they begin to categorize their own world.

If, instead, they observe us flowing with our reality without tightness or heavy-duty mental activity, they learn to respond to their own life the same way. By modeling an attitude of trust, and approaching life with gracious ease based on this trust, we teach our children to draw wisdom from all of their circumstances, instead of viewing some aspects of life as "good" and others as "bad."

Life is to be *experienced,* not fought against, run from, or engaged halfheartedly. Though we may wish to make changes in the future, to be conscious is to be *with* an experience as it's unfolding, rather than thinking about how we would like to change it. Taking charge of our life so that we alter the quality of our experiences in the future comes *after* an experience.

When we embrace life itself as a wise guide, we dare to entrust ourselves to it completely, free of evaluation, judgment, or analysis. Leaving behind any feeling that life is somehow a threat to us, we commit ourselves to its flow. When we allow ourselves to really *feel* each experience as it happens, then—instead of trying to attach ourselves to it— release it into the flow of the next moment, we free up psychic energy that would otherwise be squandered on resistance and reactivity. This energy is then available for us to bring engaged presence to our relationships, especially with our children. As our children also learn to experience their experiences without the need to "do" anything about them necessarily, they ease into life *as it is.* They see the pleasure in the simplest of experiences and reap the rewards of being fully present in the moment.

So that my daughter learns to own her experiences in their *as is* state instead of wishing them away, I am honest with her about my own feelings about the situations I encounter. If I'm exasperated, I say, "I am exasperated right now." The fact is, I am in a mood at such a moment, and I am *allowed* to be in a mood, though not to take it out on others. Hence I *acknowledge* my mood, but I don't *react* to the situation, don't fight it—don't act out the feeling. Rather, I embrace all of my feelings. As I do so, I find myself spontaneously shifting into full acceptance of the situation.

Similarly, when we are in a traffic jam, I say, "We are in a traffic jam right now." I desist from labeling such experiences as "good" or "bad," refusing to impose on these present experiences clutter from my past, let alone my imagination of how the future ought to be. The point is to cease trying to bend reality to our will.

As our sense of who we are deepens, our inner being proves spacious enough to include everything life sends our way.

IS IT POSSIBLE TO *TRUST* LIFE?

Trusting that life's messengers come to us with secrets to reveal about who we really are, we embrace our children for the messages *they* hold for us. We don't judge, blame, or shun them for shining the light on our unconsciousness, but learn from them in humility and with gratitude.

In precisely the package our children arrive in our life, they are here to teach us how to release our ego and embrace our authentic being. I think of Elizabeth and Matthew, who have two sons, and how the package in which each of these boys came revealed itself to Elizabeth as life's wise gift. She was able to see that to embrace her sons just as they are contained a powerful lesson for her.

Elizabeth and Matthew's older son, David, is a star basketball player, an A student, generous and compassionate by nature, and most of all a truly wise soul. Things are a little different with their younger son, Deacon. Not so academically astute nor athletically inclined, Deacon is rather sloppy, inattentive, forgetful, and sluggish. Engaging life in a nontraditional manner, he refuses to be pressured by the standard rules of life, preferring to set his own rules. Unconcerned about how he looks, what he wears, or how he comes across, he resists competition and success in the material world, preferring to spend his time tending his pets, reading, and tutoring underprivileged children. Seemingly untouched by the numbers on his report card, he regularly fails his classes, declaring that he wants to be an organic farmer or teach in a Third World country. Because he's a dreamer and nontraditional in every sense of the word, he is at times his father's worst nightmare.

If Matthew has a hard time accepting Deacon, he has an even

harder time reconciling the fact his two sons are so different. He feels proud when he's with David, but experiences humiliation and even resentment around Deacon. Categorizing his sons based on how they make his ego feel, he is unable to discover the lessons that are abundantly present for his growth.

Elizabeth, on the other hand, completely "gets it." She sees how David serves to solidify her ego, but how Deacon crumbles it. "Imagine what a horridly egotistical parent I would be if I only had David," she confessed to me. "Thank goodness I have Deacon to remind me to be more accepting of the nontraditional and different."

Your Child Doesn't Need to Earn Your Trust

Because so few really trust the wisdom of life, people tend to project their lack of trust onto their children. Consequently, our society believes that trust has to be earned.

I believe that not only do our children not need to earn our trust, but they need to know that we trust them implicitly because we see them as fundamentally trustworthy. Just by their presence, our children have earned the right to be trusted. To ask them to earn our trust reflects an insecure, power-hungry attitude that's charged with both fear and ego.

To have implicit trust in our children requires that, as parents, *we* display a basic reverence for and trust in life. The degree to which our children feel trusted by us reflects the trust or lack of trust we ourselves have. When we come from the mindset that all of life is wise, and therefore all its manifestations good, we see our children this way. We frame all mistakes as emerging out of a pure place. If this is so, where is there any room not to trust our children? On the other hand, if we are anxious and doubt our ability to transform life's struggles into spiritual gold, no matter how we assure our children that all will be fine, we unconsciously transmit the opposite message.

As parents, we communicate trust or distrust in the subtlest ways.

The questions we ask our children, the lectures we give them, and the unsolicited advice we dish out all convey trust or distrust. For instance, when we repeatedly ask our children how they are doing, believing they must be going through something or other, we unwittingly communicate our own anxiety and hence our mistrust of life. By constantly checking on our children, hovering over them, or needing to know everything about their world, we communicate a sense of uncertainty, which undermines their basic trust in themselves. The less we check in on them in an anxious manner, the more we communicate the message that we don't need to check in with them all the time because we know they are fully capable of taking care of themselves and will ask for help when they need it.

When we make decisions for our children without giving them the chance to chart their own course, we communicate to them our own powerfulness and their helplessness, which fosters a distrust of themselves. If, instead, we solicit their ideas and show respect for these ideas, even if we can't always incorporate them into our plans, we communicate a deep reverence for their ability to contribute to the discussion at hand. Our children can sense when we have a true, deep respect for their opinions and choices. It's vital we recognize that, though they may only be little, they have a valid opinion that we respect and always take into consideration. As our children see that their presence is both meaningful and important to us, they learn to trust their inner voice.

We promote trust whenever we encourage our children to speak up and be heard. They learn to trust themselves as we tell them, "I admire the way you put your thoughts together," and assure them, "I trust you to do the right thing." Should they happen to make an unwise choice, we don't allow this to cause us to indicate a lack of trust in them, but simply tell them in a matter of fact manner, "You made this decision and now you are learning from it." Lack of trust doesn't enter the equation.

I assure my daughter, "You will always be okay, no matter what circumstance you find yourself in, because this is the sort of person you are." Above all, I communicate a trust in life's ability to take care of us spiritually. Once we look at life as an incubator of consciousness, what is there not to trust?

When our children sense our respect for their ability to lead the way, this empowers them beyond measure. As they learn they are worthy of holding our trust, this will come to mean the world to them. They will naturally rise to our trust in them.

How You Draw Many of Your Circumstances to You

Life in and of itself is neither good nor bad, but neutral. However, each of us holds the power to choose the manner in which we interpret our experiences, which greatly affects the nature of these experiences.

Until we become aware, our interpretation of each of the things that happen to us is made all but automatically based on ingrained patterns. We label our world according to how we *perceive* what's happening, not because it's really so. For instance, if we feel pain, we tend to label our reality "bad." In so doing, we are *choosing* how we feel about our pain—such as whether to feel sad, angry, lost, or unloved. Our choices are the result of the years of conditioning we received as children.

When you operate from the worldview that life, in the precise pattern it unfolds before you, holds transformational lessons for you, you no longer shun experiences. Instead, you invite them in, sensing you in some way drew these lessons to you out of your innate longing to develop on a spiritual level.

When people hear that they might have invited what they see as a negative experience into their life, they are often indignant: "Does this mean I caused the cancer in my body, or the accident my child was in? How am I responsible for an earthquake or the downturn in the economy? I can't possibly be the cause of such seemingly random events." Many are confused by this.

In my own case, my confusion cleared up when I realized there are two *kinds* of events: personal, and impersonal. Personal events include marriage, parenthood, work, friendships, and the like. Through engagement with another, it's fairly obvious how we co-create the reality we experience. Personal events also include such elements as our eating habits, exercise choices, attitudes, and motivational level. Though we might like to live under the illusion that things just "happen," we help create our reality just by the fact of our presence in the dynamic.

Impersonal events are a little different and tend to feel like they really do just happen to us. I'm thinking of aspects of life such as the economy, our supervisor's bad mood, the neighbor's noisy dog, a car accident in which we weren't at fault, a flood, or a tornado. Such events often seem random and unpredictable, as if they can pounce on us without a moment's notice—and certainly without our conscious approval.

If we are in denial of life's potential craziness, imagining that somehow our resistance will magically keep things from happening to us, we will find ourselves in a cauldron of frustration, if not despair. When such events occur, it is *our response* to such random occurrences that's key. This is where we get to make a choice and give our consent.

There are times when life feels unbearably tenuous and highly unpredictable, often leaving us with a feeling of resentment, which may lead us to adopt an attitude of resignation. However, the fact there's a random element to reality isn't a reason for resignation. We do ourselves no favor by embracing a sense of fatalism, assuming no control over our life.

Neither is life's capriciousness a cause for paranoia, so that we are always wondering when we will be struck down by its extremes. On the contrary, we approach everything with full acceptance and a heightened appreciation for each moment. Accepting life doesn't mean lying down in defeat, but vigorously accepting life's *as is* nature. Accepting life *as is* requires awareness of all that is before us, then choosing how we respond. Then, and only then, do we experience the consciousness to affect the circumstances we find ourselves in.

Living life with awareness means being able to dance the fine line between assuming full ownership over our psychological health and energetic space, while always knowing things happen that may throw us off our center. It's this constant interplay between taking charge and surrendering that defines conscious living. We are aware that traumatic events occur, but we know they don't have to determine our reaction. We are all subject to life's unpredictable and sometimes seemingly cruel nature, but it's our choice whether we live as a victim.

We all want to know *why* things happen to us, somehow imagining that if we just knew the reason, we would feel more secure. The bitter medicine we all must swallow is that we don't know the "why." We could postulate that events happen due to a confluence of old karma, or we might attribute them to chance. The fact is, things happen, and we may never know the reason—if there even is a reason in many cases.

Though we may not be able to say why things happen, there are aspects we can address that are more personal and, ultimately, more relevant. For instance, we might ask, "How can this circumstance I am now in foster my growth? What am I resisting? What do I need to surrender to in order to grow? What purpose does this upheaval in my life serve for myself and others?" Such questions have the power to transform a "bad" event into a growth-inducing experience, whereby we mine emotional gold from what seems so negative. Just the asking of these types of questions has the potential to shift us from blame to ownership and authorship. Such questions empower us to transcend a sense that life has victimized us.

The choice of question differentiates a victim from a survivor. The victim whines, "Why did life give me this struggle?" The survivor asks, "How can I use this struggle for higher evolvement?" It's a matter of not allowing our identity to be defined by the events in our life. Instead, we understand that it's how we either respond creatively or react negatively that defines our fate.

You Can Break Free of Your Unconsciousness

There is a helpful technique for watching our thoughts and emotions. Writing in a journal can assist us in becoming aware of what's going on inside us, and how we ascribe unwarranted interpretations to things, because it enables us to create a little distance between our inner being and our thoughts.

For such journaling to be really effective, it's beneficial to use an "automatic" approach to writing, which means we don't think about what we are going to put on paper, but simply record our stream of consciousness. Setting aside time each day, we write in a free, associative manner.

Such writing loosens the hold our ego has on us. As we see our thoughts laid out on paper, we are able to separate our identity from them. We realize, "These are just thoughts." Because they are just thoughts, we don't need to feel overwhelmed by them any longer. Through the rigorous practice of writing every day, we learn to allow our thoughts and the emotions that often accompany them simply to exist, not making more of them than they are. By so doing, we dip into the stillness that lies beneath them, where our true being resides.

Awareness can also be fostered by setting aside a period each day to sit in silence and solitude, with our eyes closed and our attention on our breathing. All that's required is to notice the out-breath and the in-breath, either as the breath enters and leaves our nostrils, or as it enters and leaves our chest area. Bringing awareness to our breath allows us to come into the here and now. By focusing on the breath, we observe that, like our breath, our thoughts and emotions are fleeting. We accept that they are *just* thoughts and emotions. Because thoughts and emotions are by nature impermanent, we have no obligation to hold onto them but can let go of them because they aren't our identity. This simple practice of putting a little space around our thoughts and emotions enables us to experience them with a detachment that frees us from the compulsion to act them out. We sit with our thoughts and emotions in a nonreactive manner, having no need to dump them onto our external reality. In this way, we free ourselves and others from the emotional entanglement that comes from being in the clutches of our past conditioning.

How does this affect our children? Imagine that, as a parent, the thought occurs to you, "My child isn't listening to me." Or you begin to feel, "I'm being disrespected." Instead of interpreting this to mean, "My child is disrespectful," or, "I am a hopeless parent," you sit with your thoughts and emotions. "Why am I feeling triggered?" you ask yourself. Perhaps you come to the realization that you feel helpless in some area of your own life that's unrelated to parenthood, and your child is simply activating this feeling. Or maybe you realize that your child is triggering the feelings of helplessness and powerlessness you felt when you were a child. By becoming aware of these feelings, you don't act out what you are thinking or feeling with your child, but instead respond from a more centered place. Even if your child needs to be corrected, the way in which this is delivered is less blind, less personalized.

By learning not to react to your every thought or emotion, you demonstrate to your children that their thoughts and emotions don't have to call forth a reaction, but can be used to teach you something about yourself. As your children discover the power of sitting with their thoughts and feelings, their own inner space opens up so that they create a connection to their true being.

From watching our own thoughts and emotions as they arise and subside, we move into watching the world around us. This entails learning to see that reality simply *is*, which enables us to respond to it from a neutral state. After all, reality *is* neutral, allowing us to interpret it any way we choose.

As we focus on our breath, we ask ourselves, "What about reality's *as-is-ness* am I unwilling to accept and surrender to?" When we check our internal thermometer before we act, we empower ourselves to come from a conscious place. We allow reality to unfold because we no longer experience a pressing urge to impose our "I" onto it. In such a state, we are free simply to experience.

When we cannot deal with life in its *as is* form, we are likely to engage either in behavior that harms others, such as control or anger, or in self-defeating behavior such as overeating, overworking, over-exercising, drinking too much, self-medicating, or using illicit drugs, while we wait for things to reach their "should be" form.

By learning to respond to life *as it is*, the most ordinary of moments become teaching tools that show our children how they can detach from the force of their own willful ego. For instance, if we break an egg by mistake, we say, "Ah, the egg broke. I realize I wasn't paying attention." If we are sitting in traffic, instead of complaining, we say, "This happens sometimes and we have no control over it. So let's enjoy the time by playing a game, singing a song, or just resting." In this way, our children learn not to feel threatened by the downturns of life. They discover that not only is it possible to sit in this space without feeling anxious or emotionally reactive, but it can also be an enjoyable place to be.

Having said this, I want to be clear—as I emphasized earlier—that I'm not talking about approaching life in an "I'm so happy" manner, which isn't at all the same as being real. I'm talking about accepting that a situation *is what it is*. We then discover how we can best use the situation for everyone's benefit. The fact is that some-times life presents us with unfair situations.

A case in point is the day I took my three-year-old to the doctor's office for an appointment scheduled for 7:30 AM. When we had to wait two and a half hours before the doctor saw us—a long time for a three-year-old—I spoke up. The doctor apologized profusely and promised he would ensure this wouldn't happen again. It was bene-ficial for my daughter to observe me speaking from a feeling place.

To respond from a neutral state of mind doesn't necessarily mean our response is neutral. Rather, our response has an *as is* quality that's tailored to an *as is* situation, untainted by heavy-duty past conditioning. For this reason, it's easy to let the matter go once we have truly resolved our emotions in the here and now.

How can we differentiate between when it's appropriate to speak up and when it isn't? The difference lies in the place from which we are coming. Are we coming from an unconscious egoic state, so that we impose our past conditioning onto our present reality? Or are we making an authentic present-moment response that's fitting for the situation before us?

My comments to the doctor weren't based on an unconscious past, but on a situation that crossed the boundaries of propriety and fairness. I was honoring my limits. Because I wasn't blindly triggered based on my past, I was able to speak softly yet firmly. I neither felt personally injured nor had an urge to hurt the other. After I had expressed my feelings, I was able to let the matter go. When we either experience a compulsion to change another's mind, or allow them to trigger us into a state of overwhelming emotion, we are no longer conscious but in ego.

Learning to detach from our thoughts and emotions, and consequently from our external circumstances, can be disconcerting. We wonder, "Does this mean I'll stop loving others? Will I no longer care about anything? Am I going to become cold and unfeeling?" To find ourselves bereft of emotional drama is initially perturbing. Becoming comfortable with this new state of internal affairs, getting used to living a drama-free life, requires us to pass through a period when life may feel empty. This is because we feel like we are losing a sense of connection to the real world. In due course, we realize we aren't losing anything, but instead increasing our connection with the whole of reality.

When our children observe that we are less attached to emotional drama, they follow suit. They discover that thoughts and emotions are simply thoughts and emotions.

IT'S ALL IN THE INTERPRETATION WE GIVE IT

Let me share with you an example of how the way we frame our experience makes a world of difference. A sixteen-year-old suffers from autism-related difficulties, which are accompanied by acute panic attacks and paranoia. His panic attacks make him so anxious, he finds it extremely difficult to trust anyone, which leads him to either act out or withdraw. Consequently, he has a hard time socializing with his peers, and even with leaving the house. Taking him out is a huge ordeal as the panic attacks strike anytime, anyplace, while leaving him alone in the house is never an option either. On a good day, he can be fun, easygoing, relaxed; unfortunately such days are rare.

This teen's parents are the most dedicated parents I have ever met, having altered their entire life to work around their son's disability. Though they are with him 24/7, not once in the two years I have worked with him have they lost their patience or shown any sign of frustration. I asked the father, "How are you so patient, loving, and giving? Don't you ever want to rail and scream at the world and yell, 'This isn't fair?'"

He looked at me, puzzled. "What isn't fair?" he asked. "That my son is who he is? He is my child, and I accept him completely. If he is difficult, this means I need to be more patient. If he is scared, I need to be gentler. If he is anxious, I need to be more comforting. I give him what he needs from me because this is what I'm here to do."

Here was a man who had chosen to live his destiny willingly. Not in any way playing the role of a victim, he had made the choice not just to survive, but to thrive in the face of this challenge. Fully understanding his responsibility and role in the dynamic, he knows that his approach to his son has the power to define their joint reality. As a full-on participant, he regards his life as an adventure, no matter what the odds.

Winners in the adventure of life don't focus on *why* life presents itself in the ways it does, but instead focus on their desire for growth. Accepting reality as it is, they realize that life is like the ocean, with waters that are sometimes calm and other times tumultuous, and contour themselves to go with the flow. Assessing the energy around them, they surrender their agenda of what their life "should" look like and respond to their situation in its *as is* form with emotional flexibility rather than rigidity. Foregoing intellectualization, they come from a place of intuition, with a wisdom that recognizes one can never know the "why." Instead of seeking to impose their will onto reality, they learn from it, approaching everything that happens to them as students instead of as victims. They know that it's often when reality works in the opposite way from our decrees that the jewels of courage and hope sparkle. They know how to frame their experiences within a philosophy that values failure as life's biggest teacher. When everything is viewed as an opportunity for growth, the "good" and the "bad" form two sides of the single coin of self-evolvement.

When we frame our experiences in a manner that allows us to extrapolate higher meaning from them, we view all of life as a wise teacher. Even the worst of life's offerings are regarded as a call to become our highest self, so that our weakest of moments become our most transformational.

If we look at life as a wise guide, every circumstance is replete with opportunities to teach our children giving, receiving, humility, patience, courage, and love. We just have to be willing to identify these opportunities amid the grime. When we teach our children to find the emotional lesson behind every experience, we teach them to own their life with zest. No longer do they need to see themselves as victims. Instead, they are able to hold onto a sense of empowerment.

When we are confronted by situations or relationships we least expect and may not even want, we have a chance to activate our ability to create meaning and purpose. Often this requires a leap of faith that what's happening is for our benefit. In any situation, there may be hidden opportunities to make new discoveries about ourselves and our world. There are certainly opportunities to become more patient, humble, and compassionate. For this reason, we ought to explore with our children questions such as:

How has this experience opened you up?

What needs to happen for you to surrender
to this experience?

Is there something you are resisting, or something of
which you are afraid?

What will you carry from this experience into your
next experience?

When our children watch us process our experiences and deal
with life as if it were full of rich meaning and opportunities for
growth, this is how they will approach their own challenges. They
will learn to befriend their experiences and trust that these experiences exist to take them closer to authenticity.

Approaching parenting with such a philosophy, we impart to our
children the assurance that life isn't to be feared and resisted, but
that it possesses infinite wisdom in all its shapes, colors, and dimen-
sions. We teach our children to embrace situations without reacting
to them, fighting with them. In this way they learn to become peaceful co-creators of their life, viewing it as a partner to grow with, not
as an enemy to conquer.

Life is here to be our teacher, our guide, and our spiritual partner. We are here to uncover our unconsciousness and integrate it.
For this purpose, our past reappears in our present. Our ability to
release ourselves from its shadows will determine how free our future
will be. Every experience appears before us to teach us more about
ourselves. When reality doesn't go according to our expectations,
instead of reacting, we tell ourselves, "Surrender, let go, detach,
examine the expectation." Our thoughts and emotions are a reflection
of our inner state and require observation, not reaction.

We forge a connection with our inner being on a moment-by-
moment basis. Unafraid to sit in our solitude, we invoke inner stillness.
This enables us to pause before we interpret something and react to our
interpretation. Sometimes reality presents us lessons in harsh and
severe ways, but we embrace them calmly and trustingly, knowing that
such times have come to teach us what we need in order to grow. Instead
of choosing what we like or don't like about our reality, we are grateful
to all of reality for being a wise guide, even its challenging aspects.

When we can see in others what we see in ourselves, we realize we are all connected and all desire greater connection. We are therefore humble before all, knowing we are no more and no less than others, and that when we serve others, we serve our inner being. Indeed, the best way we can give to others is by entering into our inner condition and integrating it.

The most valuable lesson you can teach your children is that life is about the unfolding of the conscious self. When you show them that the key to fulfillment lies in embracing the wise situations life places us in, you give them a great gift. With this perspective, they will forever befriend life, knowing that it seeks to be of benign service to them, even when its lessons may seem severe. As they come to see that they can transform each experience into one that increases their self-awareness and promotes their growth, they learn to regard life as their friend, an intimate partner on their journey to self-awareness.

CHAPTER 7

THE CHALLENGE OF A LIFETIME
Infancy and the "Terrible Two's"

In the dance of parent and child, we affect each other in complex ways, shaping each other and imprinting ourselves on each other's psyche. For this reason, each of the developmental stages our children go through provide abundant space for the evolvement of both parent and child, offering us gateways to a more conscious experience of ourselves as parents.

Visits to the pediatrician's office don't generally involve conversation about the inner connection between parent and child. Neither do they focus on the imperative we have as parents to become aware of our unconsciousness and how it affects our children's development much more than how early they learn to read and write or which school they attend. Even more in the shadows is the fact that just as there are physical and intellectual milestones we want our children to attain, the parenting journey presents us as parents with spiritual milestones we too need to attain.

The emotional and spiritual significance of each stage of our child's development is often obscured by what we think of as more "practical" concerns, such as nutrition, sleep patterns, and behavioral issues. For this reason, to identify these milestones our eyes need to be trained to look at each developmental stage in a manner that transcends the physical and cognitive, instead going to the heart of the matter—the spiritual relationship between parent and child.

The transition to parenthood is complex, requiring us to surrender to an irrevocable loss of our identity as we have thus far known it. To create the internal space required to embrace the tending of a new spirit, the pillars of our old lifestyle have to crumble. Who we were before becoming a parent doesn't and cannot exist with the same ferocity. Once children enter our life, their impact is indelible, and we are required to reinvent ourselves in response.

If we view the various stages of our child's development not only through the lens of how our children are progressing according to a scale or comparison with others, but as an opportunity for spiritual and emotional growth for both them *and* us, we begin walking this path as spiritual partners, finding kinship in what each offers the other.

We will look at the spiritual lessons of raising our children in two sections. In this chapter, we'll examine the years up until they go to school. Then in the next chapter, we'll address the school years.

THE LESSONS OF INFANCY FOR THE PARENT

No sooner do we arrive at our front door with our bundle of joy than our lifestyle changes. Just the fact that we feed our infants on a schedule not subject to our circadian rhythms is a huge shift. As we move from being individuals in our own right to being in the service of our infant, our boundaries elasticize beyond anything we could have imagined. To draw upon our capacity to love and serve another is both deeply moving and a shock.

In the infant stage, the primary spiritual agenda revolves around oneness and togetherness. This is when the deepest bonding takes place. The child and parent infuse each other, rhythmically synchronizing their body and mind to the other. The child's breath, cries, and gaze merge with the parent's original biological and psychological signature, creating a new template. The parent's mindset, including fantasies, fears, inhibitions, and courage, are registered in the infant's body at a cellular level. Everything is stored, enriching the blood, making the skin smoother, strengthening the muscles.

The way a child's parents burst into laughter or smile only hesitatingly, welcome the rain on their face or run for cover, embrace their fears or cower in shame, invite challenges or succumb to doubt, panic or calmly soothe their infant when it cries—all of this is noted by the infant, who is soaking it in. This is where the bricks and mortar of the infant's sense of self are laid, and where the parent first forms its identity as a caregiver and nurturer.

Infancy is about psychological security and physical comfort. The child learns the first vowels of its spiritual language and inscribes the first imprint of its spiritual signature. How its parents or early caregivers respond to its mainly physical needs and create a sense of oneness sets the stage for all later parent-child dynamics. Not yet possessing a clear sense of what its physical boundaries are, the infant needs to be kept close to its parents' or caregivers bodies in order for it to feel secure and protected. In this way it learns to trust its external world and develops a sense of security.

Through give and take, child and parent learn how to be in a symbiotic union, each contributing to the other's growth. Although it appears the relationship is mostly one-way, with the parent serving the infant, it's through our constant service that our infant affords us access to our spiritual depths. The demands of caring for an infant cause us to dip into our core, where we discover that we do indeed have the capacity to give, serve, and nurture with the intensity required. Thus our infant shows us our ability to transcend our own selfish wishes and become present for another. In this way, infants are reflections of our deeper humanity.

In this stage, it's as if our being were saying to that of our child, "I no longer know where you begin and I end. Days and nights blend into a haze of brilliance and fatigue. I am elastic, rubber, and wax. I bend to your will with no resistance, no boundary, transparent like glass. Even when you aren't with me, I am with you, imagining you. There is no moment in which I exist separate from you."

A JOURNEY OF SELF-DISCOVERY

Whatever images we may have held of what the parenting journey would be like—fantasies of rosy moments filled with the scent of our infants' bodies, the undeniable pleasure of holding them, the feeling of having created a sense of family and continuity—when parenthood descends upon us, we find our fantasies crashing around us daily.

Because an infant needs a caregiver 24/7, the early years of parenthood are as exhausting as they are exhilarating, as ordinary and routine as they are spectacular. To give to our infant on demand is an enormous psychological and emotional responsibility that has the potential to drain us of energy and sanity, especially if we have no additional help. If we are also juggling a career, it can exhaust us beyond all conceivable limits, pushing us to our psychological edge. As we discover that our time no longer belongs to us, we come to the profound realization that our very *life* is no longer ours to call our own. Someone else is in the driver's seat, someone else's needs more pressing.

The relationship we share with our infant can only be described as a deeply intimate energetic dance in which souls unite and destinies merge. As we open to this realization, with tiny steps our infant then waltzes us straight to our core. We feel with a new intensity: love, guilt, fear, heartache, confusion, insecurity, unbelievable exhaustion. Never having had to care for another being in this way, we are thrust into the orbit of incessant giving, which confronts us with both our highest and lowest self. We discover parts of ourselves we didn't know existed— our capacity to love, give, and serve, and correspondingly our desire for control, power, appreciation, and perfection.

Since infants live in the moment, free of any agenda or desire to manipulate, we can't hold onto fantasies of what "should" be happening if we are to engage with them. Because for an infant each moment is radically new, there's no agenda and no predictability. Up for hours one night and sound asleep the next, colicky and irritable one moment and gurgling in delight the next, a baby's first six months especially mandate that we open ourselves to constant upheaval and chaos until a routine develops. Infancy is truly an *is-what-it-is* landscape, where being attached to wishing it were otherwise is a hopeless quest and huge waste of energy. As helpless as infants may be, it's they who are in full control of their schedule and needs. We exist simply to serve.

In serving, we do ourselves a service. Through the daily tending of our baby, we discover the boundless expanse of our heart, touching upon our limitless capacity for compassion and unconditional love. Because we are unaccustomed to living in the present moment and unused to being attuned to the needs of another in such an intense manner, the invitation to become present for our infant is challenging. Addicted as we are to our incessant focus on our own needs, to be present for our infant can be intimidating, overwhelming. Those who muster the courage to take up the challenge discover that the act of giving loosens their grip on their ego, offering them a chance to live in the zone of non-self. As our children take us beyond our ego's narrow needs, we become intimate with our potential for *selflessness*.

To own our capacity for selflessness is particularly crucial during this stage of our child's development because an infant's reflection in its parents' eyes is its only validation of its inner experience. Imagine if the infant is upset, but instead of reflecting back concern, the mother begins to laugh or becomes angry. Such a child experiences severe dissonance, becoming confused. If its parent empathizes with it through their reassuring tone of voice and secure embrace, the infant feels validated in its emotion and will allow itself to be calmed. In this way it learns to be centered.

Due to our own mental preoccupation, at times we may simply be unable to respond to our infant authentically. We may be too worried about our own problems to be truly present with our child. For instance, if we are sad about something, we may be unable to reflect back a sense of joy. At such a time, we may find ourselves asking, "How can I calm you when I am a storm inside? How can I return your smile when I am weeping within? How can I soothe your fears when I quiver myself? How do I let you find yourself when I myself am lost?" Such times are bound to descend upon us occasionally. Raising an infant often demands we put our throbbing headache, aching heart, or injured spirit on the back burner for the time being and focus on our child's needs. At such times, the way out of our pain is *through* it. We simply allow our pain to be what it is and just *be with it* to the best of our ability.

Parenting consciously isn't about "getting it right" all the time, but about evolving together. Children are immensely forgiving, and neither are they irreparably damaged by those times when we come up short. On the contrary, they learn to accept their own limitations through seeing us accept ours.

When we serve our children in a reasonably consistent manner, respectful of their dignity as our spiritual partners and friends, we enter a state of humility and gratitude. We give back because we have received so much. In so doing, we create a circle of lasting kinship and spiritual regeneration.

A CHANCE TO RECOVER YOUR RHYTHM

With a baby, we need to be there when it's thirsty, hungry, cries, needs changing, wishes to play, and wants to go to sleep. This can be challenging, especially for those of us who are attached to the traditional ways of living and relating, which are centered on verbalizing, intellectualizing, and performing. Infancy is anything but these.

Because infants operate not in the realm of the verbal and intellectual, but in a dreamlike existence suspended between sleep and wakefulness, neither here nor there, we are unable to communicate with them through traditional means, which makes our task all the more challenging. To respond to this challenge requires us to suspend all previous ways of knowing and relating, and instead enter our infant's pure energy.

An infant exposes us to a rhythm of life that has been lost to us. The need to experience oneness with our infant requires us to look at this early stage as a time of slowing down. We have to still ourselves and hold ourselves steady while we nurse our baby, rock it to sleep, or change yet another diaper.

A period of non-productivity, this stage in our child's development asks us to drop all attachment to where we have been or are going, instead clamoring for our realization that *this moment, here right now, is the only moment of relevance.* A baby invites, "I am here. Be here with me."

To be fully present to our infants' needs requires us to rank all other demands with a lower priority. Only by complete surrender to our changed situation can we embrace the beauty of the place we are now. Those of us who respond discover there is nothing of greater significance—not our hobbies, friends, lifestyle, or career.

Because of an infant's slow pace and tiny developments, we are challenged to change the speed, intensity, and direction of our entire way of living. We quickly realize that "success" in an infant's life is measured in an entirely different way. A "big" thing is a smile, the shaking of a leg, or holding a rattle. These are milestones.

For some parents, reconfiguring their sense of "big" and savoring the tiny and ordinary can be a leap indeed. Yet it's in this dismantling of ego from its attachment to the extraordinary, the wonderful, the dramatic, and the loud that our infants offer us our most-needed spiritual lessons. In their ability to draw us into an attentive state of receptivity, focused on their little burps, sighs, soft and non-resisting bodies, miniature fingernails, and wide-eyed gaze, we learn to enjoy the abundant extraordinariness of the simple moment.

No stage in your children's development offers you a better opportunity to learn the power of moment-by-moment *being* than does infancy. Unparalleled in its ability to take the most ego-driven parent to a deeper state of soul, even if only for a few moments at a time, the apparent emptiness of just being with your infant is rich with spiritual fullness. *This is your window for changing your spiritual vibration.*

Infants, by their ability to engage in their world in such simple yet awakened ways, compel us to enter into a state of engaged presence. Our infants ask us to coo with them, make faces that mirror theirs, and hold them close for no reason other than that they wish to be close. If they understood our language, we might say to them, "You demand I look at you with complete attention, toss aside my weariness, worries, preoccupations, and be fully here, body, mind, and soul. I never knew this could be so incredibly difficult."

If you fail to embrace the spiritual lessons of the first year of your child's life, you lose the opportunity to access new parts of yourself. Holding fast to your established ways, you commit only a piece of yourself to this venture. To truly be able to access the jewels of this deeply spiritual stage of your child's development, you need to take a deep breath and plunge into the ocean. The degree of internal transformation you experience will be directly proportional to how deeply you immerse yourself.

Once you are able to enter the sacred space of infancy with a reverence for its spiritual significance, you will reap the fruits. Not only will your infant grow, but you will grow. As you are exposed to a different way of being, through which you are enabled to connect not only with your infant but also with yourself, you will uncover your deep connection to all life. You will be exposed to what it *really* means to live in the present, unencumbered by the past and unfettered by tomorrow.

TODDLERHOOD: A PLANET ALL ITS OWN

In the emerging dance of individuality and oneness, separateness and togetherness, our children first learn to enjoy simply being in the secure embrace of the parental cocoon. As they move toward the age of two, they increasingly begin exploring their individuality and separateness. Then, in the school years, they slowly learn how to put being a part of the whole and being individuals within the whole together in a balanced way.

As a child's desire to express its uniqueness kicks in, it heralds a trying time for parents. Children in the two's can be exasperating, draining us of patience. We tell them to go here, and they go there. We tell them up, and they choose down. We tell them no, and they scream or wail until we experience unbecoming fantasies of what we would do with them if only we could get away with it. Unpredictable and impetuous, manipulative and attention-seeking, they can be moody, sullen, clingy, defiant, rowdy, and tempestuous. We spend hours taking them to activities, arranging fun times with friends, preparing for their birthday party, and yet they are ungrateful and exploitive. Ravenous in their greed, they love us when they want something, whereas the next moment it's as if we didn't exist.

Toddlerhood is a planet all its own. Nothing prepares us for the onslaught of its wrath or the endearing confusion of its budding independence. Reactions seemingly emerge out of nowhere, then either disappear just as fast or linger on and on through lunch, playtime, and dinner. The child who is perfectly angelic one minute can turn into a raving lunatic the next. The sweet-tempered tot can become a finger-biting terror in an instant.

The toddler isn't just emotionally volatile, but often maddeningly inconsolable. Though a toddler's fears are primarily imagined, they are perceived as so very real. A toddler has the most remarkable ability to remember what it wants and to persist until its demands are met. Yet it has the amazing ability to ignore the things in which it has no interest. Just about everything in a toddler's life is over-the-top—over-the-top frustration and over-the-top excitement. Toddlerhood is a chaotic phase of a child's life both emotionally and physically. Messy, undefined, disorderly, ever-changing, and unpredictable, there are no neat and tidy answers here. No broom is wide enough to sweep away the dust, grit, and grubbiness of toddlerhood.

While this phase often feels impossible for both parent and child, it's truly magnificent to witness. This is the phase in which the child's sense of self begins to blossom, as it begins to explore its creativity, curiosity, and independence. Toddlers are spectacular, invincible in their fantasies, limitless in their potential. They want to fly high in the sky, sail the seven seas, explore the world, and stay awake until dawn.

When a child begins to understand itself as a separate being with unique desires, it's a revealing moment for both parent and child. A toddler's ability to separate from your secure embrace rests heavily on your ability to release it from your clasp. The manner in which you negotiate the delicate dance between *letting go* and *still being present* determines how easily your toddler will be able to define itself as both connected to you and separate from you.

As the initial symbiotic bond is released and space created for parent and child to intermingle as individuals, a child's unique identity begins to flourish. As this identity blossoms, you are likely to find yourself thinking, "Your temperament is bursting forth. It shakes, rattles, and astounds me. You are truly your own person. Any illusion I had that you were *my* creation is dissolving."

Like infancy, this stage of development presents parents with an opportunity for their own spiritual development. The first mandate of this stage is to recognize who your youngster is growing into, as opposed to who *you* think your child ought to become. To this end, truly connecting with the particular temperament of this unique individual is crucial.

Toddlerhood is a tricky stage indeed. It's the first time a child is able to exercise authority over its world. In its quest for self-discovery, the toddler will bump into plenty of external obstacles. However, its greatest hindrance will be the obstacles it faces in the guise of our unrealistic expectations.

In its journey toward independence, what little a toddler can do for itself is often denied it by our impositions. We seldom allow it to be in charge of its own progression. Instead, we either push our children all the time or we hold them back. When we hover, prod, and cajole to get the results we think matter—making our toddlers kiss people they may not want to kiss, asking them to perform like puppets so the world can see how smart we parents are, and demanding they be responsible when they may not be ready—we rob them of their spontaneity.

Imagine being a toddler in today's complex world. Everything is fast-paced and multilayered. It's so easy to forget that toddlerhood is all about open spaces and empty boxes—about unleashed imagination and unencumbered play. In our hurry to see our children walk, talk, and potty-train themselves, we miss the delight of staying in the moment.

Toddlerhood doesn't offer us secure places in which to sigh and rest, as our toddlers swing from clingy and whiny to brazen and defiant. Constantly reeling us into their world of need, then tossing us aside once they have been nurtured, they teach us not to attach ourselves to any fixed set of ideals and expectations.

Because the hallmark of toddlerhood is constant evolution, one of the major spiritual challenges for parents with a toddler is to live in the unknown, the state of pure discovery. We can only do this if we are comfortable straddling *what was* and *that which is still evolving*. If we are wise, we learn to live in the unknown, for life with a toddler is a constant invitation to the spontaneous, undefined, and unimagined.

Responding to the moment in an ingenious way at every instant, our toddlers invite us to bravely embrace new worlds, challenging us to be fearless in the creation of a more authentic identity for ourselves. As we watch our toddler's insatiable curiosity for life, we are reminded that we too can engage the moment with full abandon, living in wonder and awe.

Toddlerhood is the Time to Sow the Seeds of Containment

Just as we must allow our toddler to exercise its right to limitless adventure, we must also provide it with an understanding of its limits. Nestled between infancy and childhood, this stage knows no logic or reason. Everything occurs at an instinctual level, which means that impulses often run amuck. Imposing a sense of guidance amid all this energetic discharge is a challenge, but this is the stage in which we must sow the first real seeds of containment.

Thoughts that come to us at this stage in our child's development run something like, "You are testing me constantly to discover how far you can push before I yield, how loud you can scream before I stop you, how bratty you can be before I hush you. You are discovering the boundaries of your world. At times I hesitate to let you know that you come with limits. I see your desire to be a superhero and your full faith that you are. I want to let your imagination be on fire. Yet I must also stop you and tell you that no matter what you believe, you cannot fly out of the window."

As the first foray into the realm of boundaries, containment, and negotiation, toddlerhood can be as much about a battle of wills as can the teen years. How are we to best impose limitations on our toddler's curiosity when a situation becomes dangerous? Where does the line get drawn? How much is too much, how little too little?

The parent quickly realizes that the needs of a toddler are vastly different from those of an infant. When the first "no" is uttered by the parent and metabolized by the child, the idea of acceptable and unacceptable behavior is introduced. Whether this "no" is appropriately delivered and consistently applied sets the stage for all later behavioral dynamics between parent and child.

Unlike in infancy, our role as parents is no longer simply to nurture and *be,* but is also about being firm, consistent, and—if this is what's demanded of us on occasion—the "bad guy." If we fail to sow the seeds of containment when our children are toddlers, we will find it all the more difficult to do so when they are twelve.

Containment, which is a topic we will cover in depth in a much later chapter, requires building muscles of awareness. Discipline is ultimately all about the creation of moment-by-moment awareness. To the degree this is in the forefront of our mind, we are able to function as our toddler's container in a manner that's spiritually regenerative, exercising our authority in a conscious, engaged, nurturing way.

For instance, when our toddler throws a tantrum, we can either walk away (assuming we are in a place it's safe to do so), or we can stay very present and calm, simply bearing witness. Which route is most beneficial in a particular situation depends on how we judge our toddler will tolerate our actions, which will be dependent on their developmental level and individual personality. Either route offers the possibility of alerting our toddler that it has boundaries. A keen awareness will guide us as to which approach to take.

What do I mean by "containment?" When a toddler bites something it isn't supposed to or throws a tantrum, we need to bring its focus to this and say, "No, this isn't okay." We may find we are constantly saying "no," but don't believe for a moment that this is an exercise in futility. Though it's important to be gentle, we must be consistent and firm in laying down boundaries. Mindful of the fact that our toddler still exists in a somewhat dreamlike state, we don't want to shock it out of this state, yet we do need to start building the container within which it will live.

It's essential to realize that a toddler only kicks and bites us because it doesn't know how to say, "I'm mad at you." Though it cries and flails as if we have deprived it of food for months, what it's really saying is, "Help me, I'm miserable."

If displays of emotion frighten you and make you anxious, you will be unable to help your toddler cope with its internal world. This means teaching your toddler how to deal with the emotions that rise in its body when it's denied something it wants. Thankfully, your child's vocabulary is now expanding exponentially. Using the bridge of language, combining role-playing and storytelling, you can invite your toddler into the world of imagination and help it make sense of its world. As you do so, your toddler learns that it can survive intolerable emotions and return to a centered calm.

Even though toddlers want to believe they can climb mountains and reach the moon, the truth is that they simultaneously feel helpless in the face of the enormity of life. To alleviate this feeling, toddlerhood needs to be a time during which routines are further established and boundaries more firmly set. As a schedule evolves, toddlers learn to walk, talk, eat without our having to feed them, potty train themselves, and sleep in their own bed. In due course, as they attend preschool, they will separate further from us as their parents.

Having enjoyed oneness with us in the first year or so of life and explored their individuality as toddlers, our youngsters are now ready to begin the journey of learning to be both separate and connected in the wider world around them. Thus it is they enter the school years, and with these years come fresh opportunities for us as parents to develop spiritually alongside them.

CHAPTER 8

FROM CENTER STAGE
TO SUPPORTING CAST
A Parent's Opportunity for Spiritual
Growth in the School Years

The early school years are when our children learn volumes of information on a daily basis, some of which may prove overwhelming, while other aspects turn out to be liberating.

Children at this age go through phases of regression during which they cling to their parents, alternating with phases of rejection of their parents as they only want to be with their peers. They are as needy and clingy as they are autonomous and free-spirited. They are as rebellious and defiant as they are obedient and angelic. Still extremely temperamental and moody, in other ways they can manifest a maturity that's inspiring.

When my daughter entered this phase, I found myself musing, "Suddenly you have discovered friends. I am not as important, and for this I am both relieved and nostalgic. Now we will discover how sturdy our connection to each other truly is."

In this time for socialization, our children learn to get along with their friends without our help, obey the norms of their school, engage a curriculum, and regulate their own emotions. Our youngsters get to see who they are vis-à-vis their friends and teachers as they come to rely on themselves and people external to the home to reflect back to them their sense of identity.

As much as this is a time for experimentation, it's also a time when fear tends to abound—a time that's about confusion as much as it's about enthusiasm. Parched for a sense of right and wrong, our youngsters are even more thirsty for connection. This stage can be annoying for us because we find ourselves wedded to our children's school, friends, and teachers—elements of their life that may be quite different from our preference. However, if we are awake, this is also a stage in which we get to shape our children's behavior in profound ways, encouraging the virtues we wish them to exhibit: generosity, compassion, empathy, awareness, and focus.

If you are a wise parent, you will fulfill the background role of offering a grounded perspective of who your child is, for these are the years in which children first experiment with the adult roles they will later inhabit. As you engage with them in the drama of life, it's vital you contour their personality toward wholeness. You cannot blame them later for what you fail to teach them now. As you provide the support they require, they gain a sense of their individuality, competence, and worth—and also of their limitations.

Since it's in this stage of their development that children first spread their wings, you especially need to be sure you don't clip them as a result of your own needs and biases. Yes, you may influence the direction in which they fly, or even the speed of their flight, but the fact remains they are ready to fly.

MIDDLE SCHOOL: THE CHALLENGE OF "BEING THERE" FOR OUR CHILDREN

The middle school years are a time of tremendous transition, often painful and wrenching for us to witness. We see our children's pain and confusion, their exhilaration and energy. Though we try to shield them from what is to come, they boldly run forward, wanting to taste it all.

During these intermediate years, our children's sense of who they are undergoes a dramatic overhaul. Their identity is now in flux, leaving us in equal unrest. We watch how their development suddenly takes a different turn as they grapple with the uncertainties of their maturing body and budding intellect. Their body doesn't care for psychological timetables, which renders them mentally unprepared for their physical maturity. Abuzz with hormonal surges and riddled with insecurity, they feel groundless. Where before the world was so clearly black and white, now they are unsure which colors paint their life.

Your children belong less to you now than they ever did. They are growing and need the space to do so, which requires you to retreat from your dominance and emerge in your kinship. No longer can you be the ever-powerful parent, but must instead become an ever-present partner. Your children need you to hold their hand, but without leading the way. They need you to be there when they cry but cannot explain why they are crying. They need you to respect their privacy even while they cling to you. They need you to accept them when they reject both themselves and you, and to understand them even when they make no sense. They need you to swim with them in the treacherous waters of their chaotic emotions, even when they keep throwing their life jacket away. They need you to be calm when they take you to the edge of your sanity, to be quiet and listen even when they beg you to give your opinion, and to simply be there without heed to your own ideas or interpretations. They need you to forgive them for their forgetfulness and distraction, understanding that this is hormonal. They need you to cut them some slack and let them defy you a little, knowing this is part of healthy development. They need you to let go of them as your babies and tell them, "You are ready to walk in your own shoes, no matter how scary."

It's at this time in their lives that children are exposed to cliques, as well as to romantic crushes, in an environment of social politics that will require them to endure the pain of betrayal, rejection, and a broken heart. Each friendship will leave a mark on their personality as they morph into who they think they need to be in order to fit in. Your task is to sit with them and be the container for their angst, holding hope while never minimizing what they are experiencing. Your children need you to be there, stalwart in your presence, as they swim through wave after wave of emotion. It's essential you don't try to "fix" their life, but simply understand the chaos of these years. In this way, your children learn to manage their emotions and create their own coping strategies. It's as if you were to say to them, "Even though you feel anchorless, abandoned by your body, lost to your soul, I will sit here with you and reflect your essence."

If you become caught up in your children's whirling emotions, swept away by your own anxiety over what they are going through, you will be unable to help them navigate the hardships of this phase. They require you to remain steady, despite the fact you may feel frustrated and impatient with their constantly morphing sense of identity, knowing this is exactly where they need to be. Trivial as these things may seem to you, they are meant to care about how they look, how many friends or enemies they have, whether teachers praise them, how clever they are or perhaps aren't, whether they are invited to a birthday party or asked to be someone's prom date. If you tell them they shouldn't worry about such superficial matters, you alienate them. They will also believe it's *they* who are superficial. In other words, your spiritual obligation is to reflect back to them the normalcy of their state and admire their shining courage.

The other aspect of social politics is the whole idea of the groupie. In their desire to be part of a clique, our children may sell their soul. So desperate are they for a sense of validation, they will forsake their own truth and begin to imbibe the values of others. As we watch them morph into a member of the "chic squad," trying so desperately to be one of the popular kids in school, we will have to stand quietly in the shadows as they dress, listen to music, and cop an attitude alien to their authentic self.

Our children may come to us filled with demands for the latest gadgets and fashions. They may argue that their friends "all have these things" and that without them they will be ostracized. In our desire to have our children fit in, we may fall prey to their never-ending demands, and in so doing communicate that external factors such as possessions or the opinions of those who are popular have great importance in sustaining a person's sense of self. However, if we can resist our children's urges and teach them instead to rely on their inner sense of worth, not their acquisitions or standing in a social group, they learn not to blindly follow the crowd.

HIGH SCHOOL: THE NEED FOR UNEQUIVOCAL ACCEPTANCE

As our children mature beyond the middle school years, we get to see the effects of their upbringing. As all that we never thought would or even could happen to us now descends on us, we experience humiliation, defensiveness, guilt, and outrage. We are at the mercy of these children for whom we sacrificed so much! Is it any wonder so many of us call a professional to medicate or therapize our child?

During the mid to later teen years, we are forced to reconcile our hopes for our children when they were young with the fact we are now having to deal with the problems we thought only visited other people, such as having our children diagnosed or pulling them out of restrooms because they are drunk and throwing up. Indeed, whatever our relationship with our children may have been prior to these years, it may appear to have no bearing on their often bizarre behavior now. Yet it has everything to do with what's unfolding. So much so that when parents wonder who their children have become as teens, I respond, "They are the same people. They didn't morph into someone else overnight."

Our children burst forth like never before at this stage, with more personality, more attitude, more self-assertion. However, a difficult teenager doesn't sprout up overnight; the seeds were being sown all along. At this stage, our children are able to pay heed to their unmet needs. Unfortunately, if they have been starving for authentic parental nurture, chances are they will now go about seeking this in unhealthy ways.

If you were too strict with your children, the teen years are a time when they break free. If you were too permissive when your children were growing up, so that they failed to learn containment, they now go wild. If you were neglectful of your children or absent, they now refuse to connect with you.

Let me reassure you from my experience of working with parents and teens that it's still not too late for healing. It will just be harder to achieve since teens are wary. In such circumstances, parents are asked to endure the pain their teens inflict on them, knowing this is a reflection of the parents' failure over the years to connect with their child as a real person like themselves. The parent has to be willing to admit, "I haven't been there for you, so please teach me what I need to do to repair our relationship."

On the other hand, this is the stage in which you also get to reap the fruits of your investment in your children. If you were able to listen to their authentic needs and nurture their essence, you will be delighted by their ability to do the same. It's my prayer that, as a result of this book, countless parents will be able to say of their children's entry into their teens: "Now you rise taller, brighter, grander than I was able to. Deeply connected to your essence, you are powerful. I am in awe of who you have become."

These are years in which you must trust. Ah, this is a true test indeed! Your teens are going through a maelstrom of emotions. Continuing to develop at alarming rates, they are negotiating a semi-adult world, taking on jobs, embarking on trips to foreign lands on their own, and entering college. Falling in love, breaking up, being dumped, and testing all sorts of physical and psychological limits are also a part of the maelstrom. *More than ever, they need your acceptance.*

WHY IT'S IMPORTANT TO RESIST
THE TEMPTATION TO CONTROL

Although the behavior of a teen in high school may at times tempt us to increase control, this is the moment for us to occupy a space in the wings. Now is the opportunity for our children to manifest all we have taught them, all the morals and values we have instilled in them. They need to flap their wings and fly, at least around the block. We have to encircle our teens with our embrace, but in a manner that's loose. They need to know they can always come home, but what is more important, that they are free to fly.

I know that as my daughter reaches her teens, I will need to resist the insertion of my ego. I can already hear myself saying, "I still have so many opinions to share, so much insight to impart. However, I recognize that my time for grand speeches has come to a close. It's your time to write your own."

The choice of courses our children study at school, the friends they make, and the hobbies they pursue are now less our business and more their own. Of course, our fear is that they will make poor choices and become subject to detrimental influences. This is always a risk, but the options left to us as parents are now limited. If our teens are failing in school or unmotivated, it's because they are trying to tell us that something is wrong, which leaves us with only one way to respond: *acceptance*. We can then take appropriate action, such as getting them extra help if they wish it, but especially giving them the emotional support they need.

If your children are making poor choices concerning relationships or other pursuits, at this point in the game your strategy must be that of acceptance. If you respond with control or dogmatism, you will push your teens further away. The less rigid you are with them, the more likely they are to maintain a relationship with you. If you are overbearing and possessive, this will serve only to catapult them further into negative behavior.

Parents naturally ask, "Does this mean we just let them take drugs or drop out of school?"

I explain, "The time when they are going to seek our permission has passed. Our teens will do exactly what they wish, which is directly related to how they were raised. At this point, we have to remove ourselves from any illusion we can control their life. The only way to gain access to them is through rebuilding our lost connection."

The key spiritual lesson for parents during these years is that we must reorient our relationship with our teens to one of true kinship and partnership. I repeat: the key is *trust*. This isn't a time for fear and anxiety on our part, but for confidently assuring ourselves, "Now I can sit back and enjoy you like never before. Finally, we can release each other from our old roles. Are you ready to create a new relationship with me—one in which I can partner with you?"

Your teens will shut you out if you don't respect their need for privacy and space. They will turn a deaf ear to your wisdom if they feel you overstep your bounds. They will stop coming to you with their problems if all they hear is caution and lack of trust. It's therefore imperative they know wholeheartedly that you don't harbor a desire to impose your agenda on them. They will only come to you when they are able to sit in your presence and feel your unconditional faith in their ability to handle their life.

If there's any age at which the issue of safety is paramount, it's the teen years, which are when children are at greatest risk from peer pressure and the potential of immature acts of self-destructiveness. Nevertheless, we can't jump in and try to control our teens' lives. If we do so, they are resourceful and will find a way to lie to us and do precisely as they wish—and then we are likely to feel helpless and perhaps enraged. The more intrusive we are, the less our teens will confide in us. During this period of their lives, to trust them is our spiritual discipline.

Once we own the limits of our influence in our children's lives, paradoxically we continue to be hugely influential. Exuding total and unconditional acceptance in our daily presence and conversations with them encourages them to come to us when they need to. Our best chance of keeping them safe and empowered is to validate who they intrinsically are.

CHAPTER 9

THE INSANITY OF PARENTHOOD

While acknowledging the wonderful aspects of the parenting journey, the conscious approach to raising children also embraces the madness of this journey, with full awareness of the level of psychological, emotional, and spiritual commitment it takes to raise a child—and the potential this has to alter forever a parent's self-understanding.

Because the parenting journey is one of extremes, it can bring out both the best and the worst in us. For this reason, it behooves us to face just how difficult this can be for many parents, especially the mother. While recognizing that not all parents face the severe challenges that others do, it's nevertheless the case that *all* parents go through a profound emotional and psychological transformation.

As we began seeing in the last two chapters, no one really explains to us what a life-altering event becoming a parent will be. No one tells us that the love between a parent and child has the potential to tear open our heart, leaving us at the mercy of the destiny of our children. No one explains that if we are going to parent consciously, life as we know it will no longer exist, and the individual we believe ourselves to be will evaporate before our eyes. No one tells us we will have to endure the death of our old self and that we will have no clue how to develop a new sense of who we are.

Parenting is one of the most difficult endeavors a person ever takes on. Ask any mother of a child who refuses to go to sleep at three in the morning, while she has another on her breast, and she has to be at work at nine in the morning—not to mention that her husband expects her to be a temptress in bed and look beautiful for the world. Ask any father who has to do homework with his inattentive son, constantly trying to bring him back to task, while being on time to pick up another child from soccer practice, before tackling work brought home from the office.

More than perhaps any other role, parenthood causes us to second-guess ourselves. We question our competence, our worth, and even our sanity as we ask ourselves, "Now, just why was it I thought I wanted children, when all I want is for them to go to sleep and leave me alone?"

Having said this, if you can recognize the spiritual potential of the parenting journey, you will be equipped to enter its depths without resisting or becoming stuck in a state in which you are utterly overwhelmed and confused as you attempt to grapple with its complexities. For this reason, rather than feeling guilty about the feelings that arise as you move along the path of raising a child, you are asked to *embrace* the insanities of parenthood, *capitalizing* on the way having a child opens you up—or rather tears you up, shreds your old identity, and replaces it with an expansion of yourself.

THE PARTICULAR ROLE OF THE MOTHER

Both parents undergo a transformation in their identity during the years of raising children. However, for women the parenting journey holds an especially emotional and spiritual significance because we house this growing child within our body for the first nine months of its existence. These months of gestation render the mother-child bond particularly unique in its intensity, leading to a complex relationship that's highly symbiotic and profoundly personal. This is one reason mothers are often invested in their children in ways that fathers sometimes aren't.

Expanding not only our skin but also our psyche as we participate in the emergence of a new spirit, during these nine months we witness our sense of who we are start to alter as we grapple with this miraculous event taking place within us. Our identity comes into question as we understand that our life is no longer ours to own, but is betrothed to our child. We watch our heart surge with a protectiveness that's as invigorating as it's unfamiliar.

We know we aren't the same woman we were pre-birth, but neither have we articulated who we are post-birth. Consequently, we get lost in our role as mothers, giving to our children with the zest and zeal only a woman possesses. In this giving, our sense of self fades, and we find ourselves increasingly alienated from who we intrinsically are. We feel as if we are in a no-man's land, neither here nor there.

True, we feel purposeful, but mostly only in our role as a mother. Our children grow up, our spouse climbs the corporate ladder, yet we who have in many cases put our life on hold find ourselves without an anchor in the world around us, let alone a sense of individual purpose. As the years go by, we may long to feel secure in an identity separate from our children yet tend not to recognize the gateway to any such identity. Part of us may desperately want to recapture who we were, while another part realizes who we were has died. Though terrifying, this loss of our identity can also be potentially regenerative.

In the course of raising our children, many of us become almost unrecognizable to ourselves when we look in the mirror. We see in the lines around our eyes the incident when our child slammed the door in our face because we didn't buy them a video game, the occasion they fell and broke a limb, and the day we thought we had lost them at the fair. If we look closer, we also see in these lines the joy and awe of all it means to be someone's mom.

We may find we can't help ourselves when we grumble about our children while washing the dishes, complain about them to our own mother, blame their inadequacies on our spouse, or bemoan our luck that we, of all the people in the world, produced such a "difficult" child. Only another parent knows what the eye roll truly means, resonates with "who knew children were so much work," understands "thank goodness the house is empty for a while," and can appreciate "I've got a few hours to myself."

For many mothers—as well as for fathers who bear the brunt of raising a child—parenting can be emotionally, psychologically, financially, and physically draining, yet few of us ever honestly share how exacting, incredibly tough, and emotionally burdensome we find it. So invested are we in being "good" parents that we would be embarrassed to share our feelings with friends and family. Because of our fear of being judged, we tend to hide the degree to which we feel torn asunder, shredded, and psychically distorted by the demands of our children. Consequently, most of us walk the path of parenthood feeling alone, truly believing we are abnormal in our occasional longing to be who we were before we became a mother. However, were we to reach across our mantles of perfection, we would discover a kinship with other parents and realize we aren't at all unusual for having such feelings, just human.

No one understands the mix of devotion and anguish a parent experiences unless they have gone through it. Sometimes languid with unquenchable love and at other times haggard from inextinguishable fatigue, there are moments when we are so committed to our children that we forget we even exist, while at other times we fantasize about running away, leaving them in their dirty clothes amid piles of homework and a messy room. Of course, the moment we begin to dream of lying on a beach sipping margaritas, we are likely to feel ashamed of ourselves.Children preoccupy a mother, or a father who fulfills a similar role, almost a hundred percent of the time they are together. We are either taking care of them, entertaining them, or worrying about them. Little wonder our relationship with our spouse undergoes drastic change. Our body becomes unfamiliar territory, our emotional equilibrium at times resembling that of the insane as we find ourselves sleep-deprived, short-tempered, financially drained, and on occasion transformed into a tyrant.

The day inevitably arrives when the realization comes to us, "Gosh, I'm just like my mother!" Or, translated, "I have become a control freak." All those times our mom yelled, "Why can't you just do as I say?" suddenly make sense. We can also empathize with every parent who has lost their temper with a screaming child on an airplane. Before we became parents, we exuded a superiority that said in effect, "If I were a parent, my child would never behave that way!" Now we feel sympathy for the parent and want to take the child and lock it in the bathroom.

Whether we like it or not, every one of us is destined to be triggered by our children in some profound, elemental way. We are going to, at some point or another, just "lose it." We are going to shout, even scream. We are going to call them a name we never thought we would. It's important to accept that if we are triggered by our child, this is normal. I tell myself that, when I'm triggered, I will own the aspects of my shadow that feel threatening and embrace the lessons my child teaches me about myself. In one way or another, each of us will have to confront our "shadow parent," with its overwhelming desire for control.

Having acknowledged that we will at times react, to repeatedly lose our temper in the most childish of ways is humiliating. It doesn't feel good to yell at our children. When we are on the verge of losing it in such a way, hopefully our parents allow us to drop them off, preferably for the next year.

The reality is that as much as you need to be present to your children's emotions, you absolutely need to be present to your own, allowing yourself to metabolize what you are feeling. Only in this way can you avoid projecting your emotions onto your children.

In situations in which you feel you are coming apart at the seams, it's tempting to revert to the traditional hierarchical form of the parent-versus-child model of raising children. However, if you take this route, you are likely to pay a heavy price in your children's teen years and beyond. To become conscious in the way you parent may be painful initially, but in the long run it's by far the preferable choice.

RAISING A CHILD IS AN INVITATION TO SURRENDER TO A DIFFERENT PACE

Learning to surrender to the nature of our life with children takes some getting used to. Children by their nature test our patience—it comes with the territory. As our children grow into teens, they try our patience even more, albeit in different ways. Now it isn't a matter of waiting for them to finish their cereal or tie their laces, but having a monosyllabic conversation and waiting in line behind all their friends to gain access to them.

The development of patience is more than a necessary response to our children; it's an opportunity to surrender to the present moment. When our children require our patience, we are asked to drop our agenda, breathe, and let go of the demands of our ego so that we can appreciate the present moment more fully. For this reason the development of patience is a spiritual practice, with our children at the helm, challenging us to take life at a slower and more conscious pace.

Having said this, I also recognize that there are times when we have no time for patience, literally. We simply *have* to get from one place to another without delay. It would be a shame if this became the way we functioned on a regular basis though. With their slower tempo, children offer us a priceless jewel, since a child's natural rhythm is much closer to a soul rhythm than that of most adults. For this reason, it's helpful when we are in a hurry to remind ourselves there is no place to be but where we are at this moment. Instead of rushing, we need to allow ourselves to become present with our child's soul. If we find ourselves feeling anxious and not really present, the best service we can render to ourselves and our children is to enter into quietness and stillness until we restore our sense of calm.

When our children aren't following "the plan," we are wise to remind ourselves they aren't *meant* to, since this isn't what they are on earth to do. At such times, we may wish to consider whether we ought to change *our* plans, instead of always requiring them to abide by our wishes.

If a child is truly being difficult and you are in danger of losing your patience, it's vital to listen to the voice within you that whispers, "Don't use your children as the receptacle of your frustrations." When your child exasperates you, you are wise to hold an internal conversation in which you ask yourself, "Why am I being triggered right now? Why am I so unhappy with my child? What is my child exposing in *my* internal state of being?" The smart thing may be to take a deep breath and leave the room. This affords you an opportunity to regroup, as you remind yourself, "It's not my child who needs help right now, but me."

If at times you lose your patience and project your frustration onto your children, either through harsh words or a clenched jaw, take a deep breath and forgive yourself. Then let it go and begin over. If you find yourself losing your patience frequently, the situation invites scrutiny. There's simply no reason to lose your patience on a daily basis unless your life is stretched too thin, in which case it's time to evaluate your circumstances and if at all possible restore a balance. At such a juncture, restructuring your life may need to become your spiritual focus.

Because ending the cycle of how pain is passed from generation to generation is such an important aspect of conscious parenting, we will go into it more deeply in the next chapter.

CHAPTER 10

PARENT FROM WHOLENESS
INSTEAD OF YOUR WOUNDS

When parents are so wrapped up in their own pain that they can't respond to their children's needs in the way each child deserves, children grow up feeling not just empty within but split in pieces. This is because their essential self isn't something that once existed and became lost, but is something that was never developed. Consequently, they forage the Earth looking for a mirror of their true being, seeking anything that holds out the promise of completing them.

Because it's so incredibly hard to create an internal mirror of our true being once the parenting relationship has failed to provide such a mirror, we are likely to feel not only lost, but even severely depressed. This depression tends to manifest itself either as a dark withdrawal or through an addiction of some sort. Because our substance of choice temporarily soothes our heart's pain, we may be seduced into believing it provides us with our lost mirror and feel we are receiving the validation we missed out on long ago.

I think of Samantha, a woman in her mid-fifties who is intellectually brilliant, holds a doctorate, and is a nurse at a local hospital. Since her dream of becoming a mother is connected to finding a spouse, which hasn't panned out, neither has her hope of motherhood.

From a broken home, Samantha never knew what it meant to have parents who were stable and present. Her mother, a doctor with a busy practice, was mostly unavailable, and she never knew her father. This meant that Samantha spent her childhood taking care of herself. Feeling guilty for even suggesting to her mother that she attend her first play or her high school graduation, it took her a long time to understand that her mother wasn't really interested in her, preferring to save the world instead. The result was that Samantha saw life as untrustworthy, which caused her to believe the way to survive was to squash her own needs.

When Samantha's mother remarried, it was to a physically abusive man. Samantha couldn't believe how a strong and competent woman could allow herself to be humiliated in such a way. The moment Samantha graduated from high school, she ran away, hanging out with a crowd that did drugs, engaging in promiscuous sex, and living mostly on the streets.

After six years, at age twenty-four, Samantha hit rock bottom and was taken to a hospital suffering from drug-related heart palpitations. It was in the ER that a light bulb went on, as she realized she was becoming emotionally paralyzed like her mother. Finding a job, she enrolled in school. Her natural brilliance saw her through college, a masters degree, and a doctorate. By the time she was forty, she was drug-free and financially stable.

Although Samantha appeared successful, internally she was in pain. At work, she took care of people all day, a role she was comfortable filling because she found intimate relationships suffocating. Unable to trust any man and ready to feel betrayed at the least opportunity, her longest relationship had spanned only five months, which meant she was intensely lonely most of the time. As she felt herself slipping into depression, she lamented, "I have nothing to look forward to. I have run as far as I can from the circumstances of my childhood, yet I still hurt as if I were five. Inside, I'm still that little girl. Doesn't this pain ever go away?"

The sad fact is that no matter how much our external world may change, the pain of childhood lingers in our heart, as it did for Samantha, until we heal our internal landscape. No matter that we own jewels, earn degrees, or are worshiped by a spouse, nothing can compensate for the yearning of a child who seeks nothing more than unconditional acceptance from its parents.

Most of us are grown children who weren't "met" for the individuals we are. For instance, if we grew up with parents who were disconnected from their authenticity, when we looked up into our mother's or father's face hoping to see our own essence mirrored back, all we received was either a blank stare or an emotional response that had nothing to do with us. Because we didn't see a reflection of our authentic self in the eyes of our caregivers, we learned to feel less than we really are.

There are a variety of ways in which parents who parent from their wounded psyche, with its tortured thoughts and turbulent emotions, mark their children for life. It's helpful to examine some of the more common effects of such parenting.

IF YOU GREW UP FEELING YOU WEREN'T GOOD ENOUGH

Jonathan, now in his forties, is a person who missed out on the validation he needed to receive as a child. The result is that, despite the fact he's smart and articulate, he can't hold a job longer than a year. Though he has dabbled in professions ranging from corporate positions to private businesses and teaching children, nothing proves satisfying. In every work situation, he manages to find an enemy who turns against him, leading to his departure. He's now at a dead-end because no one wants to risk hiring a man whose resume reveals so much instability.

Drowning in pain, Jonathan drinks to excess, chain smokes, fights with his wife, and is abusive to his children. "He's going to hurt himself, I know it," his wife told me on the phone. "He not only doesn't trust anyone, but he's alienating himself from me and the kids. He feels as though the world has shut its doors on him."

Were Jonathan to look within himself, he would discover that it's *he* who shuts people and opportunities out, all because he has felt unwelcome in the world as far back as he can remember. Just as Samantha saw life as untrustworthy, Jonathan's take on life is that it's cruel and unfair. He feels this way because not once has he stopped to examine his expectations, which are based on his own dark fears of betrayal. Expecting to be betrayed, he repeatedly sets himself up for this. Based on his inflated sense of entitlement and grandiosity, he imposes unattainable standards on the people in his life. Since these standards can never be met, he rejects opportunities that come his way. Thus the cycle of disappointment continues. Such an approach comes from the emptiness he feels inside. Because he experiences an internal void, all he can focus on is what he's getting or not getting, not what he's capable of *giving*.

When we grow up feeling we aren't good enough, we displace this feeling of inadequacy onto the world around us. We do this by creating a persona of grandiosity, as Jonathan did, in an effort to overcompensate for not feeling good enough. As a result of this grandiosity, we project an energy that treats others as less than ourselves. We walk with an overbearing sense of entitlement or put on an air of being better than others, when the truth is we suffer from a lack of self-worth.

Jonathan carries this energy into his parenting role, pressuring his children to excel at their academics, urging them to pursue those activities he determines worthwhile and judging their performance. Since he's only comfortable in the role of a "powerful" parent, his children fear him. As a result, his oldest son has turned away from him. Never home, Joshua is failing classes and wants to drop out of school. Giving up on himself is easier than living in constant fear of disappointing his father.

Many of us exude an energy that screams, "Life better satisfy my needs!" Driven by this energy, we seek to extract pleasure from life in the exact package we think we require. Because we are steeped in this demanding energy, anything that doesn't meet our expectations feels worthless. Even when something precious is offered us, we find no value in it. Highly judgmental, we resist not only life in its *as is* form, but also our children in their *as is* form. Of course, our resistance gets us nowhere because life remains true to its essential nature, flowing in its own way. If we are wise, we recognize this and start flowing with it rather than fighting it.

The lack of self-worth that hides behind a facade of grandiosity is sometimes the result of insufficient acceptance from our parents, so that we are left hungry for more. In other cases, it may be the result of being coddled and praised beyond what was appropriate. Or perhaps we felt as if we were our parents' puppet, here to fulfill their ego needs rather than meet our own needs.

Natasha is an example of someone who displaces her desire to feel self-worth onto her surroundings. Accustomed to living in a beautiful mansion in a coveted neighborhood, for years she prided herself on the clothes she wore, the jewels she possessed, the friends she kept, and the cars she drove. Then her husband lost his job. Within a year, they had to move into the home of Natasha's in-laws—a situation Natasha deemed beneath her. Natasha became emotionally undone, so depressed that she was unable to be present for her children. Deciding that what had happened was a "horrible" thing, she projected her insecurity onto her husband, belittling him for his inability to maintain his job.

What Natasha was going through was admittedly difficult, but it was nowhere near as cataclysmic as she was making it out to be. Though her new situation wasn't what she had been accustomed to, she still enjoyed a decent, safe, steady life. Only her attachment to her ego kept her from seeing this.

So convincing was she of how awful her situation was, she created a loyal following. Her husband became depressed, her children began doing poorly at school, and her health began to suffer. Now the situation really nosedived, as her husband stopped looking for work and they had to pull their son out of school because he was failing in every subject. The entire household had become invested in Natasha's misery.

"Tell me how I am supposed to react to such pain?" she demanded of me. "Should I jump around? Throw a party? Tell the universe I love this and want more of it?" In the clutches of unrelenting fear, anxious about where her next meal would come from, she couldn't see how she was creating the disaster she dreaded. Not for a second did she imagine there might be another response to her situation.

Natasha had grown up with parents who exuded great anxiety around money. Her father worked all his life to save, while her mother constantly worried about not having enough. Although the family wasn't poor by any means, Natasha inherited the message that one's sense of worth is intertwined with how much one possesses. Her parents were never able to pursue lives that were true to who they were because of their attachment to their savings account. Forever penny pinching, restraining themselves, they spurned life's bountiful offerings because of their pervasive anxiety about the future. In this parental life-script lay the roots of Natasha's attachment to luxury and extreme fear of ordinary simplicity.

Once Natasha was able to realize that this script was part of her parents' legacy, she chose to accept her reality as it was. From this place of acceptance, she then crafted an authentic emotional response. Realizing her rejection of her husband was a reflection of her own inner terror, she reached out to him again. Together they started a nonprofit organization to help single women get back on their feet. Although they never achieved the financial status they previously enjoyed, their life was abundantly blessed with the gratification that comes from making a difference in the lives of others.

IF YOU LEARNED TO PLEASE OTHERS TO EARN THEIR APPROVAL

Children who are raised by parents who sidestep their authenticity, camouflaging their true feelings for the sake of fitting in, learn to emulate this phony way of living. Watching us alter ourselves to gain the approval of others, they become pleasers, catering to the needs of others for the sake of approval.

When our children see us place the needs of others before our own, they learn that they are to value others more than themselves. Because they are highly oriented toward relationships, they also base their sense of identity on their relationships. But beneath such inauthentic service of others lies a simmering resentment, since no one can sustain such giving unless they have first given to themselves.

When we please others to gain their approval, we may also begin to please our children. Seeking their approval, we cater inordinately to their needs instead of teaching them to take care of their own needs. Overindulging them, we send a message that it's okay to take advantage of us. Out of our own low sense of worth, we allow them to imagine themselves the center of our world, which is an emotionally unhealthy, obsessive way of attempting to assuage our own lack. It's also a recipe for bringing up narcissists who imagine the world revolves around them.

When we are unable to create healthy boundaries for ourselves, our children learn to disrespect the boundaries of others. Observing us fail to claim ownership of our space and our needs, they come to believe their space and their needs are more important than those of others. Because we constantly give to them without saying "no" when appropriate, they fail to learn the importance of accepting that life itself sometimes says "no" to us. Consequently, they develop a grandiose sense of themselves.

Anita grew up as the youngest of two children. Her father, Stanley, died when she was seven years old. Anita's older sister suffered from severe mental and physical limitations, which meant she was confined to a wheelchair. The girls' mother, Louise, focused her attention on the older sister, forever consumed by her daughter's disability. Faced with such a situation, Anita learned her place in life quickly: she was second best. Nothing she could do grabbed her mother's attention away from her sick sister, and she felt like a greedy monster for even wanting this attention.

Since her mother noticed her only in the context of her ability to serve her sister and help carry the overwhelming burden of raising a sick child, Anita adapted to this role well, becoming the consummate caregiver. As a result, her mother increasingly leaned on her, while simultaneously pushing her to be everything her older sister couldn't be. Fulfilling all her mother's expectations, Anita became a successful pediatrician and took care of the family both financially and emotionally.

Marrying late and giving birth to three children, in her new family Anita continued to do what she did best, giving her all to her children, who grew up to be competent and accomplished. In her zeal not to inflict on them what she had endured as a child, she capitulated to their every demand, allowing them to use her as she had been used by her mother.

Anita's husband, Steven, was no less demanding in his expectations of her. Petty, jealous, and possessive, he drained her of her emotional energy. As a result, Anita spent her adult life shuttling between her mother, sister, children, and husband, which she appeared to do effortlessly until the day she was diagnosed with breast cancer.

With no more fight in her, Anita broke down, becoming depressed. At the very time she needed to be her strongest, she just gave up. This woman who had given to others her whole life, when she was asked to give to herself, had no ability to do so. So low was her sense of worth that she couldn't "show up" for herself.

Anita counted on her mother to pick her up. Because the situation evoked so much anxiety in the mother, instead of being compassionate and caring, she was furious with her daughter. Belittling her repeatedly, she refused to accept that Anita was in a needy state. Anita's children, who were also unable to cope with their mother's deterioration, began to deteriorate too. Her husband, unused to being the emotional leader, started staying away from the house, which he described as "too morbid." So it was that, just as she had been in her childhood, Anita found herself abandoned.

Only after months of therapy did Anita awaken to the fact she was *abandoning herself* as a result of being abandoned by her own parents long ago. She now saw how she had attracted a husband who was just like her mother, narcissistic and negligent. She realized how, by constantly giving to her children, she had fostered in them an inability to cope emotionally with the hardships of life. In her desire to protect them from suffering the same kind of things she had experienced in her childhood, she had overindulged them, causing them not just to lack empathy, but to be callous. So determined had she been not to inflict on them the responsibilities she was required to shoulder in her youth, she had unwittingly brought them up with a disregard for duty.

Like Anita, many of us find ourselves contouring ourselves to earn another's approval. In our bid for acceptance and validation, we transform ourselves into someone we aren't. Raised by parents who were unable to allow us to enjoy our natural self, we learned that to gain our parents' blessing, we needed to alter our desires and inhabit a persona— a false self of which our parents could approve. Tailored to suit them more than it suited us, this persona masked our authentic way of being.

When we are raised by parents who, because of their own unconscious upbringing, make us feel ashamed for expressing who we are, we experience guilt for wanting to be the unique individual we are. If our parents make us feel guilty whenever we stray from the beaten path, we learn not to trust our instinctive response to life, instead experiencing a deep ambivalence toward our life choices.

Guilt is a murky emotion that coagulates our true voice, leaving us with the aftertaste of inadequacy and insecurity. Children who grow up with this imprint don't trust their inherent wisdom. Consequently, they live either forever suffocated by the guilt imposed on them or seek to displace their feelings onto others by judging and guilt-tripping those around them.

With this emotional imprint, our reflexive tendency is to view the world according to these orientations:

> I am bad for expressing who I am

> I don't owe myself the emotion of happiness because if
> I am happy, I abandon those who are unhappy

I am unworthy of emotional freedom

I am the cause of my parents' pain

I am "bad" for having caused my parents discomfort.

Children who are raised with such an imprint grow up to be parents who are unable to find their calling in life because of a sense of guilt that if they pursued what they really want to do, they would somehow let others down. Parents with this imprint are unable to allow their children the freedom to live their own life. Because these parents don't believe in their own competence, they also tend to have a hard time disciplining their children or providing an appropriate container for them. The children of such parents are often spoiled, as well as aggressive in their own quest for boundaries.

Were You Unable to Be Yourself?

We have seen that to gain attention, children who were wounded by their parents' self-absorption adopt a persona. Unable to own who they are and what their true needs are because they are in service to their parents' ego, they don't exercise their authentic voice and only ever express themselves indirectly, instead employing devious means to get their needs met. Seeing themselves as victims, they displace responsibility for their feelings onto others, since blaming someone else enables them to absolve themselves of all responsibility and allows them to adopt a "poor me" stance.

When these children grow up to be parents, they are unable to allow their own children to be themselves. If their children dare to be authentic, such parents see themselves as victims of their children. Or they take on the role of a martyr, leaving their children feeling guilty for doing nothing more than attempting to be themselves.

Let me tell you about Martha, who grew up as one of eight siblings and learned early that her parents' attention was divided among many.

Feeling shortchanged, she figured that if she wanted more of her parents' attention, she needed to be special in some way. Consequently, at times she tried to play the part of a diva, acting dramatically, coming across as louder than her siblings, even appearing brighter. At other times she took on the role of a hypochondriac, claiming aches and pains. No matter how hard she tried, the painful reality was that her parents only had so much attention to give their eight children.

Always feeling wronged in some way or other, Martha grew up to be a woman with many grievances. Marrying a man who was more interested in making money than he was in her, she found herself left to raise her son on her own when her husband turned out to be a philanderer. With no other receptacle for her emotions, her son Nate became the center of her universe. Seeing him as the one who would make her feel all the specialness she had longed to feel, she nurtured his wishes, grooming him to become the man she wished she had married.

Nate's friends envied all the attention his mother showered on him, little realizing that he felt anything but lucky because of the unimaginable sense of pressure he lived under. Expected to be the man his mother couldn't find either in her own father or in her husband, he felt guilty every time he thought of breaking free from his mother's clutches and claiming his own life.

Martha played her role of martyr to the hilt. Anytime Nate disagreed with her, she reminded him of all she had done for him, how much she had sacrificed for him, how she had dedicated her life to him, controlling him with tears and evocations of pity. Nate's father even blamed him, albeit in the most subtle of ways, for taking his wife from him.

Feeling beholden to his mother, as if it were his responsibility to make her happy in the way her own parents and husband failed to do, Nate felt trapped. Although he wanted to study abroad, he remained within a two-block radius of his childhood home, dating only those girls he thought his mother would approve of, because he sensed that to move away would kill his mother. Believing himself to be her only salvation, he was a victim to her victimhood, a martyr to her martyrdom.

When Nate eventually fell in love, it was with someone who was as controlling as his mother, with the ability to evoke a mountain of guilt in him just as his mother did. It was only a matter of time before his wife and his mother were competing for his attention. When he became a father, his mother was even more threatened and played endless games with his mind, resorting to her childhood ways of seeking attention, such as hypochondriacal states. Laying claim to her son's attention in any manner she could, Martha's self-absorption, coupled with Nate's inability to create a healthy separation from her, eventually precipitated a rift in his marriage.

Many women especially grow up with aspects of the martyr role. We unconsciously imbibe the belief we are supposed to take care of others, drawing our sense of purpose from doing so. When this eventually leaves us dissatisfied, we exaggerate this dissatisfaction to our advantage, thereby binding the object of our care to us. Since to own our emotional state and take responsibility for it would be frightening to us, we express ourselves through indirect means such as claiming we are taking care of another, all the while using them to help ourselves feel needed and therefore valued. In other words, our service is motivated by a longing to fill our own emptiness.

As a result of the damage I have seen so many children inflicted with at the hands of unwitting parents, I suggest we remove ourselves from the pedestal of approval-giving by telling ourselves each day, "I ask to be released from the notion that I have any power or jurisdiction over my child's spirit. I release my child from the need to obtain my approval, as well as from the fear of my disapproval. I will give my approval freely as my child has earned this right. I ask for the wisdom to appreciate the sparkle of my child's ordinariness. I ask for the ability not to base my child's being on grades or milestones reached. I ask for the grace to sit with my child each day and simply revel in my child's presence. I ask for a reminder of my own ordinariness and the ability to bask in its beauty. I'm not here to judge or approve my child's natural state. I'm not here to determine what course my child's life should take. I'm here as my child's spiritual partner. My child's spirit is infinitely wise and will manifest itself in exactly the way it's meant to. My child's spirit will reflect the manner in which I am invited to respond to my own essence."

"Bad" Behavior Is Really a Search for Our Inherent Goodness

Tony, a dear friend of mine, is introspective, creative, and worldly. He's also a tortured soul. A twin, he was sent to live with his grandparents in another town when he was ten years old. He recalls, "They just sent me. One day I was going to school, and the next day my mom was packing my bags. She said I had a negative effect on my twin brother. Because I was too strong for him, he was developing a complex."

Tony's mother assured him he was only going to be away for a few months while his twin found himself again. "You are the strong one," she told him. "You always have been. You will be fine." A few months turned out to be a year and a half.

"I saw my parents once a month," Tony remembers, "and they always told me, 'Your twin is coming out of his shell. He's doing better now that he's on his own.' Then they were gone until the next visit. Although they said I was strong and would be fine, I never was. Why was I the one who had to go away? From that time on, I decided that I would no longer be this 'strong, okay' person."

Tony began acting out, indulging in negative behavior to attract attention, imagining this would cause his parents to notice him in the same way they did his twin. Instead, his behavior angered them, which led to attempts to control him with threats that they would never take him back. "I just became worse," he laments. "I got into drugs and alcohol, and dropped out of school. All of this, and they still kept protecting my twin, never coming to my rescue. So from being the 'okay' one, I became the 'bad' kid, a label I still wear. To this day, if I explain to them that I didn't become a rebel just because it was in my blood, but because it was the only way I could get their attention, they laugh at me.

They tell me they sent me away because I was always the bad one. Maybe they are right and I was a bad child right from the start."

The rebel role can result from several family dynamics, at the root of which is the issue of acceptance. In the most typical cases, the parents are either too rigid, overprotective, or overbearing. The child feels squelched in its authentic expression, as well as feeling burdened by the expectations of its parents. Much "bad" behavior is a child screaming for help. The message the child seeks to get across is that it isn't getting its needs met in the normal way, which is why it resorts to extremes of behavior. Another possible response is for the child to cave into the demands of the parents, in which case it may become "the star" or "the pleaser."

Because "bad" behavior triggers all of our fears as a parent, we admonish our children, guilt-tripping them, even shunning them in the hope they will reform. They rarely do. Instead, we perpetuate their behavior until it escalates out of control. When children receive negative attention for negative behavior, they learn that if they behave badly enough, their parents will finally notice them.

Some children who are rejected by their family grow up as receptors of all the failings of a family. Therapists refer to these children as the identified patient of the family. When parents don't own their own shadow, they inevitably project this shadow onto one of their children, who becomes the container for all the family's unexpressed, split-off emotions. Occasionally, the projection encompasses more than one child. Such children grow up with a strong sense of guilt and the feeling that they are intrinsically "bad."

When these children become parents, they either project their feelings of "badness" onto their own children or onto their spouse, casting them in the role of the "evil one." If they are acutely sensitive to their own rebellion, they may be ever-vigilant of signs of rebellion in their children, which causes them to become either too permissive or hyper-controlling. Such parents don't realize that both approaches result in the creation of a rebel.

Your Brokenness Doesn't Reflect Your True Being

None of your pain or brokenness, whatever particular form it may take, is who you really are. None of it ever touches your essential being. For this reason, whatever may have happened to you in the past doesn't have to define you today.

Despite all the pain of life, your true being, with its inherently loving joyfulness, never goes away, though it fails to develop and consequently becomes layered over and lost from your view. What better place to uncover your essential being and integrate the unintegrated aspects of your psyche than within the parent-child relationship? In so doing, you benefit not only your children but also yourself.

Few of us are blessed to have been raised by parents who are in touch with their inner joy. Those children who are so blessed grow up with a lightness of spirit and an intuitive trust that life is good and wise. They know that life isn't to be feared, but embraced. These children watch their parents harness a connection within themselves that transcends the physical, and in this way learn to harness their own unique connection to their source.

CHAPTER 11

A HOUSEHOLD BUILT ON *BEING*

As adults, we are preoccupied with constant activity. Many of us fill our every moment with some activity or other. The foundation of our self-esteem rests on the amount we do, how much we earn, how good we look, and how socially connected we are.

Our children don't operate from this manic state until we teach them to be this way. For this reason, to parent consciously is to operate under a different constitution than society dictates. A child's success is measured by different criteria. Instead of being inundated with activities and pressured to succeed in a world devised by adults, children are allowed to live in the moment and celebrate the organic nature of their existence. In this approach, grades and external measures of achievement are regarded as but a tiny facet of a grander picture.

Encouraging the simple enjoyment of life requires us not to over-schedule our children. Instead, we allow their early years to be about play dates and lazy hours. If children are caught up in a buzz of constant activity from morning to night even before they reach the age of five, how will they ever connect with themselves?

The truth is, many a modern child's hectic schedule is more about the inability of *parents* to sit still than the child's need to do so much. We have been raised to live in a state of constant "doing." It isn't just physical activities such as working, exercising, or running errands that keep us occupied, but also our ceaseless mental labeling, categorizing, evaluating, and theorizing. The modern mind is so busy, we have lost our ability to meet a person or a situation with *neutral* energy. Instead, when we face an "other," be it a person or an event, we immediately impose on the individual or the situation our preconceived ideas of right and wrong, good or bad.

Witness the parent who responds to uncomfortable aspects of their life with anxiety, frustration, anger, and cursing. Sit in traffic with them and observe how they judge and label their experiences. They are unable to calmly note the fact they are sitting in traffic and be at peace with this, unable to find themselves in a difficult situation and just note that it feels difficult. Such a parent leaves a legacy for their children that mandates all life experiences be judged and labeled, especially the "bad" ones. When we are unable to meet our children's reality from a state of *being*, they learn that life cannot simply be experienced *as is*.

All of this "doing" is an attempt to assuage our sense of incompleteness, as can be seen from the example of a mother who gives up her own life to be with her children, only to engage in endless activity "for her children's sake." Outwardly, she may appear a devoted mother, taking her children to ballet classes and baseball games, cooking and cleaning for them constantly. However, because her sense of self is predicated on what she does for her children, her giving is conditional. Since her helter-skelter schedule is driven by her need to soothe her own angst, she is *unable* to be present to her children's needs and instead uses her children vicariously to fulfill her unfulfilled fantasies. If her children fail to contort themselves to her requirements, she can't tolerate it, which leads to an even more unhealthy dynamic of manipulating her children to get them to be "good."

I watched this happen with a mother and her two children. A fashion designer who left her career to become a full-time mother, this woman's focus was her children, to the point that her entire day revolved around them. Over-zealous and over-involved, they were signed up for activities every evening, which meant she was constantly in her car running back and forth to pick them up and drop them off. That they excelled in their academics and activities was of utmost importance to her. Since her daughter was a star swimmer and her son a stellar pianist, this mother couldn't be more proud of them and lived for their moments of triumph. The first parent to arrive at all their events, it was these occasions that made her feel worthy as both a mother and a human being.

Then one day the school guidance counselor called this mother to say that her daughter had confided she had become bulimic. The little girl had broken down, declaring she was terrified of her mother finding out, and kept repeating, "Please don't tell my mother. She will hate me. She will be so disappointed in me." The daughter was just eight years old when she became bulimic after feeling pressured to look thinner in her bathing suit.

It was at this point that the mother slammed the brakes on all their lives. This was the first time she had considered the toll the endless activities were taking on her children's emotional wellbeing. Until now, she had presumed she was doing the best she could for them. She would never have imagined all the pressure might have an adverse effect. How could she know? When she was a child, she wasn't exposed to activities or given much attention by her parents, who traveled a great deal, leaving her with her nanny. By doing things her own mother never did for her, this mother imagined she was being a devoted parent. Ironically, her desire for her children to have the childhood she was deprived of resulted in her children feeling as lonely and neglected as she had. Only, in her children's case, they had buried their feelings beneath their busyness because they sensed they had to keep performing for their mother's sake.

The lesson is that if we teach our children to predicate their sense of identity on "doing," they will be unhappy every time life fails them in some way.

ARE YOU AWARE THAT ANXIETY IS A FORM OF "DOING?"

One of the most common forms of "doing" that we use to cover up our inability to just *be* is anxiety.

When parents react to their circumstances with doubt, hesitation, pessimism, or distrust, unable to sit calmly in their present reality, anxiously seeking answers to how their future will look, children orient themselves to life in the same way. Because such parents don't see life's difficulties as an invitation to connect to their resilience, instead developing an attitude of "woe is me," their children develop the same emotional response to their own difficulties. Inheriting the anxiety imprint creates a feeling of victimhood and a desire to play the role of a martyr.

Similarly, when parents interact with the present moment in such a way that they focus on what they feel is missing, lack becomes their children's lens on the world. This is the result of feeling such emptiness that, when we look at the world around us, we focus on what's familiar, which is all the things we think are missing. We are so unused to operating out of a sense of abundance that we can't recognize the abundance in the universe.

In some of us, anxiety fuels a need to be "perfect," which leads to a compulsion to "fix" ourselves, all of which is driven by a longing to garner everyone's approval of us. In others of us, anxiety fuels just the opposite of a desire for approval, which takes the shape of a spirit of rebellion. We still feel we ought to be perfect, still have a yearning to fix ourselves, still want approval, but these are overshadowed by our actual behavior.

More than anything, anxiety tends to surface as a need to control. When we are unable to be with ourselves just as we are, we forsake a kinship with our own authenticity. In place of authenticity, we either seek to establish some sense of being "in control of ourselves" by bending to the will of another, or we try to feel in control by dominating someone else, especially our children. In an attempt to reduce our anxiety, we are driven to order the circumstances of our life, dictate the outcome of situations, and organize the people among whom we live.

Worrying gives us a reassuring sense we are "doing" something, fooling us into imagining we somehow have some control over things. By engaging in mental "doing," we feel we are taking action. However, since worrying is focused on the future, on things not yet developed, it deflects us from initiating positive action in the present. The truth is, worry is a mask for our fear of being "present" in our *present*.

Paradoxically, when we are caught up in anxiety, we are afraid of actually *taking charge* of our situation in a way that might change things for the better. In fact, when we examine anxiety closely, it's really a *passive* state—a distractor that allows us to fill our head with busy thoughts that appear to be active responses to our situation but in reality are powerless. Though we seek to impose control through the stance we take on an issue, by means of our thoughts, or by seeking to impose our will on others, we rarely take the action required to alter things.

The anxiety generated by the thought of surrendering to our reality manifests itself in a variety of ways. It's worth exploring some of them. For instance, whenever life doesn't turn out the way we want it to, we experience an overarching sense that we are "above" life, which means that things are only supposed to go wrong for other people, not "special" individuals like ourselves. We tell ourselves, "This wasn't supposed to happen to me. This can't happen to this family. I can't believe that I, of all people, have to go through this. I need more from life. This isn't what I bargained for. This isn't what I worked so hard for."

Others of us indulge a pervasive sense of victimization, even martyrdom, when things turn out in a way we didn't anticipate. We think of ourselves as unlucky. "This always happens to me," we may say. "I always lose in the end. I can never win." We might even come to believe that everyone is out to get us. Taking this a step further, we can begin to believe that the world isn't only unfair, but also unsafe.

Our internal dialogue runs something like, "No one cares about anyone but themselves. It's all so competitive. I hate living in a world that revolves around money, not love. People do such mean, cruel, vengeful things. You can't trust anyone because human beings are untrustworthy. The world is a hellish place to live."

Some of us blame ourselves for our misfortune, which only compounds our misery. "It's all my fault," we tell ourselves. "I attract bad things into my life. I deserve this fate." Or we may turn our sense that we are being victimized outward, telling ourselves such things as, "They never really loved me. They should have paid more attention to me. If only they would have cared more. They set me up for this failure. Why don't they listen more?"

With such a mindset, life's challenges are met with a constriction of feeling rather than a sense of expansion. The anxiety that results then fuels a sense of despair and distraction, which in turn leads to failure, which results in lowered motivation, which then spirals down into yet more anxiety and the paralysis that accompanies such anxiety. Out of our fear of committing to life because of our fear of failing at it, we create one obstacle after another. Confronted with a tough situation, we see only problems, not solutions.

Many of us repeatedly create situations in which we sabotage ourselves in order to feed our "I can't" mindset. For instance, we start preparing for examinations late. When we fare badly as a result of our procrastination, we translate this into a belief that we are "incapable." Or we start projects but don't finish them because we not only succumb to distractions but also place hurdles in our way, which feeds our belief in our incompetence. Even if at some point we initiate positive change in our life, we experience such change as discordant because of its unfamiliarity, which generates so much anxiety that we abandon the change and return to our passivity. Believing we need to know the outcome of a situation before getting into it, we embark on a venture only if we are certain of how it will turn out. Without certainty, we feel too vulnerable, too exposed.

If you grew up with parents whose primary reaction to life was anxiety, this is what you too will pass on to your children unless you watch yourself closely and consciously undo this pattern. Your children will come to view life as intrinsically threatening. They will learn from you to fear the very gift that can empower them to face life's dangers triumphantly, which is their inherent trust based on their inner "knowing." Coming to doubt themselves, they will buy into the illusion that unless they worry about something or find something to dislike about their life, they jinx themselves in some way.

A cycle of this kind, passed from generation to generation, is only broken when we discover that *worrying is a mask for a fear of being present*. By becoming present, we can help our children develop their trust in life as inherently wise.

WHAT'S THE SOURCE OF OUR FEAR OF THE PRESENT?

Many of us are terrified to sit with ourselves and truly experience our solitude. To come face to face with our total aloneness scares us. This is why we fill our days with projects and gadgets—why we seek endless ways to insert ourselves into our children's lives.

Of course, the root of this fear is our fear of death. This is a reality we are unprepared to accept, which is why we live our life pretending death will evade us. Until we come to terms with our mortality, we clutter our life with noise and drama, which heighten our sense of being "alive." We control our children, fight with our spouse, and create unpleasant situations in our place of work for the same reason. Through the throb of activity, we assure ourselves we are "alive." Without all of this activity, we would be terrified that we would not only *have* nothing, but *be* nothing. Entering the void is our greatest fear.

This fear is compounded when we hold a belief that life and death are two ends of a linear spectrum. Such a perspective generates anxiety, accompanied by the feeling we must rush through life at all costs. However, if we embrace the perspective that life and death are just points on a continuum, we can allow our maniacal attachment to "this" identity, "this" life, "this" role to be subsumed within the understanding that life continues. As a result, we loosen our grip on our egoic state and allow ourselves to glimpse our true being.

No matter that we try to hide from the reality of our mortality, we all know that life is tenuous and extremely fragile. We live with this understanding despite our attempts at denial. Even though to truly confront what this means is harrowing, wouldn't we be better to be real with ourselves? Embracing the tenuous, moment-by-moment nature of our existence is ultimately empowering. Instead of warding off this realization by creating emotional drama, we are wise to simply sit with life's *as is* quality.

Fear of death keeps us attached to the ego, so that our sense of "I" is that of an isolated monad. In contrast, once we accept the impermanence of life, we awaken to its total connectedness and everyday wonder. This is where the parenting journey becomes enlivened. Cherishing every moment of our children's existence, we enjoy each experience, especially those that seem ordinary. We stop wasting time and energy on endeavors that ultimately evoke no joy. We cease squandering our existence on impersonal material things, realizing that what matters is a connection to ourselves and the relationships in our life.

It's no easy matter to accept that, ultimately, this journey of life is only ours to call our own. We fear we'll feel isolated and lonely if we really claim our uniqueness. This is because, to the degree we are strangers to ourselves, we feel ill-equipped to nourish our own self. Little do we realize that it's only through the experience of our unique path that we can experience both personal fulfillment and oneness with all beings.

Our children can lead us into authenticity because they instinctively know how to *be*. They intuitively know how to live within their body and respond to their spirit. They are fully aware of the need to meet reality as it presents itself and are able to respond in a manner that we adults often aren't. This is why it's from our children that we can learn how to really *live*.

Basically, we are afraid to surrender to life *as is*, and this fear keeps us in reaction mode. Yet surrendering to our children's spirit is imperative if we are to raise them with an ear to *their* true being. This we do by diving beneath our reactions, intellectualizing, and even know-how, simply meeting our children as they are, *being* to *being*.

BEYOND LIVING BY "DOING"

The great ailment of modern society is our grave inability to be with ourselves. We are so anxious, perplexed, and lacking peace. Why? Because we are disconnected from our essence. If we were connected to our inner being, we wouldn't destroy each other, and now the planet itself, in our manic quest for power. When we are simply being, the need for control is relinquished for a sense of oneness and personal empowerment. By paying attention to our inner being, we automatically develop a reverence for life and compassion for all beings, especially those with less power.

Once we realize that the answer to our children's anxiety isn't found in the external world but in their internal landscape, rather than encouraging them to seek immediate external gratification to calm their anxiety, we teach them to engage their imagination. If we are a conscious parent, we are patient and therefore in no hurry to impose every activity and piece of knowledge on our child. We recognize that childhood isn't the time for the fruit to come to fruition, but the time to plant seed. We also understand that it's our children's choice to water whichever seeds they will, guided by their innate wisdom and sense of destiny. In other words, a conscious parent trusts implicitly the child's intuition concerning its destiny. To live consciously means to focus not on the outcome but the process, not on the perfection of an activity but on our courage to learn from our mistakes. It's to be aware that the present is the only moment of relevance. It's to trust life to be a constant, willing, and wise teacher.

To live in a state of being requires you to connect to your inner pulse. When you work from this centered, still place, all activity that arises is simply a manifestation of your deeper purpose. Coming from this place, you no longer engage in one pursuit after another, but instead devote your energy to awareness of your inner stillness. This inner stillness manifests as *presence,* and presence is the core characteristic of the awakened, receptive, accepting spirit of a conscious parent.

As parents, unless we learn to live from being rather than doing, listening to our inner voice instead of being driven by external factors, the parent-child journey will be fueled by anxiety and drama. When we shift from egoic doing to authentic being, our worldview changes. We find ourselves no longer focusing on need, but on service; no longer feeling internal lack, but experiencing abundance; no longer feeling stuck, but flowing; no longer locked into the past, but present now.

While this is an essential shift if we are to parent consciously, it isn't an easy one for a parent to make. We engage in doing because we find it easier to say yes to those aspects of life connected to our child's performance in society than to their authentic being. However, if we shift our own axis to a delight in simply being, so that all our activity flows from this childlike state, we spontaneously find ourselves honoring our children for those qualities that may be less quantifiable but that are infinitely more essential—qualities such as authenticity, awe, joy, peace, courage, and trust.

When we are invested in where our children will end up in life, we impart to them the sense that "time is money," instead of teaching them that time is infinite when experienced in the present. Parents who live in a state of being teach their children to live for their inner purpose, which is born of their spirit, not for money or image. Children are as content with a little fruit for dinner as they are with a gourmet meal. Their eyes don't search for things to attach to, but for things to let go of. Instead of imposing their will on life, they flow with the stream. Life is seen as a partnership in which the external world enriches the inner life, and vice versa.

THE MOMENT IS NOW

Our children won't stay around us forever but will soon move on to their own lives. It's during the few short years we have them to ourselves that we can help them awaken to the fullness within them, because it's into this inner cup that they will dip when they are alone at college and under pressure, in a relationship and struggling with intimacy, or in a financial crunch and anxious. To prepare them for this, their spirit needs to be nourished on a daily basis.

Many of us look to when we are out to dinner at a restaurant or on vacation together to connect, but it's in the ordinary moments—giving a bath, seated at the dining table, waiting for a bus, driving in the car, standing in line—that emotional connectivity best flourishes. Unless we understand the potential for connection in each moment of each day, we will miss countless wonderful windows of opportunity for interaction with our children.

When your children speak to you, it's helpful if possible to set aside anything you are doing and give them your full attention, looking them in the eyes. In the mornings, it's important to greet your children and engage them for at least a few minutes before the rush of the day takes over. When rushing to get ready to leave the house, you can engage them in song, share jokes, or join in a game of who can get ready first.

You can also connect in all sorts of other little ways throughout the day. For instance, when you pass your children in the hallway, you can briefly touch their skin or perhaps squeeze their hand. At random moments, reach out to them and tell them how crazy you are about them. When you greet them out of school, do so with complete acceptance, never criticism, and invite them to share their stories. When waiting in line at the store or at a traffic light, connect by tickling them if they are very young, or by telling them about your day and asking about their day if they are older. Also, while they are gone during the day, you might write them a letter or just a short note telling them you thought about them and missed them.

It's vital you enjoy your children's humor and make sure you laugh with them at least once a day. You can also allow them to teach you something about yourself or themselves each day. When evening comes and it's time for bed, treat this time as sacred, allowing them to ramble and unwind in your arms if they wish to. In this way bedtime becomes a welcome ritual.

Since we are all unique individuals, how each of us manifests our connection with our children will differ. The key is to be attuned to our children's inherent rhythms. When we flow with their natural way of being, we find we are able to be more present, open, and engaged.

Watch a child, especially an infant or toddler, and you will find the secret to living a conscious life. Children naturally inhabit the present moment. Even though infants or toddlers are touted as having minimal consciousness, it's they who most embody the elements of conscious living. How? By their ability to respond to life in its *as is* form, without the encumbrance of egoic liabilities such as fear, guilt, attachment, or a need to control. When we raise them unconsciously, we take them out of this natural habitat and cause them to feel the pressure of the future. Jolting them out of presence and into the mind, we cause them to exchange their spontaneity for the predictability of habit.

Very young children especially are able to reinvent themselves on a moment-by-moment basis. Intrinsically spontaneous, they are unafraid of a fluid way of approaching life, which renders them open to change. They see a flower and stop to gaze at it, or notice a cloud and are able to drop what they are doing to admire its shape. Because they have boundless imagination, rooted in a lush inner landscape, they can play in the sand for hours, needing no gadget or machine to entertain them. Always consciously in their body, they honor its needs without shame, so that when they are hungry, they eat; and when they are sleepy, they sleep.

To respond to our present as if it were the only moment of relevance can be scary because, instead of interpreting a situation according to our past, we are asked to see the newness of each situation in the way a little child does. We have some rather clever ways to disguise how we obsess about the past and agonize over the future. Regret, remorse, guilt, and nostalgia sound so honorable, but they are simply a preoccupation with yesterday. Similarly, worry, fantasies of what will be, and excessive planning and organizing can sound like we are just concerned for things to go right, yet they are forms of preoccupation with tomorrow.

When we are blinded by our past or yearn for our future, we miss the opportunities that are evident to the eye of wisdom but invisible to the overcrowded, over-analytical mind. Before we know it, we lose our connection to our authentic self and therefore to each other. The authentic self only develops through awareness of the present moment. To raise a child to be conscious, it's essential we parents begin living in the time zone of the present. No matter how messy or unbearably painful the present moment may be, only our *judgment* of it makes us want to avoid it, not the present moment itself.

No matter what has passed or what may come, in this moment at least, you can look at your children differently. Right here, in this moment, you can inhabit an altered consciousness. Even if you can only do this for a few moments each day, these moments have the power to affect your children's destiny. Awareness isn't an all-or-nothing phenomenon, and each moment in which you are aware holds great power. Every additional moment you connect with your children is one more than yesterday.

CHAPTER 12

THE WONDER OF THE ORDINARY

We all want our children to be special because this makes *us* feel special. But at what cost to our children? So anxious are some of us to raise the next Einstein, Michael Phelps, or Julia Roberts that we push our children to excel at some activity or other. We want them to be not just good at something, but *great* at something. We all know the surge of pride we feel when we announce to the world that our child is an "A" student, a star swimmer, a prized actor, a brilliant tennis player, or has been "accepted to Harvard." Especially when they are young, our children are attuned to this and push themselves to quench our ego's thirst.

One reason we are so hungry for our children to be a success is that we tend to seek validation through them. We measure them against their peers. Are they doing better or worse than our friends' children? Are they better or worse readers, better or worse writers, better or worse on the sports field or the court? We are impatient to maximize our children's potential.

Although our children are born with none of these worldly concerns, they learn early that they are part of a competitive world that's sharply divided between the performers and non-performers. They learn that they are measured by criteria external to themselves: grades, teachers' remarks, how they are seen by their peers.

Unfortunately, they also learn about labels: ADD, PDD, learning disabled, bipolar disorder—and, at the other end of the spectrum, gifted and talented. They learn that their behavior is constantly under scrutiny. Should they fall short of some socially accepted criteria, they find themselves subject to humiliation.

When we teach our children that their success in life is dependent on their performance, childhood becomes geared toward the future instead of being experienced simply as childhood. Children learn that who they are, *as they are*, isn't enough in the adult world. Little wonder that childhood is shrinking, so that even eight-year-olds are now being labeled bipolar, while fourteen-year-olds are experiencing eating disorders, attempting suicide, or becoming parents themselves.

I see anxiety all around me. Almost everyone is rushing toward the future. There is little presence, little time to savor the extraordinary in the ordinary.

Do You Revel In Your Child's Ordinariness?

A parent who was denied the experience of ordinariness during childhood will be unable to tolerate their child's ordinariness. The child will grow up under pressure to always be extraordinary, which will come at the cost of authenticity. Instead of putting all this pressure on them, can we enjoy our child's ordinariness? Can we find specialness in their ordinary state?

Parents say to me, "But we want to expose our children to the best of everything. What's wrong with that? Why shouldn't we send them to ballet and tennis and swimming classes?" I'm not advocating that parents restrict a child's desire to explore. To encourage exploration is a way of honoring a child's being. I'm stressing the importance of helping our children understand that their *sense of worth* isn't predicated on achievement.

Although it's natural to want our children to excel, this is preferably never at the expense of failing to revel in their ordinariness. When we deny our children's ordinariness, we teach them to be enthralled only by exaggerations of life. They come to believe that only the grand and the fabulous are to be noticed and applauded, and hence constantly pursue "bigger" and "better."

In contrast, when our children learn to value the ordinary, they learn to inhabit *life itself*. They appreciate their body, their mind, the pleasure of sharing a smile, and the privilege of relating to others. It all starts with what we as parents teach them to appreciate.

I suggest you highlight for your children the following quite ordinary moments:

The touch of our skin when we hold hands together

The quiet of the mornings when we first wake up

The warm rush of the water in the shower
   when we bathe

The smell of the laundry when we fold it

The togetherness of the family when we sit to eat

The light of the sun as it sets

The quiet of the moon when we shut out the lights
   for bed

The grip of our child's hand on the pencil as they write

The excitement of starting a new book

The taste of our favorite foods

The wonder of every element in nature

The excitement of a friend sleeping over

The thrill of summer's first ice cream

The crunch of fall's withering leaves

The starkness of winter's bare cold

The smell of the dough baking as we pass the pizza shop

The untold secrets within a library's walls

The glee of finding a lost penny.

When your children learn to revere such moments, gone is the madness for more, flashier, bigger. They grow into adults who are able to focus their attention on *what's before them* as opposed to *what isn't*. Then, free of your expectations, they enjoy their ordinariness and reach for expectations that spring from their *own* center.

THE FALLACY OF THE OVERPRODUCTION OF LIFE

When we aren't solidly grounded in our own essence, we tend to compensate by creating an external life in which just about everything becomes a "big deal." Lacking an adequate sense of our intrinsic value, we feel a need to exaggerate, bend over backwards, and overanalyze.

For instance, our child gets lice and we act as if a tsunami has occurred. They receive a bruise and we rush to medicate, often way overdoing it. They earn a C and we call in a tutor. Another kid hits them and we're ready to take this kid's family to court. They tell us a lie and we go ballistic. They are bored, so we buy them more gadgets whose entertainment value will be as limited as the ones they already have. They turn thirteen and we throw them a party fit for a wedding.

Believing that more is better, bigger is brighter, and expensive is greater value, many in modern society have lost the ability to respond to life without turning it into a major production. Consequently, our children grow up believing life is to be lived fast and furiously. In their everyday existence, drama trumps simplicity, excitement beats out stillness. They grow up addicted to a life of highs and lows, unable to rest in the ordinary and with little perspective on how to glean enjoyment from the mundane.

Children learn who they are and what they really enjoy if they are allowed to *sit with themselves*. Inundated with activity and subjected to lesson upon lesson, how can they hope to recognize their authentic voice amid the din of all this "doing?"

One day my four-year-old daughter was in a restless mood. Jumpy and hard to please, she kept saying she was bored and had nothing to do. My first instinct was to rescue her—and, in the process, myself! Isn't a "good" parent supposed to schedule their children's time? As I contemplated whether I should turn on the television, do a project with her, or take her to the park, the insight came to me, "How will she learn to navigate her way through her boredom if I rescue her all the time?"

Our children develop emotional sturdiness when they manage their emotions without the assistance of an external aid. So I told her, "It's okay to be bored. There's nothing wrong with feeling bored. Keep being bored."

She looked at me not just with great disappointment, but as if I were slightly mad. As she left my room, she muttered loudly to herself and kept on muttering long after she was out of view. After several minutes, I noticed her complaining seemed to have died down. When I went to her room, I found her humming contentedly to her dolls.

Imaginative by nature, children are able to respond to the *as is* with body, soul, and spirit. Our children only need an empty room, their imagination, and a willing partner-in-crime. They don't need expensive gadgets and a room full of toys, just their creativity born of their still center. Once they are in touch with their center, they learn to be happy with whatever they have, realizing that contentment arises not from the outside but from what's within.

Watch any young child and you will marvel at their ability to make something out of nothing—their ability to turn an empty room into a canvass for their fantasies and transform the most ordinary of moments into the most magical. I wait with my daughter by the bus stop and within no time she is playing shop, selling wares to her imaginary customers. Me, I am fretting and fuming, wondering when the bus will ever come, unable to imagine any other reality besides my own anxiety-ridden state. I go with my daughter to buy vegetables, in a hurry over which ones to choose, eager to get in and get out. She, on the other hand, is delighted to touch each one. "This tomato is round like my cheeks," she shrieks, "and this eggplant is shaped like my tears." I look at her amazed. How can she see nothing but potential, when all I see is fatigue and hassle?

Our children at this stage are true pioneers, sculptors, singers, actors, playwrights, hairstylists, fashion designers, and race car drivers. They are potters, chefs, gardeners, painters, and scientists. They inhabit entire worlds within them. What happens to this creative potential once they hit middle school? Where does this unrestricted, kinetic burst of magic disappear to? How much of its loss are we responsible for?

In innumerable subtle and not-so-subtle ways, we chip away at our children's ability to think the impossible, thereby limiting them to live in boxes that are comfortable for us. We tell ourselves this is for their own good, but in truth it's to quell our anxiety. Steadily, we erode their sense of life as magical in the service of "reality." Listen to some of the things we tell them:

"You can't be a race car driver; it's too dangerous"

"First learn to sit still, then talk about being a scientist"

"You don't have an ear for music, so how can you
     be a singer?"

"Acting is for dreamers"

"People in our family don't become gardeners"

"You are too short to be a model"

"I think you should be a teacher"

"I think you would be a wonderful doctor."

When children are full of confidence, seeing only abundance, opportunity, expansion, and adventure, they have an oceanic faith in the goodness of the universe. It's our spiritual obligation to allow them to foster and nurture their innate capacity to engage life. It's too early for us to burst their bubble. Let them dance and not worry about the performance at the end. Let them draw and not concern them- selves with how good or bad the product is. Let them go to school and not be anxious about the grade they get, realizing that when we are overly invested in grades or how well they do at a certain hobby, they begin to lose interest in the learning and focus only on the perfection of the outcome. Let them fly in their imagination without us telling them they are impractical for doing so.

Having said this, I'm not unaware of the growing body of evidence that a child is subject to profound influences in utero, which can affect the child's demeanor, temperament, and capacity to embrace life fully. Also, for not all women does pregnancy occur as a welcome event, a factor that can have a profound effect on the developing child. Because any chemical bath the mother generates while pregnant flows instantly into the bloodstream of the infant, including negative stress hormones, to parent consciously as early as possible in a child's life becomes all the more important. Still, any step toward conscious parenting, no matter when this step is taken in a child's development, is better than none at all.

At every opportunity, encourage your children to listen to their inner voice, love the process of learning, enjoy the mastery of a skill, revel in taking a risk, and laugh at themselves when they fail. This is how you teach them to manifest their true creative potential. More than this, they will teach you how you can unleash *yours!*

Surrender the Urgency to "Do"

The inability to value the spaciousness of free time is *learned*. Our children pick up restlessness by osmosis as we teach them to rely on being busy all the time. They then grow up to be adults who can't enjoy being alone in their own body, but must instead always be at a nightclub, with friends, or working.

To be able to flow from state to state, children don't require gadgets or other forms of distraction. They are able to adjust from one state of being to another quite easily once we cease our interference. Indeed, when we fill our children's lives with countless activities or artificial trinkets, we rob them of their imagination, and hence of their ability to create their own pleasure.

When we empty our life of clutter, noise, and distractions, prioritizing our schedule around the creation of space, we open the way for vital experiences. For instance, we gaze at a beautiful sunset and it almost takes our breath away. Unable to take our eyes off the ever-changing rainbow of colors, we find ourselves at a loss for words. So present are we with the experience, all urgency to "do" is surrendered, replaced by awe and a transcendent awareness of our connection to all of reality.

At such a moment, there's no room for hatred, hostility, or a critical attitude, which are swallowed up in the serenity of the vast expanse before us. Completely in our body, yet in a heightened state of consciousness, we are enjoying a foretaste of what it means to truly enter into our experiences.

BACK TO BASICS

One of the easiest things to do to help our children return to their innate fluidity is to reduce the amount of television or other forms of screen time. I'm not suggesting that television or computers are bad for our children, only questioning the role they play in their everyday life. There's a world of difference between allowing our children to enjoy cartoons, shows, or games (especially at weekends) for leisure, and resorting to these things to distract us from being with ourselves. If a screen is used to comfort restlessness or boredom, our children learn to be dependent on external aids to allay their anxiety.

Television and computers often serve not only as a band aid whenever children feel bored or upset, but as a replacement for relationships. Used in this way, they rob our children of the opportunity to learn how to sit with their emotions and navigate their feelings themselves. As the child becomes buried in the noise of the program or game, its emotions are blunted. Television or the computer soon become an obsession, so that our children want them to be on at all times, in their numbness feeling strangely comforted by the presence of a screen.

Another step we can take is to exchange *purchases* for *experiences*. Instead of buying a gadget, we take our children to the zoo. Instead of buying a video game, we accompany them on a bicycle ride. Rather than buying them a fancy car on their eighteenth birthday, we send them on a trip to a Third World country, where they have to earn the money for a car.

Our children first and foremost need us to give them our attention, not our money. The gift of our attention is so much more valuable than anything money can buy. If from a young age our children are taught to value our relationship with them over the things we buy them, we set the stage for a reliance on their inner being rather than externals. A human will always choose relationships over gadgets or other possessions, provided we haven't corrupted their natural instinct.

On weekends, my daughter is allowed an hour of television or an hour on the computer. One Sunday, since my husband and I were both at home, we decided to play a board game together. As the game proceeded, I realized it was going to take longer than I had anticipated, which meant it would be bedtime before my daughter could enjoy her hour on the computer. "Let's stop this game," I suggested, "because I promised you an hour of computer time." I imagined she would race out of the room, thrilled to be by herself with her computer games.

Surprising and humbling me, she responded, "I don't want to play on the computer. I want to play this game with you." It's we who rob our children of their natural desire to be close to us—and then we bemoan the fact that, in their teens, they want nothing to do with us.

Instead of rushing to buy our children the latest video game, computer, or jewelry—especially if they are under the age of twelve—we help them best when we encourage them to live a simple life. If they see us become flustered, promising to buy a certain toy for them when they complain they don't have it, they come to believe such things are really important. However, if they receive no reaction from us, they learn to appreciate what they already have.

We help our children develop their resilience when we don't panic at every opportunity. They are going to fall ill, receive bruises, get into a fight at school, come home with a B (or heaven forbid a D!), and in general mess up. They are going to eat too much candy, forget to brush their teeth, wear their shirt inside out, lose their cell phone, break our television remote, and violate our rules. This is the nature of childhood. If we develop an over-exaggerated response to our children's follies, they learn to have over-the-top reactions like our own—reactions that, in the teen years, can include suicide.

While many parents put tremendous stress on their children, others try to rescue their children from stress. The reality is that children need stress in order to grow. Learning to tolerate the pain of seeing them deal with stress, allowing them to sit in the discomfort of their imperfection, staying out of it while they are forced to decide between two equally desirable or undesirable choices—all of this is essential for a child's development.

During times of stress and tension, the ability to think outside the box can so easily become constricted and wither away. This is why it's crucial you teach your children to engage life from an authentic sense of a deep calling, as opposed to fulfilling an ego-desire. Once they hold within them the power to transform their hardships, they will never find themselves at a loss for sustenance because they will know that the source of everything is within them. They will make rubies out of rubble because they see this is how you live your own life.

When you foster your children's creativity on a daily basis in the same way you supply them with the right nutrition, you teach them one of the most valuable lessons of all: to rely on their inner being to solve life's problems. They have an intrinsic ability to think outside the box, and only your anxiety causes them to doubt their inner voice.

A LIFE THAT MIRRORS WHO YOUR CHILD IS

As part of expressing their unique being, a child's life needs to mirror who the child is. Their room should reflect them, their wardrobe be personal, their hairstyle individual. Little do many of us realize how we narrow our children's vision, teaching them that following the beaten path is to be preferred over beating out their own path. For this reason, we are wise to solicit our children's input on decisions regarding all these areas of their life. In this way, it's *their* choice how their inner world manifests itself.

Parents often argue that their children would make unwise choices. Let me be clear that I'm not advocating we allow our children to decide which city we should live in or which school they will attend, although they can certainly give their input on these issues. It's important we don't pretend our children are mini-adults, capable of acting with reason and wisdom. As parents, it's our responsibility to keep things in perspective. Hence we present our children with choices that are *appropriate* for their age and in alignment with their ability to discern wisely. For instance, we allow them a voice in determining the clothes they wear for the most part, unless of course they want to go around in a bikini in the dead of winter. They also have a say in the activities in which they participate, including such things as the restaurants the family eats at. And, too, we give them the freedom to disagree with us when they have a different viewpoint. In this way, they learn to engage life as a creative process that's always in flux.

How wonderful if every parent would convey to their child, "You are a creative person. Be free with your imagination. Take me to places in your imagination so I can visit and revel. Imagine all you want, and express yourself without fear. How else will you know your limits? You have the capacity to place your unique imprint on the universe. At the same time, there's a sense in which you are at once many beings in a single being, so don't marry yourself to a single way of expressing yourself too soon. All you need to be is *you*, and you can express who you are in any way you choose as you develop. Don't worry so much about the 'logic' of a project. If you believe in it, do it. Life isn't about the money you make, but is a matter of engaging in things for the sheer joy of it."

Perhaps more than anything, you promote your children's well-being when you demonstrate joy that springs from your own being. When they observe you living from pure being, content to exist as you are without the need to forever be in production-mode, they locate this capacity within themselves. They realize they are ultimately responsible for their own internal state and learn to access their own joy, which journeys with them no matter what their circumstances.

Your children are well on their way to consciousness when they realize that to simply be with themselves and with you, connected at a deep level—human being to human being, without interference from outside distractions—is the source of fulfillment. Mastering the art of simple living in this way, they grow up to appreciate all that life has to offer. Appreciating life for *what it already is*, not for what they imagine it ought to be, the *ordinary* in themselves, others, and life itself takes on a magnificence of its own.

CHAPTER 13

SHELVE THOSE GREAT EXPECTATIONS

I'm often asked, "What do you want your child to be when she grows up?" This question always puzzles me because I have no idea what my child should become.

I answer, "She already *is*. I only want her to know her own wholeness as it flows from her inner stillness. Once she knows this, she will own the world."

Children come to us full of the what *is*, not what *isn't*. When we see our own reality for all it *isn't*, we teach our children to operate from lack. When we see our children for all they are yet to become, barely recognizing all they already are, we teach them they are incomplete. For our children to see a look of disappointment in our eyes sows in them seeds of anxiety, self-doubt, hesitation, and inauthenticity. They then begin to believe they should be more beautiful, competent, smart, or talented. In this way, we strip them of their enthusiasm for expressing themselves as they are *right now*.

As I tucked my daughter into bed the other night, I said, "I'm so proud of you." When she asked why, I responded, "Because you dare to be yourself."

When you celebrate your children for their ability to be true to themselves, you encourage them to trust. You inspire them to follow their insight and have faith that they will be held if they fall. You show them they don't have to create a safety net because their safety net is already in place within their own being. You teach them to experience life for the sake of the *experience*, nothing more and nothing less. This is how to raise children with courage and resilience.

In other words, your duty as a parent is to mirror your children's inherent wholeness, out of which they will manifest who they are becoming. By mirroring their wholeness, you help them realize that who they are here and now is *already* their greatest achievement.

HONOR WHO YOUR CHILD IS

As parents, we can so easily superimpose on a child expectations that have nothing to do with *who the child is*. Because these expectations emanate from our own conditioning, we often don't even know we hold such expectations. Nevertheless, these expectations and demands fail to honor *what is*.

If we knew how to honor our own life and feelings just as they are, we would automatically honor those of our children, who need to be given opportunity after opportunity to dazzle with their natural state of being. Instead, we tend to put so much pressure on them that they feel unable to match up to our expectations. In this way, rather than creating opportunities for them to shine, we set them up for failure.

If we are preoccupied with becoming a "success," the state of our finances, and our achievements, we automatically communicate this stressful, anxious way of approaching life to our children. We push them as if they were extensions of our own desperate ego, all the while telling ourselves we are pushing them "for their own good," so they will have a better future.

More and more of us enroll our children in academic enrichment classes before they are of school age, in the hope of giving them a push ahead of the curve. Since we know how important social networking is, we also begin to monitor who they associate with. Many of us also fall into the trap of gearing their after-school activities not according to their interests, but according to how such activities will look on a college application.

Never having learned to sit in stillness and appreciate their intrinsic *being,* the children of parents with great expectations of their offspring are desperate for a sense of value. These are the parents who have prestigious college applications in their drawer before their child turns seven, pushing their children in a predetermined direction without listening to whether this is truly their child's destiny.

When activities oriented toward getting into a top school become the focus of our children's day, they don't have the luxury of allowing their essence to develop. Floundering internally, they determine their worth according to the yardstick of accomplishment. If their ability to accomplish fails to hold up, they are likely to question their value, their talent, and their purpose.

Especially in their early years, our children need the space to delve into their natural inclinations and practice expressing what they find there. Our task is to respond with delight, conveying through our eyes and our smile that they are most adored when they are in the act of *being.*

Whenever you feel the need for your children to excel by engaging in an overload of activities, you might ask yourself whether your motivation is truly to enable them to become who they authentically are, or whether you have a need to bask in their glory. If your child doesn't perform to perfection, does it trigger in you a sense of your own inadequacy? If it does, masking this feeling by appearing to be a dedicated parent can never address your sense of lack. The consequence is that your children grow up to orient their worth around external barometers such as grades, their appearance, their peer group, possessions, career, wealth, or a spouse.

HOW TO SET THE BAR FOR YOUR CHILD

As parents, we may believe that one of our duties is to set the bar for our children. Consequently many of us create vision boards when they are nine years old and cut out pictures of how we want their college years and career to look. We believe it's our responsibility to have high expectations of them, as this is how they will learn to have high expectations of themselves. We tell ourselves that if we embed within them where they have the potential to go, they will develop the inspiration to do just this.

When our children flounder despite all the "help" we've given them, we wonder why. At this point, instead of going within *ourselves* to find the reason, we usually push them even harder, believing they are failing because we aren't challenging them enough. We enroll them in additional classes, hire tutors, and send them for therapy.

Setting the bar too high and too early undercuts a child's potential. Children who grow up embracing our vision of them as a lawyer, doctor, or scientist develop an inordinate sense of themselves as inadequate. When the bar is set so high, how can a child feel anything but dwarfed?

Parents protest, "So we shouldn't expect great things for our children? We shouldn't encourage them to try for a top university?"

What if your children are incapable of being accepted at one of the coveted schools you choose for them? Are they to believe that attending a state college is inferior? What if your child wants to take a year off and join the Peace Corps, travel the world, study fashion design, become a monk, or learn animal husbandry by living on a farm in Montana?

Precisely because there's no one we call "ours" in quite the same way, our children have the power to unleash our ego unlike anyone else. For example, I sit in the ice-rink and see a beautiful seven-year-old figure skater. Then I notice her mother on the edge of her seat, following her child's every move. I think to myself, "Gosh, why can't I be like that mother, here for her daughter day after day?" Then I realize I could never be like this mother. Why? Because I happen to know through friends that this mother is pushing her daughter out of her own egoic need to have a "star" figure skater in the family.

As much as I see this mother and am amazed by her discipline, I also know that at some level she is so very lost—lost to both herself and her child. She has projected all her unmet needs onto her child.

It's so important that you don't need your children to heal a damaged part of yourself, and that you have your own life instead of devoting every minute of your day to your children. If you are content with the *as-is*—content to let hobbies be hobbies, and to let your children's pure being remain free as they enjoy such activities—you won't need your youngsters to earn medals and tiaras.

I think of a parent who cried in my arms because her daughter didn't get into a particular university, then told me, "All those activities, all those medals she won—they have been useless. She might as well have done nothing." This mother nullified her daughter's successes simply because they didn't materialize into the precise future she hoped they would.

Children with 101 averages are being rejected by Harvard. Children with 2200 SAT scores are retaking the test over and over to obtain that perfect 2400. So many children cry in front of me, lamenting the fact they only attained a 93 on a test. The parents, unflinching in their dogmatism, argue with me over the shoulder of their crying child, "You don't understand how important it is to be an alumnus of a prestigious school." They look at me with condescension.

Such parents don't realize that when we set a trajectory for our children's education, romantic life, or career, we immediately limit who they can develop into. They have the power to manifest realities we haven't even begun to imagine. It's not for us to endorse a medical career over an acting career, a marriage at twenty or a marriage at thirty—or even a marriage at all.

Many a clever parent knows how to disguise their dictates as "guidance," though in reality what we have to say is laced with a hidden agenda. Our children aren't fools. They know what we want from them even before we utter a word. Our lips may say, "Follow your dreams," but they realize we often mean, "Follow mine!"

Let your children *want* to attend a fancy school, then work hard for it, rather than you being the one who wants it for them. True, it might frighten you to engage your children in such a "hands off" manner. You may believe such under-involvement will prove detrimental to them, whereas the opposite is the case.

Having said this, there *are* areas in which you can set the bar for your children:

> Set the bar for speaking from their authentic voice
>
> Set the bar for engaging in daily dialogue with you
>
> Set the bar for engaging in acts of service
>
> Set the bar for sitting in stillness on a daily basis
>
> Set the bar for manifesting imagination, creativity, and soul
>
> Set the bar for being kind to themselves and others
>
> Set the bar for delighting in learning
>
> Set the bar for expressing emotions in a direct manner
>
> Set the bar for demonstrating curiosity and a state of receptive openness.

When you resist setting the bar in a manner that's oriented to who you want your children to become, and instead set the bar in ways that embody who they already are, you teach them to trust their innate sense of value and competence. From this foundation, they will devise their own standards of excellence—standards that mirror their *internal* state of excellence.

What Can You Realistically Expect of Your Child?

What do you have a right to expect from your children? I identify three elements: respect for themselves, for others, and for their safety.

Beyond these basics, your children own the right to manifest who *they* want to be, even if this isn't what you wish for them. Anything more presumes ownership of who your children should be. Your expectations are yours to keep and yours to know, not for your children to hold just because they were born to you.

What are some of the things you can hope for your children? Allow me to suggest a few:

>Not that they will be a good achiever, but a good learner

>Not that they will obey you, but that they will respect you

>Not that they will blindly follow your dictates, but that they will seek your counsel

>Not that they will be a star, but that they will master the art of being

>Not that they will follow your vision, but that they will create their own

>Not that they will achieve "success," but that they will live a life of purpose

>Not that they will find direction, but that they will find meaning

>Not they will be your puppet, but that they will be your spiritual partner

>Not that they won't experience pain, but that they will find the means to become whole

>Not that they won't fail, but that they will find the courage to start again

>Not that they won't hurt others, but that they will find the grace to ask for forgiveness.

Again, the first step to releasing your children from the snare of your unrealism is to free yourself from your own. You are a human being first, then a parent. As such, you are on a quest for spiritual development and still have a lot to learn, which means you have emotional blind spots that are yet to be uncovered. You aren't perfect—and if you are wise, neither do you seek perfection. Perfection is banal. Rather than hankering for the "fabulous," you find yourself delighted by the ordinary.

It's important to be able to laugh at your idiosyncrasies, which helps you release your children from the grip of your ego, allowing them to find their own center, separate from yours. You don't need them to make you feel better about yourself, since you realize this is a solitary process. You have the ability to be selfless as much as you can be selfish. And while you have the capacity to give, you also need to receive.

FOCUS ON THE PROCESS, NOT THE OUTCOME

We are well aware that, if a person is in many an ordinary job, technology is fast replacing this person's services. Looking to the future, we worry about how our children will survive when they grow up. We tell ourselves they will endure a life of hardship unless they become star achievers.

When we teach our children early that they are to work toward something, schoolwork becomes tied to mastery of concepts. Activities are geared to becoming better at things, instead of something our children participate in for pleasure. In all of this, our focus is on where our children are *going,* instead of on where they *are.*

By shifting our perspective from the future to the present—letting go of questions such as, "Then what?"—we free our children of the fear of how they will look or how they will perform, and instead allow them to learn without inhibition. It's because of our incessant focus on the end product that our children fail to learn the skills necessary to tolerate ordinariness, frustration, and even failure.

When my daughter was six years old and it came time for parent-teacher conferences, all the moms and dads signed up for a conference time, but neither my husband nor I were able to work our schedules around the openings on the sign-up list. At first I thought, "My daughter's teacher will think I'm irresponsible." As time passed, I realize I didn't need to be so attached to what her teacher might think of me, or even to what her teacher was going to say about her. Not that her teacher's comments wouldn't be helpful; after all, we can all learn from another's perspective, especially when they spend so much time with our children. However, because for the most part I knew how my daughter was doing *as a person*, I didn't need to concern myself with whether she knew her math, reading, and writing. Rather than knowing how good a student she is at school, my focus was on how good a student she is at *life*. I would rather know about her *process* in terms of living than her *progress* in terms of grades. I'm primarily interested in whether she's kind and compassionate, emotionally flexible and resilient, expressive and playful, spontaneous and authentic—elements I already see around our home. I know that if my daughter is successful as a person, she'll take care of the other aspects of her education in her own way and at her own pace. As it turned out, my husband and I were able to arrange a later appointment with the teacher.

A mother confided in me her concern that her four-year-old daughter was off the developmental track because, although she was controlling her use of the potty, she often still wet her panties at night. Reassuring this mother, I encouraged her to let go of her investment in her daughter being on track and instead realize that this would be the first of many occasions when she would need to reconcile herself to her daughter's inherent differentness. The mother called me within two weeks and shared that her daughter had begun doing much better now that she had backed off making this an issue.

So excited was this mother that she wondered whether it would be good to buy her daughter a gift. I responded, "Of course," adding the caveat that instead of simply praising her daughter for reaching a goal, the gift is most beneficial when it represents praise for all the things they learned about each other through this experience. She might explain that she had been worried, but that she was now sorry not to have trusted her daughter, and how wonderful it is that her daughter was able to set her own timetable and be strong about it.

When we focus on the achievement of a goal instead of the learning process, our children miss many opportunities to develop their self-esteem. Rather than telling them, "Good job. Here is your gift," it's important to highlight their character development, sharing with them how proud we are that they showed patience, determination, and bravery. We might also praise them for their ability to demonstrate a relaxed attitude when we couldn't—that, unlike us, they felt no pressure, but honored their own body and its rhythms. In this way our children discover joy in learning, quite apart from reaching a destination.

A little boy of five was using the potty throughout the day, but at night slept in diapers. Realizing the importance of allowing his child to self-regulate, the father said not a word. On the eve of beginning kindergarten, as the father was getting out a diaper at bedtime, his son announced, "I don't need a diaper. I'm a big boy now. I'm going to school tomorrow!" Not once did this child have a nighttime accident. This is the kind of self-mastery we want our children to develop.

When our children come to us with anxiety about an exam, a conscious approach isn't to give them a pep talk about how well they will do on the exam, but to help them handle their anxiety. We need to reassure them that it isn't so important how they perform, but how much they enjoy the material. When the focus is on their willingness to engage the topic and become one with it, we give our children permission to *relish the process* of expanding their understanding. If the focus is on how well they perform on an exam, we send a signal that their unique process is only relevant if they produce *results*. We say we want our children not to fear failure. Yet fear is precisely what we teach when we focus on where our children *need to be,* instead of on where they *already are.*

When we enroll our children in a class or see their report card, we have to remember that it's through how we respond in our body language, voice, and signs of pleasure or displeasure that we communicate what we expect from them. Is our purpose to communicate that only high grades evoke a positive response from us, whereas poor grades don't? Do we communicate that getting an A or coming first in something is the measure of their worth?

When I was twelve years old, I earned A's in every subject. Excited by my report card, I flew into the house and straight into my mother's arms. With her typical exuberance, my mother danced with me, matching my happiness with hers. I imagined my father would also dance, shout, and jump up and down with glee. Instead he smiled and said, "The A's are fine, but what's more important is that you feel you learned the best way you could."

My jaw dropped, my shoulders drooped, and my mother grumbled at him, "Why can't you just say you are excited and show her how happy you are?" I couldn't understand why my father had to be such a spirit-dampener.

It was only when I was in my late teens that I realized what my father was saying. You see, this was *always* his response, regardless of my grade. Even when I got a C, he would say, "The C is fine, but what is more important is that you feel you learned the best way you could." Of course, when my grade *was* a C, his even-tempered response came as a relief! In the most subtle of manners, he was teaching me not to attach myself to the A or the C, but to focus instead on the process of learning.

Simultaneously, I was learning from him to determine my own internal hallmark for success rather than relying on an external standard. I was discovering that embracing the task of learning is what really matters. Since it was abundantly clear that my father's approval of me was unaffected by the grades I brought home, I never felt any fear when my report card came out. Since my father had no great expectations of my grades, the absence of fear that I enjoyed allowed me not only to derive pleasure from learning, but also *to surpass my own expectations*.

This approach is bound to generate anxiety in parents. We are afraid that by not having clear expectations, we will produce unmotivated, lazy children. However, rigid standards only serve to make our children anxious.

When we focus on the process, not the outcome, our children develop their innate curiosity, which causes them to show interest on their own initiative. In this way, we embed in them a thirst for learning that surpasses the fleeting pleasure they derive from gaining our approval through grades. They reach for their own calling, kindling their own desire to live not just a successful life but a meaningful one.

We need to teach our children to approach life not with their focus on how much praise or how many accolades they can *receive*, but with their focus on *what they are putting into it*. Life reflects the internal state with which we enter it. Our children need to know that the quality of their inner life will manifest in their external circumstances.

USE THE RIGHT KIND OF PRAISE

When things don't work out in the manner our children expect, instead of wasting energy on disappointment and resentment, to parent consciously means we focus on the qualities that were allowed to emerge as a result of the process. "Look how much you learned about yourself," we might say. "Did you see how brave you were to put yourself out there? Did you notice how you were able to persevere when you felt defeated at times?" Next we might ask, "How does it feel now that you have overcome your fear?" Such an approach shapes an adult who is unafraid of life's outcomes. They celebrate every experience because it's rich in self-learning and increased awareness.

When we teach our children to disregard grades and instead focus on their courage to sit still and try, we strengthen their inner life. We encourage them to take a risk, as well as to persevere in the struggle. We teach them it's okay that they have limitations, explaining that their desire to exert effort is far more important than their ability to master something. We show them that learning to live with their limitations with ease is a far more important lesson than being attached to perfection.

If we teach our children such values, they grow up to be adults who are unafraid to venture into new territory and live with the unknown. Because they are comfortable with the possibility of failure, they find the gumption to scale their own personally chosen heights.

To help your children realize the abundance they already exude, you can tell them such things as:

> You inspire me
>
> I am in awe of who you are
>
> I am amazed by your spirit, which knows no bounds
>
> You take my breath away
>
> Your capacity for kindness is huge
>
> You are a true person
>
> Your ability to imagine and create is extraordinary
>
> You are blessed with so many talents
>
> You are rich from within
>
> You have so much to teach me
>
> I learn how to be a better person from you.

REALIZE THAT YOUR CHILDREN IMITATE YOU

When we own that our fears about our children's future are our own fears and not really about our children, we don't feel the need to project these fears onto our offspring. Consequently, we encourage them to live in a manner that's oriented to their authentic being.

I want to emphasize that the most profound way in which we can teach our children to access their inner abundance, empowerment, and purpose is if we have accessed our own. When we have, our *presence* becomes our most potent parenting tool.

Our children sense when we are either connected to or disconnected from our stream of purposeful living. When we are connected to a constant flow of fulfillment of our own, we radiate this energy, which serves to ensure our children won't be used to fill an inner void or in some way complete us. Through osmosis, they then begin to inherit a way of being that's similar to our own. They soak in our presence and imitate our ability to relate to ourselves and our life. In this way, simply by embodying our essence in our daily interactions, we help our children find their way back to a sense of fullness, which enables them to identify the abundance in every situation.

As parents, we may feel guilty if we put our needs on a par with our children's. We may feel ashamed to ask for time and space for ourselves, independent of our children. If they watch us constantly sidestep ourselves, perhaps by sacrificing our own needs for those of our spouse or friends, they will learn to devalue themselves in favor of others. If they see we are hesitant to embrace life in whatever shape or form it presents itself, they will imitate our indecision. For this reason, we do our children a spiritual service when we develop our ability to fulfill ourselves and take care of our emotions on our own.

When we don't look to our children to make us happy, but find our happiness elsewhere, we liberate them to be true to who they are. They are able to bask in our happiness without the burden of being the reason for it. Doing something we love, connecting to our inner being in stillness and solitude, honoring our body by taking care of it on a daily basis through the food we eat, the exercise we engage in, and the way we are at peace with how we look are all ways of teaching our children to value themselves.

A friend described growing up with a mother who was always eager to be the "best" housewife and hostess. Whenever guests came, she went to extreme lengths to tidy the house, decorating it throughout with flowers, fixing her hair to perfection, and preparing elaborate meals. However, when no guests were expected, she did none of these things. So great was the contrast between the two states that my friend came to believe others were far more important than ourselves. Perhaps only six or seven years old at the time, she remembers the exact moment she realized that "if mommy bends over backwards to please others so much, they must be more important than she is, since she nearly kills herself each time to take care of them."

You need to teach your children to be unafraid of owning their voice, their space, and their needs. They thrive when they feel free to stand up for themselves and set boundaries, without any hesitation to defend their rights. At the same time, they need to be able to give to others. True giving, which is fundamentally different from giving because it fills an empty space in your life and is therefore a form of neediness, comes from awareness of inner abundance. There is no giving if the inner well is dry. Authentic giving originates from a well that overflows.

Coming from this inner connection, encourage your children to live from their essential being. Released from the snare of your fantasies, expectations, and need to control, they are free to live out their own destiny. Instead of shaping them in your image, you become a witness to their uniqueness as it unfolds—something you can do because you have also become a witness to your own uniqueness.

As you increasingly honor your true being, elements in your life that were previously props for your inauthentic self fall by the wayside. Other elements now enter your life to support your authenticity, as the external follows the internal. Because of your silent connection with your intrinsic being, you find yourself able to support the emergence of your children's true being. Having learned to live from an authentic place, you are no longer threatened when your children speak their truth and live their life authentically.

CHAPTER 14

CREATE A CONSCIOUS SPACE IN YOUR CHILD'S LIFE

T he years from birth to age six are especially a time when children don't need to be thinking about soaring to life's heights, but instead need the leisure to flap their wings around in play and exploration, with lots of space for rest and simply doing nothing.

These are the years in which our children can be allowed the delight of getting to know who they are. It's a time to master small tasks, reach for tiny goals, the most important of which involve exploring and enjoying their own body and spirit. They need to be allowed hour upon hour of idle play, dates with buddies, walks in the park, or rides along the beach. They need uninterrupted hours of twiddling their thumbs, painting nothing in particular, kneading dough, playing with sand, crumbling paper, and rummaging through toy boxes. They need to dress up in costumes, pretending to be kings, queens, and dragons. They need to be permitted hours to stomp in their room and make mistakes. They need the time, freedom, and absolute permission to follow their heart.

This is a period in our children's lives when our children get to sow a variety of seeds and see which take root and eventually bear luscious fruit. This is so much more fulfilling for a child than having the parent plant a single tree, then inject it with steroids so that it bears barrels of tasteless fruit.

Beyond the age of six, and especially as they reach seven and eight, our children begin to develop mentally in a way that marks a major shift from the years of relaxed play. As thought increasingly kicks in, their life becomes more complicated. When this begins to happen, we can help them tremendously by introducing them to the importance of periods of stillness in their life during which they make sense of their experiences, feelings, and circumstances.

ALLOW ROOM FOR STILLNESS IN YOUR CHILD'S SCHEDULE

As a child develops mentally, an aspect of the ordinariness of life is that it involves considerable aloneness. Unless we allow our children to become comfortable with quiet aloneness, they become strangers to themselves, alienated from their essence. When this happens, whenever they are left to themselves, they are uncomfortable and may even feel desperately lonely. With no one to fill the void with noise and distraction, they find themselves face to face with the absolute stillness of their being—a frightening experience for someone who is unaccustomed to resting in their essence.

It's helpful to encourage our children to sit in stillness, so that they learn to exist in a state of quiet without the need to converse. Periods in the car are great opportunities to create such a space. To this end, it may be beneficial not to take gadgets or videos in the car, especially on day-to-day rides, which is when the greatest opportunities for stillness arise. Of course, if we are going to be traveling for hours, having a video, toys, or games doesn't hurt at all. However, on a daily basis, when we are in the car, it's good to drive without the radio on. It can also be good to resist the urge to sing, make meaningless conversation, or play game after game. In this way, we create the space for quiet observation.

When we are in a state of constant distraction with activity, our inner eye is unable to observe our inner being. The ability to observe can only be developed through quiet moments sitting with ourselves. This doesn't mean we create so many moments of solitude that we stop engaging with our children. Rather, we are talking about becoming aware that our children only thrive if there's a balance of doing and non-doing, of activity and non-activity, of engagement and disengagement.

Moments of solitude and stillness aren't empty moments, although they may feel like it initially. They are moments of *fullness*, in which we experience the presence of our being. Such moments give rise to opportunities for contemplation and reflection. The conscious parent isn't checked out during these periods, but is tuned into their children's natural state of being.

I recently began teaching my daughter how to meditate. Eight is a good age for a child to begin developing the art of deepening their consciousness, though this will vary based on the interests and abilities of a particular child. My daughter showed an interest, so I introduced her to the practice. We make it a family activity once a week, typically on weekends, with my husband, daughter, and I sitting together for ten minutes during which we enter into stillness.

We first close our eyes and adjust to the sensation of darkness. After a few moments, I begin speaking, which I do at times during the meditation so that my daughter can learn the technique by leaning on my voice. I guide her attention to her breath as it rises and falls in her chest. Although conscious breathing generally entails paying attention to the breath as it enters and leaves the nostrils, this may be too subtle a sensation for a young child. Paying attention to the rise and fall of the chest is much easier, as this is a larger area of the body. For the next few minutes, we observe our breath as it enters and leaves the chest area: rise and fall, rise and fall. Then I introduce silence, becoming silent for a minute or two. I allow my daughter to sit in her thoughts without any sound, explaining that she doesn't have to do anything but sit and breathe. Finally, I spend the last few minutes on the practice of lovingkindness, during which she learns the importance of spreading compassion and gratitude to the universe around her by thinking compassionate and thankful thoughts.

Before my daughter was old enough to meditate, I used other means to introduce stillness into her life. I consciously sat quietly with her in her room even when she was in activity mode. I took her for walks in nature and allowed her to soak in the stillness around her. I shut off all gadgets for a consolidated time each day and simply engaged with her. I taught her to listen to silence and not fear it.

Children are well able to tune into their inner being if given guidance. Yes, even teens! However, by the time our children become teens, it's easy to feel so helpless in the face of their onslaught that we are tempted to disengage from them, which only serves to drive them even further into their world of technology. Our teens need us to guide them back to a state of stillness, which it's never too late to begin doing. But how are we to accomplish this?

For one thing, we can ask that for one hour a week they engage in a practice of stillness, such as yoga, t'ai chi, or meditation. We can ask that for one hour a week they take a walk in nature by themselves. We can ask that for one hour a week they turn off all their gadgets and talk to us. We can ask that for one hour a week they write in their journal. We can also ask that for one hour a week they paint or engage in some other form of art in silence.

Our children deserve the privilege of knowing their inner landscape. They can only achieve this by being allowed to connect with their essence, which a parent can foster—for ultimately it's the quality of our connection with our children that allows them to enjoy a sense of relatedness to themselves and their world.

CREATE A MEANINGFUL NARRATIVE FOR YOUR CHILD

All of us seek to live lives that are coherent and meaningful. We want our experiences to make sense. Our children especially count on us to help them make sense of their reality. Our task is to teach them how to extract meaning and purpose from life.

One of the ways in which we can infuse our children's days with meaning is through the creation of a narrative of their experiences. A subtle yet powerful way in which we can help develop a narrative in our children's lives is by spending time with them, since our presence brings continuity. When we are present for not only their big moments but also their small ones, we accompany them on their adventure. Our emotional connection and presence gives them a sense of coherence, order, and organization.

We also engage in narrative-making when we remind our children, "Remember when you were eight, and we went to the zoo? You fell, and . . ." There is power in weaving together our children's memories, thereby helping them make sense of their experiences.

Storytelling also provides an interpretive framework for our children's lives. I don't just mean reading stories from books, but am thinking of the power of a story such as Alex Haley's *Roots,* which became a television miniseries. We share with our children how they themselves came to be, how they make us feel, how brave they are, how kind, and so on. When children hear about themselves in a story, they are better able to absorb what we are attempting to convey than were we to teach them directly. Children love to hear stories about themselves because they are eager to create a vision of who they used to be as a baby and how they became who they are now. By relating such stories to our children, we help them weave a narrative about themselves and their place in their family and their world.

Encouraging our children to write their daily thoughts and feelings in a journal is another way to help them make sense of their experiences. Perhaps the entire family might sit for half an hour, such as on a Sunday afternoon, each reflecting on the week and recording their feelings and emotions. What a wonderful way for the family to sit in stillness and activate the inner eye!

Rituals of togetherness are an important way of supporting our children's sense of connection. Whether we gather as a family for dinner every evening, or perhaps at weekends if weekday schedules don't allow, or we join in a family cuddle every Sunday morning, rituals are a rhythmic reminder of the importance of our togetherness. When children learn to count on such rituals, they develop a sense of stability. As adults, they will recall these rituals and draw on them for meaning. Of course, it's also important for families to celebrate key life-events, the memories of which act as a binding force in a child's psyche.

Children who grow up in families in which stories abound around the table and during family gatherings lead lives that are undergirded with a coherence and continuity that's especially valuable during times of stress. Having heard hours of stories about their ancestors, they grow up with an internal narrative that lends them a sense of fortitude, resilience, and courage.

WHY EXPRESSING GRATITUDE TO YOUR CHILD IS A POWERFUL PARENTING TOOL

I tell parents, "When I teach you about gratitude, I'm handing you one of the most powerful techniques to use with your child."

To access a reverence and appreciation for their life is one of the most important lessons our children can learn. Expressing gratitude reminds them that they are never alone but always in relationship with life itself. Such gratitude also reinforces the fact that life is kind, wise, and bountiful.

Creating a daily or weekly ritual at the dining table, in which each person has the chance to express something they are thankful for, helps our children develop reflective skills, which in turn enables them to extract beauty from life. At the same time, such a practice reminds them that even as life gives to them, they too must give to life. Indeed, it teaches children to give back not only in a physical form but also in an emotional and energetic form.

The more we make it a point to reflect on aspects of our existence for which we are grateful, the more our children learn to do the same. Our ability to notice and show appreciation for the smallest elements in our life helps them slow down and take note of their own life. They learn not to take any aspect of their experience for granted, but to respect all that exists around them. Such gratitude fosters a commitment to life.

It's important to express gratitude to our children just for being who they are. Rarely do we thank them for who they are, yet we always want them to appreciate who we are. If we as parents took a moment to look our children in the eye and say, "Thank you," really meaning it, their sense of their value would expand exponentially. In this way, we communicate that they have something to contribute just by being themselves.

My friend, a thirty-year-old woman, is spunky and spritely. Yet when she's with her family, she's just the opposite—especially with her father, around whom she's all but paralyzed. Recently, I saw why. She had invited her family to her home, intending to announce that she was going to be married. At this occasion, her fiancé would meet the family for the first time. Because he followed a different faith, she anticipated there would be flared tempers. I watched her prepare for the event, observed how she couldn't keep still, and noticed her swallow two Xanax before the party, chased by a shot of whiskey. A Yale graduate and a partner in a law firm, she was reduced to a state of such anxiety that it was as if she wished she could shrivel up and disappear.

When she introduced her fiancé and the family learned he was of another religion, her father's face became full of rage. Taking her aside, he railed, "You will never marry this person. To do so would humiliate me in front of our community. If you proceed with the wedding, I will no longer be your father. You will be ostracized from the family forever."

Instead of expressing gratitude to his daughter for seeking his blessing on her marriage and being brave enough to love someone so different from her, her father shunned her. Rather than embracing the lessons he might have learned from this partnership, he rejected his daughter in favor of his rigid conditioning.

Many of us begrudge our children the right to live their own life. We would much rather have them sacrifice their authenticity than forego the comfort of our ego. Little do we realize that our children don't owe us their allegiance. This is a privilege they give us, for which we need to be grateful.

It's important to regularly thank our children for sharing themselves with us. We can thank them for the wealth of meaning they bring into our life. We can thank them for their wisdom, kindness, passion, spontaneity, and liveliness. We can also teach them to be thankful by expressing gratitude for a home to live in, food to eat, a body that's strong and healthy, parents and friends to provide us with a sense of community, and the wonders of nature to enjoy. In addition, we can encourage them to give thanks for qualities like courage, fun things to do, and the opportunity to give back. It's also important that we don't neglect to express our gratitude for all that life teaches us about ourselves each day, so that we can be more fully who we are and express more meaningfully the love that fills our heart.

When we teach our children to find the smallest of things in their day to reflect on with gratitude, we teach them that rather than needing this, that, or the other thing, they have so much already. This in turn awakens their desire to do good for others. In other words, acknowledging our bounty fires our instinctive longing to serve others.

To teach gratitude is to foster godliness within our children, honoring their divine essence. Unless we are in touch with our own divine essence, we will be unable to encourage reverence for this in our children. Having said this, let me caution that for our children to be in touch with the divine Presence in their center doesn't mean they need to manifest any special sort of "greatness." Rather, it's to be acutely aware that our children are already great in their natural, raw state of being. Only when we don't honor our own natural godliness as parents do we push our children to be something we esteem "great," with the thought that *then* we will honor them. This is actually to dishonor their connection to the divine. To recognize and express gratitude for their inherent divinity without their having to accomplish a single thing is to be in touch with the element of divinity in ourselves, and indeed in the whole of life.

If we live our life not with gratitude but with need and greed as our motivators, seeking that which is brighter, flashier, and grander in the hope of feeling fulfilled, this is the consciousness our children will absorb. However, when we enjoy the air we breathe and the shade of the tree we sit under, experiencing the divine Presence in everything, our children learn to be content with what they already have. Then, if more comes, there's no attachment to it, just further appreciation.

CHAPTER 15

CONNECT TO YOUR CHILD
WITH ENGAGED PRESENCE

Many of us mistake the *business* of parenting—the cooking, homework, dropping off and picking up—with being "present" for our children. Though we may be present for their material, physical, and even intellectual needs, this doesn't mean we are present for their emotional and spiritual needs.

Meeting our children's need for connection requires a particular set of skills. It means we listen to our children, truly hearing what they are saying, without feeling we have to fix, correct, or lecture. To achieve this, we have to observe their body, including their gestures, affect, and energy. These we allow to soak in with awakened receptivity.

Many of us have great trouble bringing our presence to our children. Without our realizing, we generally ask that our children relate to *us* and *our* state of being. Though we imagine we are engaging with our children, we are really *forcing them to engage with us*. To identify the way we subtly shift the energy to ourselves, instead of bringing our energy to our children, has the power to change a child's life.

When I ask parents who complain that their teens refuse to talk to them how they know this to be the case, they say something like, "He's always watching television and won't turn it off to talk to me." Often the parent complains, "She is forever on the phone and won't spend time with me." Or I hear, "All he wants to do is play video games. I can't stand video games. What am I supposed to do?" Then there's the parent who bemoans the fact that "all she wants to do is talk about her favorite musicians, which is a topic I know nothing about."

In each of these situations, the parents want their teens to stop doing what they have learned to do with their time in the parent's absence, and instead do what the parent wants them to do. It doesn't occur to the parents to change *their* agenda and join their teens in whatever activity they may be enjoying—not necessarily because they enjoy the particular activity, but because they enjoy connecting with their teen.

The role of a parent isn't to dictate, but to support the development of a child's inherent being. This is why, if we wish to connect with our children of any age group, we need to find a way to match *their* emotional energy. When we match our emotional energy to theirs, they are assured we aren't preparing to strip them of their authenticity and in some way change them, which allows them to become receptive.

Whether children are six or sixteen, they yearn to have a meaningful connection with their parents. If the relationship becomes about control, judgment, reprimands, lectures, and pressure, a child will turn a deaf ear. However, if the relationship is about autonomy, empowerment, kinship, emotional freedom, and authenticity, what child would reject their parents?

Engaging our children consciously enables us to issue an open invitation, welcoming them in such a manner that they can't help but feel they are being *seen for who they are*, free of our critique. The point is simply to convey the message, "I am here, available to be your witness."

Since to give our complete presence is all that's required to raise an emotionally healthy child, some parents might think this means they should be with their children almost all the time. On the contrary, a conscious parent may be extremely busy, and our children need to respect this. However, during those times when we aren't busy, can we allow ourselves to engage our children attentively? When we do so, they come to the realization, "I must be a worthy person because my mother and father have turned off their phones, stopped their work, and are now spending this undivided time with me."

In my own life, in order to enter a state of engaged presence with my daughter, I determine not to try to change her state of being, but instead join it. I attempt to find a way to align my emotional energy with her energy, instead of asking her to match her energy to mine. When my daughter speaks to me, I try hard to bring all my attention to her, listening with my heart as much as with my mind. I express respect for her voice and spirit, demonstrate reverence for her opinions even if I don't agree with them, and remain in a state of receptive openness.

I'm careful not to forget that my goal in being present with my daughter isn't to demonstrate my wisdom and superiority, but simply to connect with her. I have come to greatly value this daily time of engaging in a *being-to-being* dialogue with her, carving out at least an hour for this each day. Relating from an authentic state of love and admiration for who she is, I express how much I learn from her. During this time, we don't do homework or chores, but simply relate, either eating together, playing, reading, or talking to each other. This one simple hour has the power to fill my child's cup with her own inner presence.

How We Undermine Our Attempts to Connect with Our Children

The minute our children try to talk to us, we tend to jump in to advise them, critique them, admonish them. We are also apt to label their experiences. Why do we feel we must constantly advise our children, always impart some gem of wisdom, give our opinion on everything? I suggest the reason lies in *ourselves*, not in what our children require. We are simply unable to *be* and *allow*. We can't accept the *as is* of the situation.

Since our children didn't ask for our unsolicited opinion and didn't invite us to dominate the discussion, is it any wonder they stop engaging with us and begin hiding things from us?

As a result of the abundance of psychologically based reading, teaching, and counseling about not trying to "fix" things, some of us have become savvy. We practice the art of reflecting back to our children what we hear them saying. Perhaps you have used some of the following mirroring statements with your children, as I have with mine:

> I see you are upset
>
> I notice you are angry right now
>
> I just want you to know that you appear very irritated at this moment
>
> You feel as if no one understands you
>
> I understand you are feeling lonely today
>
> I can see you aren't in the right mood to talk right now
>
> I can tell you are frustrated right now
>
> I can see how overwhelmed you are
>
> I can see you are anxious about your exam tomorrow.

It's important to be aware that often these reflective statements are infused with our own ego, with its need to control. It isn't easy to reflect back a person's feelings and thoughts without contaminating them with our own. In fact, if we listen closely to the above statements, we will see that some of them can appear patronizing or judgmental.

For instance, if someone says to us, "I notice you are angry right now," and we feel they are coming from a place of judgment or being patronizing, we are likely to resent them for coming across as superior and clam up. Or we may explode at them for saying such a thing. In response to a statement such as, "I can see you are upset" or "I want you to know that you appear very irritated at this moment," we may similarly feel patronized and react by saying, "You're damned right I am!"

To make truly reflective statements to our children, we need to be aware of our own anxiety and ego. Otherwise, instead of allowing our children to have their experience, and being completely accepting of them as they go through it, we will unconsciously patronize or judge them, which may cause them to disengage from their feelings about the experience. In other words, when we make reflective statements, it's important to be aware of the place from which we make them. Is it our intention to *join with* our children as they go through an experience? Or is it our desire, however unconscious, to separate ourselves from their experience and consequently *deter them* from experiencing what they are going through?

When you engage your children at *their* level, words often aren't even necessary, since they can detract from the emotional connection children have with their experience. Instead, your tuned-in presence is all that's needed. Engaged presence involves simply *being a witness* to your children's experiences, allowing them to sit in what they are feeling without any insinuation that they need to move beyond this state.

Rather than "psychologizing" your children, simply *allow*. To allow and witness will enable your children to learn the art of *self-*reflection instead of fostering dependence on you.

Do You Validate Your Children's *Behavior*, or Their *Being*?

We all know the difference when someone validates our essential being, as opposed to validating a particular behavior. It's natural for us to show empathy for another by saying, "I understand." However, the reality is that often we *don't* understand. Even if we have been in a similar situation, we haven't walked through this particular situation in this person's shoes, with their unique mindset and emotional makeup. Again, it's the intention with which we make this statement that's crucial. Are we saying we understand because we have just injected ourselves into the other's experience? Or are we saying it as a way of telling them, "I am here for you," and most importantly, "I accept that this is what you are going through"? The difference lies in whether we are relating from ego or truly entering a state of acceptance of another, and in this manner being of service to their essence.

We are talking about *empathy*. The core of empathy lies in being able to allow the individual to experience their experiences *in their own way*, with us bearing witness. The first step to raising an empathic adult therefore lies in allowing our children to experience *all* their experiences, with full ownership and without our editing or control. In other words, empathy involves validating our children's sense of being, which entails communicating to them that they have every right to their feelings. We don't have to agree or disagree, but simply to allow their feelings to exist. We aren't invested in denying, shaping, or changing our children's feelings. Rather, we not only let them know they are being heard, but we also pay attention to what they are saying *beneath* their words.

Empathy requires a willingness to suspend our own feelings so we can align with those of our children. This can be hard to do when our children are experiencing a particularly difficult emotional moment, especially one of the shadow emotions such as jealousy, rage, guilt, or resentment. Indeed, if anything is truly hard to stomach as a parent, it's our children's negative emotions toward ourselves and others.

After I picked my daughter up from school one day, she asked to go to the park. I said no. Then she asked if we could go to the library. Again I said no. Finally, she asked if she could go on a play date, to which I again replied in the negative. Each time, I explained my reasoning: I had to prepare dinner, dad was coming home, we had a lot to do. She began to pout, then sulk, and then threw a hissy fit. "You are a mean mommy. You never let me do anything. I hate my day. It's a horrible day."

Instead of being able to sit with her disappointment, allowing her to feel her feelings without the insertion of mine, my ego became activated. After reprimanding her for her "selfishness" and calling her behavior "bratty," I proceeded to lecture her on the importance of gratitude. As I did so, I felt guilty. The more I reprimanded her, and the more guilty I felt, the more I sought to make *her* feel guilty.

When sanity finally returned, I asked myself, "Why was I so threatened by her comment? Was I so attached to her having only feelings of gratitude that I stripped her of her genuine disappointment?" I could have taught her these wonderful lessons after she had cooled down. Instead, I didn't give her the opportunity to calm herself, choosing instead to alleviate the feelings of inadequacy she triggered in me with her "mean mommy" comment by making her feel guilty.

Our tendency is to reprimand our children when they are in the grip of strong emotion. Hoping that through the power of our wanting, our children's emotions will magically disappear so we won't have to deal with their rawness, even ugliness, we counsel, "Don't be angry," "You shouldn't be jealous," or, "Snap out of feeling depressed!"

By making such statements, we seek to banish our children's shadow emotions to the recesses of their mind. Consequently, our children grow up disconnected from their emotions. They then pay the price of living in denial. If not in their teens, perhaps years later, these buried emotions get resurrected by an event or relationship, and our now-grown children find themselves overwhelmed because they are ill-equipped to navigate such emotions.

Our inability to show empathy for *all* of our children's emotions teaches them to live in fear of such emotions. For example, when I went to a water park with my daughter for the first time and she saw how steep some of the rides were, she said, "I'm scared." I noticed my first reaction was to brush her fear away by responding, "Oh, don't be silly. Don't you see how many children are going on the rides?" Or I might reassure her, "Nothing is going to happen to you because I'm with you." I hear so many parents tell their children,

"Don't be scared. There's nothing to be scared of."

I curbed this reaction when, after a moment of reflection, it became clear to me that she wasn't going to feel less scared just because I told her not to be scared. Instead, I said to her, "Of course you are scared. I am too. In fact, I'm very scared. But this is the whole point—to shiver and tremble, and still go on the adventure." She got it. Soon we were both waiting in line, muttering to ourselves, "I'm so scared! I'm so scared!" Instead of becoming afraid of our fear, we became excited by it. When we went on the ride and came out fine on the other side, I was able to underscore the importance of taking a risk even though we are fearful.

We think we need to teach our children not to be afraid, not to be angry, or not to be sad. But why shouldn't they be scared if they are scared? Why shouldn't they be sad if they are sad? Why would we ask them to dishonor their feelings? We help them most not when we try to banish their emotions, but when we equip them to navigate such emotions.

In whatever experience we are going through together, no matter how mundane, we can encourage our children to give voice to what they are feeling in a straightforwardly factual manner, such as, "I'm sad my friend couldn't come over," "I feel scared in the dark," or, "It's loud in here."

Just *Be* There

Many of us find ourselves taxed when our children act out. What we don't realize is that at the root of a child's acting out is an emotion that was never expressed, instead becoming split off from consciousness. If for no other reason than that it's to our advantage to encourage our children to own their emotions and have them validated, we are wise to encourage them to feel all their emotions and find appropriate ways to channel them. I emphasize the word "appropriate" because we have every right to dislike how our children sometimes express their emotions, and we can help them modify their means of expression. Just because we understand our child is angry doesn't mean we need to allow them to hit us or break things.

I recognize that this simple act of bearing witness to our children's emotional states can be extremely challenging for us. We are so heavily invested in our children, determined that they not mess up but become a success, that in our desire to be "good" parents, we find it difficult to just *be with* our children in their *as is* state, allowing whatever is happening to exist.

Imagine you are talking with your best friend about a moment in your life. Every time you open your mouth to share an opinion, thought, or feeling, your friend jumps in and comments. Though what's said is well-intentioned, their repeated statements of "I think," "I feel," "I believe"—or, God forbid, "You should" or "I would"—lead to us feeling frustrated. Wouldn't you feel like yelling, "Will you just shut up and listen?" Well, this is exactly how our children feel—and definitely what our teens are saying when they turn their back on us, turn up the television, or slam the door. Our children won't communicate with us unless we learn to detach ourselves from our *own unconsciousness* and enter a state of still and open receptivity to *their consciousness*.

As we witness our children going through their emotional states and restrain our tendency to analyze or pigeonhole a particular state, we equip them to become aware of their own inner witness. By not jumping in to tell them what they are feeling or experiencing, we open up the space for them to come to these insights for themselves. We give them a chance to hear their own voice, which is the only thing that ever changes anyone. This is much more beneficial for them than anything we can say.

When we open up a space for self-reflection by resisting the impulse to interfere, it's possible our children will ask of their own accord, "Mommy, why am I so angry?" To which we can respond, "Would you like to explore this together?" We then lead them in asking their *own* inner being what's going on with them, encouraging them to sit with their feelings without trying to answer their question, assuring them the insight they seek will emerge of its own accord—perhaps in a few moments, or perhaps at some later time, but always when it's required. To help our children sit with their feelings and wait for their own answers to come is so much more empowering than "explaining" to them.

When our children have questions, we believe we must have a neat and tidy answer, ready to bestow on them a well-packaged response. However, what if we were to simply respond, "I don't know"? This sounds counterintuitive, but here's how it works: When we present our children with our theories, well-laid-out thoughts, and already-formulated answers, we teach them to be passive recipients of our knowledge. When we confide that we don't know the answers, we invite them to allow the universe to *give* them the answers.

Each of us has witnessed our child's delight when they hit on an answer mom and dad hadn't thought of. This nurtures the seeds of initiative and resourcefulness. The smallest, "I don't know, but let's find out together," has the power to evoke the most profound of life qualities. It begins with our willingness as parents to step off our pedestal of "knowing" and enter into not knowing.

Here are some ways to enter into the state of not knowing:

> When our child asks a question, we don't jump in with an opinion or answer, but simply sit in the space this creates
>
> Even when we know the answer, we say, "Let's discover the answer together"
>
> We tell our child, "You think about it, and tell me what you find"
>
> We demonstrate that we simply can't know everything, and that we are comfortable with not knowing
>
> We teach our child there's power in being able to ask

the question, even more than in being able to
answer it. This shifts their orientation from
outcome-based to process-based

When we teach our child to value their ability to ask
the question, we teach them to connect with the
wonder of imagining.

It's important not to jump in with an answer when your child asks,
"Why does the moon shine so brightly?" or "Why do clouds look like
cotton?" Instead, capitalize on their state of curiosity, helping them
experience the priceless joy of being "about to discover." For
instance, you might use one of the following responses to encourage
your child to remain suspended in a state of curiosity:

"What an imaginative question that is!"

"I never thought of that question"

"You always want to know more about life, which is
such an admirable quality"

We repeat the question, swirl it around on our tongue,
and say, "What an absolutely delicious question!"

Rather than focusing on the answer, when you teach your children to enjoy the question, you demonstrate a love of learning and an
insatiable curiosity about life. You also teach them that reality is
inherently unquantifiable, unknowable, and can't be pigeonholed.
They learn it's okay not to have the answers and that they can still
feel competent when they don't.

My daughter asked me, "Mommy, can you tell me how babies are
born—not the stork story, but how they are really born? How does the
baby get into it's mom's stomach?"

I felt the churnings of so many egoic thoughts, such as: "Ah, here
is my chance to be the enlightened parent who gives the matter-of-
fact talk to her daughter," or, "We will have an empowering mother-

daughter conversation about the body and self-respect." Instead, I said, "Hmm, what a great question that is. Let's look it up on the internet." The reason I didn't jump in and provide the answer is that I truly wanted her to sit with her desire to know. At her age, I felt the desire was magical enough. The science behind the answer would simply diminish this.

To the degree that we are coming from ego, we find it much easier to say *yes* to our children's state of ego than to their state of being. But when we are grounded in our own consciousness and model engaged presence in everything, our children learn how to become fully present in each moment of their life.

CHAPTER 16

HOW TO HANDLE
YOUR CHILD'S MISTAKES

When any of us makes a mistake, we must first forgive ourselves, show compassion to ourselves, then let ourselves off the hook. We also want our friends to forgive us, understand we were well-meaning, and let the matter go. Well, these are exactly the elements we need to introduce in our approach to our children when they make a mistake.

Mistakes need to be regarded not as something to harangue and punish, but as windows for learning. Isn't this how we want our own mistakes to be regarded? The reality is that we make lots of mistakes in our adult life. We lose keys, leave the gas on, lose our way when driving, forget appointments, get into car accidents, overlook paying our bills, neglect to call friends when we said we would, misplace our phone, curse and yell, throw tantrums, drink too much, come home too late, eat the wrong foods, or watch too much television. In other words, we do countless things we want our children, in their young state of being, *not* to do *just because we told them these things are wrong!* Where do we come off, so high and mighty, as to judge and admonish them for doing the very things we do, only we don't have anyone looking over our shoulder waiting to reprimand us?

If you want your children to learn from their mistakes, any sense of "wrongness" needs to be removed, so they realize that no matter how much they mess up, *they* are still okay. There can be no imposing of guilt or blaming. Only when your children are free of fear can they extract the lesson they need.

Do You *Really* Know Why They Did What They Did?

When we presume we understand the motivation behind our children's actions and judge them negatively, we trigger in them a sense of helplessness. Sometimes in blatant ways and at other times in the subtlest of ways, we pile feelings of inadequacy upon them. For instance, we make fun of them or even ridicule them, compare them to their friends, and put them down in front of others. We also expect more from them than they are willing or even able to give.

Consider some of the countless shame-inducing statements we make:

> You constantly break my rules because you
> don't love this family

> You don't study hard because you don't care
> about your future

> You don't do your homework because you are lazy

> You lie because you don't care about anyone's
> feelings but your own

> You are forgetful and inconsiderate

> You are silly for feeling what you are feeling

> You are rude

> You ought to be ashamed of yourself

> I don't believe you, and I can't trust you

You purposefully hurt my feelings

You are mean

You are making things up—you are lying.

In each of these and so many other cases, we presume we know the reason our children behave in a particular way, which of course we are certain comes from an evil intention. To impose such judgments on our children causes them to experience a sense of helplessness. A verdict has been handed to them without their input.

When we approach our children in this manner, especially our teens, they soon wall us out of what they are feeling. So hurt are they by our constant judgment of them that they become immune to our input. We think this is because they "don't care," which is to further judge them, again imagining we know their intent. Little do we realize they are tired of living in shame, tired of being thought "bad."

If our children turn their sense of helplessness inward, they are likely to retreat into a shell, internalizing the belief that they are "bad." If they turn their sense of helplessness outward, they may seek to do to others what has been done to them, which is how a bully is created. A bully is a person who has grown up feeling such disempowerment that to hold it within is unbearable, which causes them to humiliate the recipient of their bullying, making this individual feel powerless in the way they themselves have been made to feel powerless. The reason children bully is only ever that they are filled with pain themselves. When bullying escalates into violence, it's because the individual has internalized such an intense feeling of humiliation that their only recourse for relief is to unleash their pain on others. Cut off from their authentic goodness, such individuals attack the goodness in others.

In other words, violence in our young people originates from the level of disempowerment a child feels in the parent-child dynamic. When our children are no longer receptacles for our blame and pain, they have less need to release their emotional reactions on others. A child who is respected and whose feelings are honored when it makes a mistake doesn't turn around and dishonor another person.

HOW YOU CAN TRANSFORM
MISTAKES INTO SPIRITUAL GOLD

Our children learn how to handle their emotions as they observe us during periods of stress. Every day affords abundant opportunities to model being at ease with our imperfections. This means accepting our wounds, fallibility, and the fact that—no matter how aware we may imagine ourselves to be—we operate from a fair degree of unconsciousness.

Our children need to see that the mess of life can always be mined for emotional and spiritual gold. Once they realize this, they are freed from fear of failure, able to accept that mistakes are an inevitable and even essential aspect of life.

As we saw earlier, the way to handle our children's mistakes is to ask ourselves how we would want our friends to handle ours. Would we want to be lectured to death? Would we want to be reminded over and over how much pain we caused them because we were late for their birthday party? Would we want them to go on and on at us? Would we want to feel as if our love and devotion were in question? Yet this is the way many of us regularly react to our children's mistakes.

Particularly when our children don't do well in school, it's widely believed that if we tell them to "try harder," "study more," or "don't give up," we are equipping them to overcome their fear of failure. In reality, we are teaching them to be attached to perfection. As a consequence, when our children are catapulted into imperfection, chaos, or not knowing, they flounder. Viewing their errors as reflective of who they *are,* they become paralyzed in the aftermath. If we then reprimand or punish them, we not only miss an opportunity to show how a mistake can be the gateway to higher consciousness, but we also set them up to become angry, even violent.

Before we can help our children uncover what led to the mistake, they need to be allowed to put a little distance between themselves and their mistakes. The conscious approach is to wait until all emotional reactivity has died down and everyone is in their right mind, then sit with our children compassionately, process their mistake with them entirely free of judgment, and show them how they can extract a lesson for the future.

To help our children understand the *why* is the most effective way we can teach forgiveness, because knowing the *why* empowers us to make changes. Unfortunately, when addressing our children's negative behavior, we often don't take the time or exercise the patience required to get at the *why*, but instead deal with the *what*. Yet only through an understanding of the why can we help our children create the pathway to change. Once our children understand the *why*, everything else is gravy. Perhaps the cause of a mistake was shortsightedness or pressure they experienced from their peers. Maybe it was a simple lack of information or just poor judgment. We don't have to belabor the point, but simply note it and move on.

When we don't take our children's mistakes personally, we communicate the vital lesson that there is really nothing to forgive because mistakes are a natural part of learning how to be our authentic self. To not take mistakes personally is to recognize that behind every mistake is a good intention, though sometimes this intention doesn't readily present itself. As parents, we need to search beneath the superficial mistake and uncover the original good intention of our children. This encourages them to have faith in their innate goodness. When we focus on a bad outcome instead of on a good intention, our children lose their enthusiasm for trying.

Suppose our child left the oven on after baking a cake. Do we focus on the good intention of wanting to bake? If our child burns the toast, can we help them laugh at themselves and, in an unflustered manner, try again? If they crashed our car while shopping for groceries, can we recognize they had the right intention by going shopping in the first place? If they forgot the last section of an exam, do we acknowledge that they were so keen to do a good job that they rushed? When we show faith in our children's well-placed intent, we demonstrate we don't judge them for what they do.

One of the reasons children fear their mistakes is that when we admonish them, we unknowingly strip them of their sense of competence. We disempower them to such an extent that they become afraid of doing anything that could possibly result in such a mistake again. If they burned a cake and almost the house, they are likely to feel inept to the point they are afraid to try baking again. If they lost their cell phone, they may feel so guilty that they conclude they shouldn't be trusted with a phone.

CELEBRATE YOUR CHILD'S MISTAKES

In our house, we often play a game at dinner time. Each of us talks about a big mistake we made during the week. We have turned this into a volley of sorts, where each tries to up the other's mistake and the conversation goes to the tune of, "You think that was a silly mistake? I made an even sillier mistake." My daughter gets a kick from hearing about her parents' mistakes. There's a sequel to this game. We pick one or two of the mistakes we made and describe what we learned about ourselves.

One day my daughter said, "I made a mistake, Mommy. I left my marker open and now there's a big stain on my bed. I'm sorry." I told her how brave she was to "fess up." Then I taught her how to clean it up. My daughter knows that I attribute bravery to every confession. So now she makes it a point to tell me every time she eats a candy she isn't supposed to or each time she and her friends hide something from their teacher. However, it must be said that when my child does lie, which she has done and will do again, this is just one of the realities of childhood (and adulthood!) that one has to accept. I don't belittle her fear when she does this, but reassure her that it's natural to be afraid to confess her mistakes. I also point out that there are times when others will reprimand her for her mistakes. However, in our house, she needs to know that mistakes are accepted, and for the most part will be treated compassionately. In this way, the mistake of lying is seen as a natural aspect of the continuum of human behavior.

You might wonder, "Doesn't this encourage a child to take mistakes lightly?" Let me share why this isn't a concern. The premise behind conscious parenting is that our children are inherently well-meaning and want to do the right thing. However, in the course of a day, it's inevitable a child will make a few mistakes either through omission or commission. If they are afraid of punishment, as already noted, they may then try to cover up their mistakes by lying. The approach I'm suggesting not only teaches a child not to fear mistakes, but also highlights that there are simply too many precious lessons to learn about ourselves from our mistakes to cover them up—lessons that enrich our life in ways we couldn't have imagined had we not made such mistakes.

By encouraging your children to let their mistakes go, you help them separate the wheat from the chaff, then throw the chaff to the winds. The true test of whether *you* have let go comes the next time you are asked to trust them with the keys to the same car they crashed last week. If you crashed your friend's car, would you want them to never hand you their car keys again?

When your children show you their most vulnerable aspects, and you show up ready to meet who they are, you indicate to them that they are worthy of being respected and received. If you betray them through your own self-absorption with the way you imagine they "ought" to be, you convey to them that they are unworthy and that the world is an unforgiving place. They then become fearful of stepping out in life.

By exercising the courage to own their errors, children learn to respect their fallibility and limitations, while demonstrating faith in their ability to move on. This strengthens their belief in their competence. With the reassurance they are still loved, they accept that each of us is a work in progress.

CHAPTER 17

THE TWO WINGS OF THE EAGLE

To develop conscious behavior, a child needs two streams of learning. I like to think of them as the two wings of an eagle. They are *authenticity* and *containment*. A child missing one or the other will flounder, never soaring to the heights of its potential.

So far in this book, we have focused on authenticity, which springs from a strong connection to our inner being. For a child, this means learning to recognize their own inner voice, which will teach them how to expand their presence in the world. As children increasingly relate to their inner being, they learn not just to *accept* themselves, but also to *embrace their own will and manifest this in the world*. They develop the ability to forge a meaningful connection with others, as well as with life itself.

Containment, the other wing of the eagle, is the means by which we absorb the will of another. While authenticity requires us to respect our own inner being and express who we are, containment allows us to contour this in relation to the will of those around us.

Our children need to learn both the art of connection to themselves *and* connection to others, which are the two pillars of all relationships. The ability to relate to another is linked to our ability to connect with ourselves, which is the springboard of authenticity and the key to our ability to maintain meaningful relationships.

Even as our children need to foster a sense of inner connection and the ability to be authentic, they also need to learn how to live in a world of rules and get along with others in the sandbox of life. For this to happen, children need to listen to their own voice *and,* in equal measure, absorb the voices of others. To foster the ability to surrender to one's own will *and* to that of another when appropriate is a key element of discipline. This is very different from just getting children to "behave."

When children have been taught to express their voice, it's only natural that this voice will at times be the cause of dissension with their parents. This is the inevitable fallout of raising a spirited and confident child. But as our children discover that the world doesn't revolve around them, they learn to tolerate frustration. They accept that, since they aren't the only ones who have wishes and needs, they can't achieve instant gratification all the time.

To the degree that we as parents connect with our children, providing for them a safe container in which they are seen for who they are, they learn to be comfortable with connection. They understand the dynamics of a give-and-take relationship and are better able to thrive amid the difficulties that arise. They can tolerate being depended upon, and in turn trust that another can be leaned on.

A CHILD CAN'T SOAR WITHOUT CONTAINMENT

Stephanie and her husband Phillip have three young boys who are out of control. Because the three are always fighting with each other, play dates are a nightmare and mealtimes a disaster. There's no order in the house, the children rule the roost, and chaos reigns. It's a household that's completely lacking in respect, either on the part of the children or their parents.

Overwhelmed, Stephanie is in tears on a daily basis. Having grown up with a controlling, domineering mother, she has little sense of empowerment and feels easily victimized. Since conflict frightens her, she does her best to avoid it. Similarly, Phillip grew up in a home where emotions were rarely expressed, which means he's uncomfortable whenever he has to articulate his own. Because both Stephanie and Phillip lead emotionally constricted lives, they are afraid to find their authentic voice with their children. Of course, this couple's children, being the spiritual gurus that children are, act in the way they do precisely to challenge their parents to address their emotional baggage.

When I observed these parents with their children, it was immediately clear there was no system to the parents' discipline. The children had no clue how they were supposed to behave. For instance, the three boys were playing in the family room when, before long, they began throwing their toys all over the room and climbing on the furniture. When Jacob, the oldest and leader of the three, began to shake the lamps, Stephanie entered the room, saying, "Please don't do that Jacob." Jacob paid no attention. Again Stephanie spoke up: "I said, 'Please.' Please stop this behavior or you will get a time out." None of the boys paid any attention. In a pleading voice, Stephanie repeated, "I said, '*Please.*'"

When this had no effect, Stephanie turned to me, helpless, her eyes begging me to understand, as she explained, "I'm trying to discipline them, but no one is listening to me. Do you see how hard this is?" A moment later, the lamp fell on the floor and Jacob hurt his foot. Now Stephanie ran to him to take care of him. Jacob experienced no consequences, only hugs and kisses.

After a short while, Jacob returned to his play, engaging in the same behavior. Within minutes, there was another mishap, this time as a result of a fight between the three boys. Again Stephanie appeared at the door and said, "Boys, please don't hurt each other." The boys continued fighting. Still standing a distance away from them, their mother again pleaded, "Please don't hurt yourselves." No one listened.

Out of the blue, Stephanie strode over to the boys, pulled them off each other, slapped Jacob across his face, and yelled, "You are a bad boy! You are always making me upset. You are in 'time out' for the rest of the day."

Not having seen this coming, Jacob was stunned. Screaming back at his mother, he protested that he was being singled out and it was unfair. His mother, still nursing residual emotion from the mishap in which he had hurt himself, became enraged, quivering and shaking. Jacob hit her. She hit him. As the other boys cowered in fear, Stephanie broke down in tears, blaming her sons for her pain as all three hung their heads in shame.

Stephanie had no idea that the present scenario was one in which she had recreated her own childhood feeling of disempowerment. Superimposing the helplessness *she* had experienced when she was young onto her boys, she was unable to separate their behavior from her own feelings at that moment. Because every move on her part was driven by emotional avoidance, she couldn't respond as the boys needed her to.

I meet many parents of older children especially who feel help-less in the face of their children's "bad" behavior. When I observe these parents, I notice that their common error lies in their inability to engage in swift action in the moment. For example, an eight-year-old girl was snatching the toys from her younger brother, but the mother ignored it, which she continued to do until it escalated into a fight. In another situation, the mother of a six-year-old watched him drop crumbs on the floor, saying nothing about his behavior until, after he had scattered crumbs everywhere, she exploded at him. Though it's often wise to wait until we are no longer reactive before we engage in teaching our children a more appropriate way to behave, there are times when delay is counterproductive. Instead of allowing a situation to escalate, the conscious parent takes action the instant it's required.

In Stephanie's case, had she been aware of her emotional patterns, she could have approached this situation with much greater firmness from the start. The moment Jacob began violating the rules of respect for the home and safety of self and others, Stephanie could have been authoritative. Coming from her inner strength, she could have declared, "Freeze, right now. Everybody stop what you are doing." With play stopped, she could then have reiterated the parameters for the boys' behavior. Telling them to repeat after her what was expected of them, she could have made sure they understood the consequences of a further violation, making it clear that any deviation from these expectations would bring a quick termination to their play. We cannot be a "pleaser" and "pleader," then expect to have any power with our children.

Afraid of owning her emotional boundaries, Stephanie let the boys abuse her. So accustomed was she to feeling disempowered that she automatically embodied a position of weakness, whereas her sons needed her to be strong and clear. Even when, having missed all the cues, she finally exploded, she was still unable to own her emotions, instead displacing them onto her children, causing them to feel guilty for "making" her so upset. Far from being "bad," the boys were just doing what boys do, whereas their mother had failed them miserably.

Stephanie's example reveals how we so easily become mired in our own patterns, which often have little to do with the behavior we are addressing in our children. Instead of responding to our *children's* behavior, we are driven by *our own anxiety*.

So many well-intentioned parents perpetuate chaos in their children's behavior. This is because stepping out of our own ego and life-scripts to discipline our children effectively feels alien to us. If we aren't alert to our ego and the scripts that drive us, we can't engage our children in the manner we need to. Unaware of our emotional triggers and our level of comfort with conflict, we react from emotional blindness.

Conscious parenting isn't about being lovey-dovey and touchy-feely all the time. When we parent consciously, we don't give our children a green light to behave inappropriately, and neither do we automatically place their needs ahead of ours. To allow our children to behave as if they were wild, without regard for how this affects those around them, is to raise little monsters. Teaching our children how to *appropriately* contain their authenticity and manage their emotions is essential. For this reason, to be unyielding when required goes hand-in-hand with yielding when appropriate. Setting boundaries, saying "no," and being firm are as much a part of good parenting as are accepting and embracing our children.

The heart of conscious parenting is the ability to be *present* in any situation that arises. Are you able to respond from a place of *awareness* rather than *attachment*? Do you discipline from a place of authenticity or from your ego?

To parent consciously means you *respond* to your children's needs, not *cater* to them. You don't indulge your children when they behave in a spoiled, undignified manner. Your task is to help them find within themselves the emotional strength to become self-sustaining and resilient. A large part of gaining such strength involves managing their emotions when they are being disciplined.

The Spiritual Approach to Discipline

Conflict is a hot button for most of us because we carry an unhealthy imprint when it comes to dealing with someone who behaves contrary to our expectations. While some of us respond by becoming over-involved and over-controlling, others feel overwhelmed and withdraw. In particular, disciplining our children has the power to unleash within us either the *control monster* or its opposite, the *emotional avoider*. Which of these reactions conflict evokes in us depends on the combination of our upbringing and our temperament.

How aware are we of our projections and our ego issues when we raise our children? For instance, are our children truly acting in a defiant way, or are we being too rigid? To discover the answer, it's helpful to ask ourselves, "What emotions are being roused within me right now? How am I being triggered? What from my past am I bringing to my present?" Once we have addressed our own internal state, we will be able to determine whether we are in a position to respond to our child in a manner that's warranted, or whether our judgment is presently obscured by our own anxiety.

One of my friends accompanied my daughter, who was three

years old at the time, and myself to the beach. During the day, my daughter behaved like a monster—screaming, flailing, and in general acting like a lunatic. I was horrified. I had so wanted to impress my friend, so wanted her to admire me as one of the "best" mothers, with a "best behaved" child. Coming from ego, I took my daughter's behavior personally, becoming livid with her for humiliating me. Pulling her aside, I gave her the snarliest, meanest look I was capable of, which predictably resulted in her crying even more loudly.

Now I became really reactive. "I will never, ever bring you to the beach for as long as we both live," I swore to her. This of course produced still more crying. Escalating my threats, I told her, "I will never, ever let you watch Elmo or give you candy again. Neither will I take you to the park, nor to eat pizza, ever again." Finally, she had the sense to be quiet and let mommy have her tantrum instead. During the rest of the day, she behaved like an angel.

Feeling personally attacked had caused me to lose my center. The result was that instead of helping my daughter regulate her emotions, I shushed her with threats for the sake of my ego, caring more about how I looked in my friend's eyes than about correcting my child's behavior. Indeed, the only thing my daughter learned was to be scared of mommy, because mommy sometimes loses it—and all because I interpreted her actions in a personal way.

If there's an aspect of parenting that has the power to truly expose our attachment to control and our inability to tolerate any deviance from our vision of the way things should be, it's when our children behave in a manner beyond the confines of our expectations. At such times, we get to see how rigid, dogmatic, dictatorial, and even tyrannical we can be. We witness the extent of our unconsciousness.

It had never occurred to me that I would have to discipline my daughter on a heavenly day at the beach. I presumed that because I was in a good mood and the weather was so beautiful, my daughter's mood would follow suit. However, the need for discipline rarely occurs at the "perfect time." When containment is required, it must be provided regardless of the situation. Correction of a child's acting out *always* needs to occur *in the present moment*. This is something we have to be absolutely consistent about. A swift here-and-now response coupled with later processing of their feelings are both key components to teaching containment.

I violated the principle of correcting my child in the present moment because I didn't want the outing to be spoiled. By trying to avoid disciplining her, I made the situation worse. Unable to stay neutral and take the right action, I was more upset that my day was being ruined than I was with the fact my daughter was acting inappropriately. This is the essential difference between merely trying to get a child to "behave" and teaching the child containment.

These days I remind myself frequently, "I will respond to my child in the here-and-now. If her behavior asks for validation, I will be present enough to give this. If her behavior asks for shaping and containment, I will be engaged and alert, ready to provide this the moment she needs it. If her behavior asks for non-reaction from me, then this will be my response."

We seem to believe we can "get by" with minimal engagement, an approach I find most common in parents of children who are extremely difficult to manage. It's a mistake to presume our children will magically learn the appropriate way to behave. When we wait in the hope our children's behavior will somehow change, all the while taking no action to help it along, our children become set in their ways and we find ourselves at a loss for what to do. Our children count on us to guide them across the continuum of time, not just when it's convenient. If we zone out for days at a time, then reenter the parenting process at our leisure, we miss the opportunity to nip emerging behavior in the bud. Shaping our children's behavior can't be done in fits and starts.

For this reason, I now welcome incidents such as occurred at the beach. Not that I enjoy them, but I know that these messy episodes bring my ego to the fore so I can confront it. When this occurs, I tell myself that my child is allowing me to witness the ways in which I need to evolve. For this I am eternally grateful.

It's at times like these that raising children has the potential to become such a spiritual process. Few other relationships evoke within us our blind hunger for control, thereby revealing our immaturity—and hence inviting us to take great leaps in our own development.

Don't Avoid Conflict—Value It

Conflicts with our children are inevitable. Although they don't make us feel good and we prefer to avoid them, they can actually be valuable opportunities for growth.

When a parent avoids conflict, afraid to take decisive action on behalf of their child, they are equally afraid of taking a stand that's demonstratively loving or protective. Such parents raise children who, because they have learned to doubt their essential being, exude a low sense of worth.

Conflict is often generated when there's a battle of wills as a result of engaging in rigid thinking. The first step to transcending a conflict is to examine our own thinking and the unconscious ways we battle for control.

Imagine it's your mother's eightieth birthday and the pretty party dress you spent a fortune on for your four-year-old is lying in a heap on her bedroom floor. Unless she's allowed to wear her old, dirty sneakers and favorite jeans, she refuses to go to the party. As she looks at you with that all-too-familiar "see what I can do" glint in her eye, her chin defiantly thrust forward, feet firmly glued to the floor, she is waiting to see whether you will retreat to the cowardly shadows of bribes or, better still, fall on your knees and plead. With your anger churning, fantasies of "really showing her who's boss" flash through your mind. Your voice rises. She cries and flails. You yell louder. She stomps and kicks. An hour has passed. She wins. She wears the sneakers and jeans to the party. You have aged five years.

Every parent has been in a situation in which they have thought to themselves, "My child is purposely acting like this, so I'm going to show them I'm in charge." When we take up such a position, it's because we feel personally attacked in some way. From this place of ego, we rarely take wise action. On the contrary, we tend to unleash our control monster and seek to dominate our children in an effort to regain some semblance of order and a sense of power. It's at such moments that we may inadvertently yell at our children or even slap them.

Instead of taking our children's behavior personally, it's helpful to understand that our children *aren't thinking of us* when they are acting out, only of themselves! To bring them to a state of calm, we need to find the strength to separate ourselves from their behavior. We need to detach our ego from how they are acting at the moment, then from a place of serenity work to halt their inappropriate behavior.

Once we rein in our ego, conflict becomes a valuable conduit for learning "give and take," the skill of negotiation, and the art of losing. Our four-year-old can be taught, right here in the moment, that this isn't a me-versus-you battle, but a situation we are in together for which we need to find a creative solution that works for us both.

To achieve this, as parents we must first detach from the desire to "win" and have it "our way or no way." So perhaps the dress is worn, but with the sneakers instead of the dress-up shoes. Or perhaps, the dress is worn, but she is promised that she gets to choose her outfit the next time. Alternatively, we let go of our need to have her look a certain way and allow her to wear what she wants because, after all, it's mainly our ego that's in the way—our need to have our child look or act like a "doll" because, heaven forbid, "what will the relatives think?"

Such a stalemate can be transformed into a rich dialogue, with abundant opportunity for practicing the art of negotiation. Of course, there are some situations in which there can be no yielding, such as safety and respect for self and others. But for the most part, the conflicts we engage in center on our massive parental ego—our desire to "appear" a certain way to the outside world.

When we teach our children the art of negotiation, we sow the seeds that will allow them to enter into intimate relationships later in life. Many a lesson is learned when we are able to stay with the discomfort of not knowing, wondering, "Should I give in, or will you?" It's a matter of being comfortable with not achieving complete resolution. Life isn't neat and tidy, but messy. It demands that we give of ourselves and let go, and that we do so again and again. By staying with the internal struggle that accompanies conflict—accepting that things aren't perfect, and being okay with feeling frustrated that we can't come up with a quick fix—we teach our children to tolerate their emotions.

Conflict offers timeless life-lessons both for parent and child—lessons that teach our children: "Yes, you *can indeed* assert your will, and you will not be punished for it. But at the same time, you need to learn how to accept and absorb another's will." Simultaneously, we parents learn to quell our need for control. Conscious parenting is a two-way transformation indeed!

If as a parent you can practice and then teach the dance of balancing the "I" and the "we," you will impart to your children one of life's most difficult but essential lessons. By learning to view conflict as a way to experience the value in "losing," the beauty of creating a negotiated solution, and the foolhardiness of living in a rigid world of either-or, you teach your children to engage life as it truly is: full of complex, competing demands, and rich with unpredictability. You teach them that "winning" in life is all about finding creative solutions, being flexible, and learning to negotiate authentically with an intimate other.

How to Discipline in a Manner that *Works*

Traditionally, the relationship between parent and child has been hierarchical and linear: the parent issues rules and orders like a military general, and children either obey or find themselves punished.

A conscious relationship is never hierarchical or linear. Conscious discipline isn't parent *versus* child, but involves a circular dynamic of parent *with* child. The *relationship* between parent and child is paramount, not specific techniques. No matter what may be occurring in terms of the *content* of the relationship, the relationship itself should always be circular in nature. Many behavioral issues can be headed off simply by altering the parent-child dynamic in this way.

If we focus only on the content of our children's behavior, we may find ourselves limited to a few strategies such as reprimands, time outs, and punishments. These not only create stress and strife, they also narrow the possibilities for self-growth. Because we turn inappropriate behavior into something shameful, our children also lose the opportunity for self-learning.

Children generally view discipline negatively. The very word "discipline" smacks of authority and control, conjuring up images of punishment. In contrast, by seeing discipline not in terms of instituting obedience based on fear, but as education in crucial life lessons, our children learn how to use good judgment and discernment, make effective choices, and create positive solutions. For this reason, I believe the term discipline needs to be replaced and suggest that something like "behavioral shaping"[1] is more in line with a conscious approach to parenting. Behavioral shaping implies we respond to *all* of our children's behavior, not just behavior we deem undesirable. Equal or greater focus is placed on the positive.

Rather than regarding times of conflict as a nuisance, behavioral shaping uses all conflict as a laboratory for learning. For this reason, shaping occurs continuously on a moment-by-moment basis instead of being squeezed into punitive time slots. The signature of this shaping is *positive reinforcement*, which is a more effective tool than punishment.

---

[1]Behavioral shaping is a term often used in behavior modification programs in which new behavior is taught through the use of reinforcement until the desired behavior is achieved. In this book the term is used to describe the ongoing, moment-by-moment attention a parent needs to devote to a child's behavior so that corrective action takes place in the here-and-now rather than in a time frame that is disconnected from the present. The term "shaping" is used to describe the continuously evolving nature of behavior, implying that there is always contouring and adjustment to be done and that there is no "perfect" state to arrive at.

Positive reinforcement means that if your child gives you a problem over brushing their teeth, you don't obsess about the thirty-one teeth that weren't brushed well but instead focus on the one tooth that was. If your child resists studying geography, you don't belabor their inability to sit and study for a whole hour but instead commend them each time they study for ten minutes. If your child has been talking rudely to one of their friends, the first time they talk politely—and every consequent time—you note this behavior and reinforce it.

When you focus on wholesome behavior, and especially good intentions, you invite your children to turn toward the light within them. Just like a flower, they have a propensity for turning themselves toward this light. The issue is: Do you believe your children need to be motivated by what's good in them or in punitive ways? How you answer this question determines your approach to the entire parenting process.

For instance, if your child earns a C in school, to reprimand or punish them fails to address what's really happening. Do they respect their limitations, and are they working to overcome these limitations if possible? Are they learning how to be humble by embracing their ordinariness, accepting themselves? Are they engaging the subject matter, enjoying learning? Are they truly present in their schooling experience? These are the primary issues at such a time, not the specific matter of grades.

When you focus on grades and developmental charts, thinking to yourself, "I know my child can do better, so I must push him or her," you project divine characteristics onto the A grade or their ability to be potty trained by two. In so doing, you fail to see the divine at work in the C grade or in behavior you deem "lazy," "unmotivated," or "attention-deficit." The *conscious* parent sees the divine in *all* of these things.

THE RULE ABOUT RULES

Many parents get into daily battles with their children over food, which clothes to wear, or how homework should be done. Most of these battles are related to our ego and its need for control. If we regularly find ourselves embroiled in frequent conflict with our children over petty issues, this could be a sign we are too invested in our children's lives.

When an issue isn't a matter of life or death and yet we insist on our way of doing things, we may imagine we are teaching our children respect for rules, whereas in reality we are teaching them to be like us—rigid and unyielding. This is why conflict continues relentlessly. Our children soon turn a deaf ear because they know we want things done our way regardless of their wishes. This is how stealing, sneaking, and lying begin.

In our anxiety, we sometimes become ultra strict without meaning to. Driven by fear we will lose control and be overpowered by our children, we become extremely stern. We then treat even healthy defiance as a sign of disobedience, a breach of our authority.

Everything can't be a rule. A house with too many rules will simply fall apart one day. Children who are brought up with an undue amount of rules, with insufficient free space to explore and experiment, are likely to swing to the wild side, unable to metabolize their parents' rigidity any longer.

When everything is treated as a rule, our children feel stifled. The worst thing we can do to their spirit is create an atmosphere in which their every expression of themselves is scrutinized for potential rule violation. If rules are to garner our children's attention, they need to be simple and few, so that our children grow up in a household in which they feel secure, familiar with the rules, and confident that new ones aren't going to be imposed every day. Whatever rules may be required need to guarantee that our children enjoy plenty of room to roam carefree and worry-free.

There's a difference between main rules and flexible rules.

Among main rules, I would list respect for the parents' authority around bedtime, homework, mealtimes, wake-up time, and so on; respect for the parents' authority when they say "no"; respect for self, including staying warm and safe; and a respectful tone and attitude toward others.

Unfortunately for us and our children, the window for learning the foundations of how to behave isn't very large. Shaping behavior carries the most weight between the ages of one and six. These are the formative years during which schedules for homework and other routines such as bathing and bedtime are consolidated. Unless we seize the chance to shape our children's behavior during these years, we will have children who act out in serious ways when they enter prepubescence. If a child hasn't learned to respect its parents by the age of eight, it will be extremely hard for it to respect its parents at the age of eighteen. If a child hasn't learned how to sit in one place and work on a project in silence by the age of nine, chances are it will forever encounter these problems.

If we want our rules to be followed, we need to be serious about communicating this. All too often, parents are inconsistent with rules or simply don't follow through with them, then wonder why their children ignore them. The rules of respect for self and others need to be set early in the game. When we fail to teach our children to absorb our will and respect it, they grow up thinking it's okay to walk all over another human being. The consequence is that we end up raising narcissistic children who don't know how to be empathic toward others. Unable to maintain friendships, they are often isolated by their peers.

Flexible rules are all the rules that make no real difference to a child's sense of wellbeing or health. Once the main rules have been laid down, both parent and child need to contribute to the list of flexible rules, which can be discussed and mutually agreed upon. Our children need to be allowed to say "no" to us in an ever-flowing dialogue in which two spirits exchange views. When our children see us use our power to lay down the main rules, but also see our willingness to give up power so that they can flex their full personhood, behavioral shaping becomes a truly spiritual exchange between parent and child.

More than the main rules, it's the flexible rules that teach our children important life lessons because they provide them with an opportunity to express their opinion. Our children learn there's give and take in relationships, and that matters can be negotiated—a vital skill for functioning effectively in the adult world. Flexible rules might cover what clothes to wear, food to eat, interests and hobbies to pursue, books to read or movies to watch, friendships to keep, and how free time is spent. Through a healthy balance of main and flexible rules, our children learn how to have appropriate boundaries as well as a respect for dialogue with another.

As children grow to be teens, they need to know they are allowed to wear what they please (unless it crosses the line into the space where it violates their sense of wellbeing and safety), express their interests and passions, and choose their own friends. If we have done a decent job of teaching them how to respect themselves and others from a young age, we need have no concern over them losing this respect once they grow older.

When we negotiate flexible rules with our children, we show resilience and simultaneously model a willingness to learn emotional lessons alongside our children. We drop our "perfect" agenda and instead learn about our imperfect self. This frees us to take a softer approach, so that potentially stressful situations can then be addressed with creativity and in a spirit of fun.

As we model a willingness to engage in a collaborative solution to a situation, we infuse the process with a sense that we are in this *together*. Our children learn that all parties in a relationship need to be heard, which leads to each getting what really matters to them. In this way, our children learn to think outside the box in order to come up with creative solutions that work for everyone. This is an especially important lesson in today's increasingly diverse world.

Why Teaching Is More Effective Than Punishment

There are times when it's necessary to confront inappropriate behavior. If your children engage in thoughtless acts, you need to bring their attention to their thoughtlessness in the here and now. For instance, if your child hits someone or behaves in a bratty manner, it's imperative that you respond in a swift and engaged manner. How you do so will depend on your child's level of maturity.

In the case of a toddler, you might gently hold them and be very present with them until they calm themselves. Because they can't be expected to contain themselves at this age, you do the containing for them. On the other hand, if your teen talks to you in a rude way, you need to become present with them in a manner that's not combative.

Sometimes it's appropriate to issue your children something akin to a reprimand, while at other times it's better to approach them in fun, with gentleness, or with praise and positive reinforcement. At other times your children need you to help shape them by simply bearing witness as they figure things out for themselves. Song, dance, acting, and play can also be effective in helping your children understand the appropriate way to conduct themselves. In these and other ways, your children internalize the norms you ask them to live by. Living in a contained manner then becomes a habit, enhancing their natural way of being.

Punishment may stop a behavior, or it may not, but it definitely won't teach a child to replace inappropriate behavior with more-productive behavior. Instead of simply punishing your children's behavior, you can use the very situations that are problematic to teach the art of self-reflection, which will open up the path to positive ways of handling situations through problem-solving.

For example, if your child is acting out and you are aware that they are tired, instead of focusing on their acting out, go directly to their emotional experience and say, "You must be so tired right now." Or if they are sad about something, ask, "Are you acting like this because you are sad?" The doorway to emotional processing then swings open. After you have identified their emotional state and entered into it with them, explain, "No matter how you feel, you simply can't act out in this way. Let's find another way to communicate how you feel." You can then teach your children to communicate their feelings in a direct manner instead of indirectly by acting out.

If children are unable to find a means to express themselves in a direct manner, their mind and body find other means of expression. Split off from their internal world, they are driven to seek what feel like their "missing pieces" elsewhere. This tends to take the form of self-destructive behavior or behavior that harms others.

When children become excessively clingy, defiant, begin to steal, cut themselves, stop bathing, or fail at school, these are all signs that something is amiss with their emotions. Often a child's emotional state manifests in symptoms associated with the body, such as migraines, stomachache, or panic attacks. This happens when children have become so split off from their real feelings that they have overloaded their body with unexpressed emotion. They may have become so overwhelmed in the role of pleasers or overachievers—or, in contrast, as rebels and "bad children"—that they finally collapse, with their body bearing the brunt of the collapse.

As parents, we tend to react anxiously when faced with this secondary means of attention-seeking. For example, if our child begins to fail in school, we become angry and controlling. If our child is experiencing an inordinate number of physical problems, we take them to see specialist after specialist. With physical symptoms, the situation is particularly tricky because there's always the possibility that such symptoms have a physical cause. The difficulty is that we may inadvertently reinforce our children's belief that something is wrong with their body, instead of tapping into the underlying emotional issue. This is why it's so important for us to carve out the space for our children to express who they are on an emotional basis.

Once you understand that your children engage in negative or positive behavior due to an underlying emotional state, you can teach them to express their emotions in a direct manner. A direct way to express their emotions would mean they are able to articulate when they are angry instead of engaging in angry behavior that's hurtful or destructive. Similarly, they can note that they are sad rather than resorting to self-destructive behavior. As you teach your children to access their emotional world on a continual basis, they don't feel the need to act out their emotions in attention-seeking ways. Because they feel heard, they have no reason to draw attention to themselves. Feeling accepted and validated, they experience no compulsion to drown their painful emotions in negative behavior.

When your children hear you articulate your emotions in a direct, matter-of-fact manner, they emulate this. To express what you are feeling, you don't have to yell and scream. Instead, when an issue arises between your children and yourself, you can say, "We both have feelings about this. Tell me yours, then I will share mine." It's crucial your children know that their feelings are as important as yours.

Whenever you invite your children to tell you what's bothering them, if the matter concerns something you have done, you might say to them, "Why don't you tell me where you believe I have gone wrong and how I can correct it. I'm ready to listen to everything that's causing you pain right now. You are free to express yourself—there will be no judgment." In such a situation, it's essential you are ready to admit your errant ways. You can tell your children, "I know how it feels when I sense I'm not respected. I'm sorry I have made you feel this way. Let's find a way whereby each of us can experience respect from the other."

If your child steals, you ask yourself questions such as: What is it about my presence that causes my child to feel the need to steal? What internal lack is my child experiencing that they are seeking to meet by stealing? This is an opportunity to identify the emotional roots of the behavior, since such behavior doesn't occur in a void but always involves an underlying emotional reason. Your responsibility is to uncover this.

Consider yourself an usher, leading your children toward living in reality in an acceptable manner, as you simultaneously move away from thinking of youself as a disciplinarian. Consistency is crucial. You cannot shape one behavior and not the next, or shape a behavior one day and ignore it the next. When you scream at your children's behavior one day, then ignore it another day, your children learn to manipulate you.

ACTING OUT REFLECTS UNMET EMOTIONAL NEEDS

Little do we realize that when our children act out in a serious way, it's likely because they are screaming, "Please help me!"

They are in effect saying, "Please stop my behavior, or I will hurt myself or someone else. I want to learn how to be contained because I don't like how I feel when I'm out of control. I don't like feeling guilty for hurting others, and I don't like feeling ashamed all the time. I'm a good person. Please help me express my goodness. I don't want to be wild or defiant. This doesn't feel good to me."

I realize it's difficult to hear this underlying plea when a child is kicking, biting, screaming, drinking, or using drugs. Because such extreme behavior frightens us, to look beneath the external manifestation to a deeper place of understanding can be difficult. However, only when we accept that our children act out because of an unmet emotional need are we able to embark on a serious process of inquiry.

Behavioral shaping recognizes that the reason our children engage in troublesome behavior isn't that they are bad and need to be threatened with punishment, but that they are good people who are experiencing difficult emotions they haven't yet learned to express in a contained manner. Until the underlying emotion is addressed, the surface manifestations of inappropriate behavior will continue. The more our children learn to express their emotions directly in a contained way, the less they engage in acting out. Emotional self-regulation is always the goal of behavioral shaping.

I want to emphasize once again how crucial it is that behavioral shaping is linked to your children's level of maturity, not the particular behavior they display or their chronological age. Hence, just as schools conduct educational assessments of your children to understand the level of their educational development, you need to conduct emotional assessments of your children on a regular basis. I'm not suggesting some kind of formal assessment, but a deepening of your understanding of their actual level through observation, rather than *assuming* they are at the level they are "supposed" to have attained.

Some children are mature for their age, while others mature more slowly. So caught up do we get in sticking to the traditional notions of age and maturity that we fail to recognize the unique temperament of each child. Pushing a child to "grow up" simply because their chronological age is more advanced is a fruitless exercise that can only destroy the child's sense of worth. When we feel ourselves becoming frustrated because our child can't "be like others their age," we are wise to remind ourselves that age is simply a construct—an illusion that, if we buy into it, can curtail our child's spirit. For this reason, it's prudent to avoid all comparisons.

Each child needs either more or less of different approaches. Some children do well with positive reinforcement and use this to charge toward change. Others do better with rules and guidelines. Still others thrive on emotional nurturance, which fosters their creativity. Depending on the child in front of us, we need to adjust our approach to meet their individual requirements.

My daughter is precocious in some emotional areas, at least two years advanced for her age. In other areas, she's average, perhaps even below average. Unless I'm able to recognize those areas in which she's advanced and those in which she's slower, I'll treat her according to how I *think* children her age should be treated. Failing to understand her particular level of maturity, my efforts at teaching her containment are likely to be inappropriate.

When your children act out, it's important to ask yourself the following questions:

> Did my child act out because of a lack in judgment due
>   to emotional immaturity, or with full understanding
>   and hence in outright defiance?

Is my child able to master the task before them, or is it beyond their capability?

Does my child require a higher level response from me because they are at a higher developmental level?

If your child is acting out because of a lack of judgment due to immaturity, you immediately begin to operate from a different place. Instead of filling the role of disciplinarian, you take up the role of educator. Rigidity, where "your way or the highway" is in operation, is replaced by a concern for what your child needs at this particular moment.

DO YOU OWN YOUR PART IN YOUR CHILDREN'S BEHAVIOR?

If your child acts out as a form of outright defiance, or if they are acting out on a regular basis, you need to accept accountability for *your* role in the perpetuation of their behavior. Children are defiant because they are accustomed to getting away with it. True, some children are temperamentally more willful, but it's through their relationship with us that they have transformed this willfulness into defiance. Unless you realize this, you will begin to believe that your child is "bad."

When your five-year-old pitches a fit, you stop their behavior in its tracks and teach them alternative ways of handling what they are feeling. When they stick their tongue out at you at six, you don't ignore it but give them a stern look and make it very clear that this isn't acceptable behavior. When they test you by asking for candy or more television time when they are seven, you end their manipulation and lay out your boundaries. When they slam the door in your face at age eight, you enter their room and calmly but unequivocally call them on their show of disrespect. When they are distracted while doing homework at age nine, you sit with them day in and day out until they learn how to still their spirit and honor their work—and you resist doing the work *for* them, helping only when they are truly unable to do something themselves. When they pretend they don't hear you or talk back to you when they are ten, you rise to the occasion and teach them that this behavior is unacceptable. When they lie or steal from you when they are eleven, you become even firmer, allowing the consequences of this behavior to be experienced. In other words, you take your children's behavior seriously.

Let me offer several real-life situations that illustrate how this approach fleshes out in practice. I'll start with a mother who asks her daughter to pick up her shoes and put them in the closet. The daughter ignores her. The mother asks her again. No response. The mother doesn't ask again, but later picks up the shoes herself.

What needs to happen in this situation? The mother offers her daughter a chance to self-correct. If her daughter doesn't do so, the mother matter-of-factly redirects her to the task at hand, either physically or verbally, without attaching any emotional interpretation to her daughter's behavior. It's vital that the mother doesn't disengage until the task has been completed. If the mother manifests sufficient presence, her daughter will respond because authentic presence is magnetic. When she does, the mother praises her for her ability to respect the need to keep the house tidy so that everyone can enjoy it without tripping over other people's items.

Now let's move on to the case of a father who asks his son to turn off the television and do his homework but finds himself ignored. The father's response is to yell. This proves ineffective, as the boy still does nothing. Even when the father calls his son names, he is ignored. Eventually the father gives up, exasperated.

Let's rewrite this scene. When the boy doesn't pay heed to his father, he is told that the next time he's asked, the television needs to be turned off. When the boy still pays no heed, the father enters his space, takes the remote, and calmly—not angrily—shuts the set off himself. He then holds onto the remote, explaining to his son that he will be trusted with it again when he demonstrates he can follow the guidelines. No amount of whining or pleading gets the television back that evening. The following evening, the boy asks for the remote and, after again clearly communicating his expectations, the father hands it to him. Because there's no battle over the television that evening, the father praises his son for changing his behavior.

Two children are at the table, busy painting. Their mother asks them to clean the table after they are done painting, then leaves the room. The children ignore their mother's instructions, but the mother does nothing about it. Instead, the maid cleans up after them. What needs to happen is that the mother remains in the room when her children don't do as she asks. She takes their paint away and tells them to clean up, after which she praises them.

The daughter, who is six years old, draws a pretty picture and runs to show it to her mother. Her mother is too busy on the phone and ignores her. The daughter then paints a bigger, prettier picture. Her mother shushes her away. The girl hits her brother, whereupon her mother yells, "You're a bad girl!"

At this point, instead of yelling and shaming, the mother could call her daughter to her and explain how being hit must feel to her brother. Instead of blowing her daughter's behavior out of proportion, she simply requires the little girl to make peace with her brother.

Ideally, the mother would trace the dynamic all the way back to when her daughter unsuccessfully sought her attention. It would have been much better if, when the six-year-old came to her mother in the first place, the mother had taken a moment to acknowledge her daughter, praising her not only for her ability to draw, but also for being so able to take care of herself and find something interesting to do while mommy was on the phone. The daughter would then have felt emotionally met.

An eight-year-old is alone at home every day after school. When his parents return, they are busy with tasks such as office work and housework. Consequently, the boy is lonely. When he starts to play with matches, no one notices. He wonders if they even care. Even when he makes a bonfire in his room, no one comes. When he makes a bonfire at school, he is suspended. His parents' response? They ground him for three months.

When the boy is suspended from his school for lighting the bonfire, his parents would be wise to take this as a red flag. They might seek counseling to understand that their son is screaming for attention. Then they could apologize to him for their negligence and try to change their working hours, or arrange for someone else to cover, so that a caring adult is at home for him when he returns. His parents also need to spend quality time with him every day.

Children aren't designed to jump at our every command, and neither should they do so. Having said this, they need to understand the boundaries of their behavior so they are clear about what's expected of them and what isn't. We can only teach them this when we feel, from deep within, our right to teach this—and our right to receive respect. This isn't a matter of demanding respect in an egoic way, but of being so *present* that we command respect.

When we are mindful of the balance between flexibility and structure, we are able to let our children play freely and be wildly expressive within the bounds of what's appropriate. If they cross the line, they need to be provided with structure. It's in the continual dance between letting go and stepping in that parents have the opportunity to teach their children to be their own container.

First, we need to be clear what the boundaries are ourselves. Many of us are afraid of stepping into our children's space and gently yet firmly taking them by their shoulders and guiding them to where they need to go. Because we are afraid of confrontation and owning our own sense of power, we let our children do as they please, preferring to be mad at them instead of taking the strong action needed to adjust their behavior.

A classic example of this is Robin, whose four-year-old daughter Jolyn never took naps during the day and consequently was a mess by nighttime. Wound up in a highly excitable state, she was extremely difficult to put to bed. Nighttime involved a great deal of stress with lots of crying and screaming. Often Robin found herself going to sleep earlier than Jolyn, who would be awake until one or two in the morning. The lack of sleep on everyone's part reduced their ability to function well during the day.

"She just doesn't want to go to sleep," Robin argued, "so how can I force her?" According to Robin, requiring her daughter to lie down during the day or at a particular time in the evening was to go contrary to her daughter's will. As a mother, she was failing to recognize that enforcing a routine was for her child's wellbeing.

Robin needed to take Jolyn by the hand, lead her to bed, tuck her in, and then make sure she stayed in bed. If Jolyn got out of bed, Robin needed to gently lead her back to bed and again tuck her in. If Jolyn got out of bed again, Robin needed to lead her back to her bedroom yet again, but without spending time this time. The encounter needs to be matter-of-fact. If Jolyn has to be taken back to bed several dozen times, this is what needs to happen—and all without any anger or irritation on Robin's part. Sustained presence, not reactivity, is the crucial factor. A repetition of this scenario may occur several evenings before Jolyn alters her rhythms to those that are most beneficial for her.

Without this kind of structure, Jolyn simply ran on empty emotionally, which was the root of all the disruption. For a young child, times to nap and go to bed are aspects of the main rules and as such are *non-negotiable*. If the parent is resolute, the child will quickly pick up that there is no argument around this issue. Robin's trouble was that she herself was unsure of how clear-cut she needed to be on this rule.

Why Delightful Children Turn into Defiant Teens

Though we have already addressed defiance in our teens to some degree, because it's such an issue today, I want to return to the topic and add further insights. Dysfunctional teenagers don't emerge overnight. They are the result of years of subjugated authenticity and false promises. They have been dying a slow death and now have to fight a daily battle just to feel alive. No teen wants to be "bad." They simply don't know any other way to be.

The child who grows up to be a defiant teen does so because of a lack of authenticity, a lack of containment, or a lack of connection to the parents—or a combination of these. For instance, children who didn't enjoy sufficient real connection with their parents may grow into teens who feel the need to act out in a flamboyant way in order to be noticed.

Whenever your children act out in a defiant manner, there's always an underlying motivation. This could either be because they are rewarded with negative attention from you or because they haven't learned to be respectful of another's wishes. They have been permitted to violate boundaries without consequences. When you face difficult moments with your children, instead of becoming reactive, ask yourself the following questions:

> Is my child behaving in this manner because I'm unable to be firm and consistent?
>
> Am I being clear that my child's behavior is absolutely not okay with me? Or am I being wishy-washy and sending mixed messages?
>
> Do I need to reexamine my expectations and recalibrate my understanding of what my child's emotional capacity is right now?
>
> Is my need for control being triggered, and am I reacting to my child from a triggered state?
>
> Am I having difficulty engaging my child with mutuality, preferring "my way or the highway?"
>
> Is my child evoking a sense of helplessness and disempowerment in me because of my past conditioning?
>
> Does my child sense I'm uncomfortable with conflict and therefore push my buttons even harder?
>
> Could it be that I don't believe in myself and therefore don't believe I can garner respect from my child?

Is my child thirsty for my attention because I have
    been preoccupied, so that I only pay attention when
    they are behaving in a negative way?

Is my tolerance for frustration so low that I can't negoti-
    ate with my child through dialogue because it
    evokes too much anxiety in me?

Am I so stretched and wired that I flip out at the slight-
    est perception of loss of control? After giving to my
    family all day, do I feel resentful and unleash my
    emotions at the least provocation?

Am I running on empty right now, so that I can't invoke
    the presence my child deserves?

Is it possible I don't know how to respond to my child's
    temperamental nature, and that this engenders
    anxiety in me?

Do I pressure myself and my child to behave in the
    "right" way, to the point that when things don't go
    according to plan, I lose my sense of perspective?

When we aren't conscious of our own feelings, we blame our children for "making us" feel a particular way, which triggers in them the
feelings we are carrying within us. To the degree we unleash our anxiety on them, they will carry our unprocessed emotions within their
body, which means they too will act from an uncentered state. Their
state then catapults us into an escalated reaction—and so the cycle
of pain continues down through the generations.

Though each party's emotional energy arouses emotional states in
the other, we have to be clear, as pointed out earlier, that no one can
cause us to feel a particular way. No matter how it may appear on the
surface, at a more elemental level no one has this power. If the seeds
of irritation, helplessness, frustration, or tension weren't already within

us, they couldn't bloom. But as long as we feel helpless and somewhat out of control, the slightest suggestion we aren't being listened to will cause us either to feel disempowered, and hence ineffective in handling our children, or lead us to unleash our frustration on them. The degree to which we become emotionally agitated by our children reflects the degree to which we are *already* agitated within ourselves.

Once we understand that no one has the power to cause us unhappiness, we can let go of our heavy investment in our life scripts and emotional imprints. This enables us to alter the energetic space we inhabit during our interactions with others, which is the end of all drama. Seeing ourselves as neither victims nor victors, martyrs nor mere survivors, we find we no longer need drama in order to feel alive. If on occasion we are still triggered, we are able to reel our reaction in before we cause hurt and trauma for others.

Conversely, we are only able to feel positive regard for our children when we already have such regard for ourselves. Only to the degree we are confident within ourselves can we engage our children from a place of confidence. This is because whatever we are experiencing internally is ultimately manifested externally. That which is manifested externally affects our children, which in turn affects us— and so the cycle continues. Because at this deep level there is no separation and we are one with our children, they become reflections of our interior being, which is what makes them suited to be our spiritual guides.

HEAVY-HANDED TACTICS BACKFIRE

Many parents believe that if they are scary, or even practice corporal punishment, children will learn what they need to. Instead, our children become fearful of us, which shuts them down to their natural desire to be the good person they inherently are. If we want to discipline our children meaningfully, we need to embrace our authority and be firm, while simultaneously deepening our emotional connection with them. Fear tactics only achieve an attenuated connection between our children and ourselves.

If you are looking for simple "fixes" for your children's behavior, prepare to be disappointed in the long run. There are no tidy answers in parenting. So-called "tough love" ultimately breeds resentment. Your task is to curb your heavy-handedness so that your children learn to depend on their internal resources to figure out the right or wrong behavior in any given situation. Though once in a while a harried parent might inadvertently scold a child, and even raise their voice—as I related happened to me on the day at the beach when my daughter was three years old—this can't be a regular pattern if we are to raise children consciously.

When you engage in heavy-handed tactics, your reprimands trigger guilt and anxiety in your children. In such a situation, they don't respect either you or themselves. When your children don't feel respect, they instead feel guilt, which in turn results in either a sense of emptiness or a lack of empathy toward others. The guilt stems from the fact that no child on Earth wants to feel uncontained and disrespectful.

Conscious behavior shaping requires a shift from a dynamic in which a child feels threatened, maligned, or lesser-than. It seeks to bring order in a manner that takes the needs of both parties into account. For this reason, the dialogue can't be one-sided. We must always ask ourselves whether we are responding to our children's behavior out of a need of our own or out of service to our children, and we must be open to their input. Discipline can't be, "I said so, and that's the way it is." It must include, "These are the rules, but you are free to have your experience of them, and I am available to hear your feelings about them." Conscious discipline asks that children follow our instructions, but also allows them the freedom to express their sentiments.

Our adult ability to tolerate frustration takes root in our childhood. More precisely, it involves our parents' ability to teach us how to handle the word "no" and cope with our residual emotion. Most parents say the word "no" but don't help their children process the emotions around this. The reason we shy away from helping our children explore their disappointment is that we haven't first addressed our own disappointment with life. We either deny our children's feelings or, equally ineffective, seek to assuage them quickly by "fixing" whatever may be wrong or distracting them in some way. This is how our children learn to run away from discomfort, which in the teen years and later life can result in extreme self-medication.

Unless our children learn early how to negotiate their emotions, especially in the context of being told "no," they will be unable to handle any sort of dismissal later in life. They will react like a two-year-old, pitching a fit—or, in a more grownup style, binge-drinking or doing drugs. Few of us realize how much of our behavior is self-sabotaging. At the root of it all is our inability to soothe ourselves and tolerate our life *as it is*.

A child's need for solace and empowerment must always be kept in mind. After any form of behavior modification, it's imperative we engage our child through storytelling, hugging, or dialogue, depending on their needs and age. Behavioral modification is never at the expense of the relationship.

Our children's behavior doesn't play out in a vacuum but is related to how well we are able to inhabit our authority—the authority not of ego, but of authentic presence. When we stay stuck at the content level and react in a traditional me-versus-you way, we lose our power, and with it the ability to be creative in our response. Our children are then felt to be depriving us of something—whether our sanity, our ability to be in control, our time, our dignity, or our honor. They become entities to be worked *against* instead of *with*.

Rather than engaging in the typical "I" versus "you" battles, were we to say to ourselves, "Everyone around me is a reflection of me," we would respond to our triggers in a quite different manner. The traditional dynamic of parent-versus-child would yield to the realization that our children are often wiser than us and able to advance us spiritually just as effectively as we can advance them.

How this works even with teens can be seen from a father and his daughter who were close when the daughter was young. Now that she was a teen, their relationship had entered a dysfunctional stage, to the point that she and her father were barely speaking and she was failing her classes.

The daughter felt isolated and criticized. "My father always thinks I'm lying and doesn't trust me," she lamented as we talked. "He doesn't even know me." Feeling misunderstood, unheard, and unseen, the daughter altered her personality to avoid her father's harsh treatment by lying. "I used to care, but now I don't even care about telling the truth," she told me. "It's so much easier to lie."

At his wits' end, the father kept repeating, "She always lies to me. She must stop lying to me." His way of stopping his daughter's lies was to up the ante by becoming even more critical and controlling. Regularly interrogating her, their time together revolved around "getting to the truth." Invested in being "the parent," he was coming entirely from fear.

When I was able to demonstrate to the father that their relationship had lost its human element and its ability to be nurturing, he began to see the importance of moving away from the linear dynamic he was caught in. By spending quality time with his daughter, he was able to forge an alliance with her. Realizing that without a strong alliance between them, discipline would only tear them apart, he began to resist going into "parent" mode, instead befriending his daughter. Within weeks of showing interest in her as a person, her behavior took a decided turn for the better. Becoming more pleasant and engaging, she now lied less often—all because she felt nurtured. There can be no behavior modification without a relationship.

Whenever you find yourself repeating a dynamic without results, it's time to stop and ask, "What am I doing that simply isn't working?" The answer will usually lie in the fact that you have become mired in a way of looking at your child that's unhealthy for both of you. When you change your approach, the dynamic changes. The question is: Are you willing to change your approach?

How to Execute the "No"

None of us enjoys being told "no." One reason for this is that for many of us, the word "no" is associated with threatening messages from our own past. It may evoke memories of a harsh and punitive parent or of a childhood robbed of empowerment.

Even though we are now adults, sometimes when we are told "no," we wish we could kick like a two-year-old, hurl our pacifier at the world, or throw ourselves on the floor and scream till we are blue in the face. Of course, we know we can't do such things, so we indulge in more sophisticated temper tantrums such as whining, backbiting, tattling, or sulking. We may even punch our pillow and curse in our car. No matter our age, the word "no" is still the hardest word to hear. Yet we utter this word countless times a day to our children without regard for how this must feel to them.

Whenever we are dogmatic and unyielding, we betray our discomfort with issuing a straightforward "no." Then our children turn a deaf ear to us or, more seriously, rebel. If we are uncomfortable with the word "no," no matter how many times we say it, it will never be heard by our children. Only when we fully *expect* to be heard will they hear us. This means we have to *expect* respect and that our boundaries won't be crossed.

In other words, just as our children need to be comfortable hearing the word "no," we as parents need to be comfortable saying it. If we aren't comfortable with "no," our children are likely to be defiant and unruly when they hit adolescence. However, the manner in which "no" is said, and the relational context in which it occurs, play a key role. Do we say "no" from a conscious state, clear in our conscience that it's an authentic response to our children's behavior and not an expression of our own issues? When we come from consciousness, we will be able to say "no" not only without feeling guilty, but also free of any wishy-washiness or inconsistency.

Sometimes we can't say "no" effectively because we feel we don't have the right to respond in this way. The reason is that our own parents long ago robbed us of the right to expect respect. Self-respect must come ahead of respect from others. Neither our children nor anyone else will respect us if we don't respect ourselves.

If, in saying "no," we aren't clear *why* we are responding this way, it will result in our children pushing and manipulating us. This is why it's crucial we *only* say what we mean, *mean* what we say, and *follow through*.

There are times when our children are in ego and need to be encouraged back to presence. At such times, we may need to project *our* presence onto them. Sometimes we may even need to impose our will. This is quite different from unconsciously imposing our *ways* onto our children with little awareness of what they require.

Suzanne is a single mother who has an out of control pre-teen, Maryann. When Maryann was young, she was an angel, so she and her mother got along perfectly. However, as Maryann began to manifest her individuality, Suzanne didn't know how to handle her daughter's budding independence. Neither did she know how to respond constructively to Maryann's natural need for autonomy and empowerment, which increasingly overpowered Suzanne's low sense of worth.

Suzanne's struggle with her daughter resulted from the fact she had grown up with a critical, abusive mother, who not only constantly belittled her but even made her feel as if she was defective at her core. As a consequence, when Suzanne became an adult, she had a string of abusive relationships and was never able to attract a partner who was respectful. On top of this, she struggles with obesity and chronic back problems.

So impoverished was Suzanne's self-authority that she simply didn't think to claim respect from her daughter. So insecure was she about her own boundaries, she didn't create any with her child. Consequently, she didn't stop Maryann when Maryann defied her rules at age seven, and neither did she say a word when Maryann hit her at age eight, or protest when Maryann broke her favorite necklace and didn't apologize at age nine. Neither did she give Maryann a curfew when Maryann went out with her friends for the first time at age twelve. In other words, without her realizing, Suzanne had created in her daughter shades of her own abusive mother. She unconsciously sowed the seeds for her daughter's disrespect because the role of invisible victim was an energetic space she was familiar with.

In any situation that calls for a response, the question to ask is: Am I coming from my own need and unresolved issues or from truly serving my child? It's this willingness to be molded by the parent-child relationship and enter a state of transformation that's the hallmark of conscious parenting.

How we communicate "no" to our children depends on a child's temperament. Children who listen readily are more sensitive and hence more malleable. Some need only one look from a parent to stop what they are doing. However, such children are also prone to pleasing their parents too readily. For this reason, parents of such children need to be mindful not to overpower their children, causing them to become hesitant in life and perhaps even fearful. Children who are temperamentally more robust may need more than a simple look. Such children often get into trouble more because they tend to be not only independent, but also stubborn, willful, and even hotheaded. In these cases, parents have to be more forceful while still being kind, a tough balancing act. It's crucial that any discipline is coupled with plenty of connection in a relaxed atmosphere.

Sometimes our children go through a rebellious phase during which we find ourselves continually having to say "no." As long as this is only a phase, it's all right for a parent to be firm with a child on a day-in, day-out basis. The problem is that many parents lose their stamina after a few days. The child, having outmaneuvered its tired parents, then feels empowered to continue its difficult behavior.

If our children are being defiant, we need to pause, take a breath, and ask ourselves, "Has a main rule been violated or just a flexible rule?" If a child refuses to heed our "no" on an issue that matters, action is required. In the case of a flexible rule, we are wise to practice the art of either negotiation or surrender.

When action is required, it may be in the form of separating the child from what they are engaged in through a timeout, or taking away the child's object of interest, such as a toy, television, or computer. We have to learn how to say "no" and really mean it, in a voice that's neither hesitant nor dogmatic. When our children observe how we match our words with action, they associate the two. Action is most effective when it's neither punitive nor tyrannical, but consistent and firm.

In learning to cope with the word "no," children need the time and space to find their own self-soothing mechanisms, which will allow them to return to being centered. I tell my daughter, "I cannot take away your frustration, and neither do I want to. But I can be with you while you work through it." The way to work through frustration is first to allow it to exist. We ride the waves as they come. By practicing awareness, acceptance, and tolerance, our children learn to regulate their emotions.

When our children are younger, we can lay a foundation that will later enable them to deal with their feelings by themselves. To accomplish this, we might use a technique such as naming the feelings. Another technique is to sit with our child while they draw what they are feeling or write about it. Yet another approach is to encourage them to breathe through the feelings.

Many times, a "no" is metabolized quickly without residual emotion. At other times, our children may have things they want to say and feelings they wish to express. If we fail to help our children tolerate their frustration, they will squash their emotions into their body. Our task is to listen to them, then let them know it's natural to feel frustrated. "Let's sit with what you are feeling," I tell my daughter. Then we watch the feelings together.

It's helpful to inquire whether there's anything to be learned from the feelings that arise when our child is told "no." One lesson might be that life doesn't always turn out the way we wish it would. This is a hard but vital lesson. However, if we can recognize it, a "no" invites creativity. If our children can't have what they want in this area of their life right now, is there a way for them to get something they want in another area of their life? When we engage in finding creative answers together, we provide our children with a powerful tool for coping with the word "no."

Having focused on how to say "no" and the kinds of things to which you need to respond in this way, I would like to suggest several ways in which you need to say an unequivocal "yes":

Say yes to effort and hush to achievement

Say yes to searching and hush to finding

Say yes to not knowing and hush to always knowing

Say yes to other ways of knowing and hush to rote learning

Say yes to struggling and hush to succeeding

Say yes to curiosity and hush to attachment to the already-discovered

Say yes to being and hush to doing

Say yes to imagination and hush to imitating

Say yes to taking a risk and hush to playing it safe

Say yes to crying and hush to holding it in

Say yes to generosity and hush to greed

Say yes to play and hush to pressure

Say yes to creativity and hush to bookishness

Say yes to playing and hush to winning.

TIMING IS CRUCIAL

One of the mistakes we often make is to try to teach our children appropriate behavior when we are in the heat of battle with them. While it's essential to *stop* inappropriate behavior when it's happening, our children may not be able to learn the deeper meaning behind their behavior until they have calmed down. This means we have to wait for a fitting time, perhaps later in the day or week, to revisit the behavior with them.

My daughter didn't want to leave a play date because she was having so much fun. Of course, she had to leave; there were no two ways about this. I picked her up and hauled her to the car across my shoulders, whereupon she cried the entire way home. I was angry with her for being defiant and tried to communicate this to her. As I lectured her, she didn't pay attention to a word I said. Overwhelmed with emotion, she couldn't comprehend why I was upset with her. A few days later, while putting her to bed, I revisited the topic. Role playing how she had behaved, I expressed all the emotions she was feeling the day of the play date and demonstrated how unreasonable she had been. When our children see their behavior through our reenactment, they have an opportunity to look in the mirror and self-reflect. This was a chance to brainstorm possible options together, coming up with a solution that works for both parties. Such a process enables our children to feel empowered, since they are being included in the process of their own discipline rather than having it handed down to them.

In the dialogue that ensued, my daughter explained, "I am sorry, but I just cannot handle leaving my friends." I responded that I understood it was hard for her to leave her friends and that this was normal. I also made it clear that, while it was hard, this didn't mean she could ignore the boundaries of the play date. Affirming that I was appreciative of her honesty, I asked her to help me find a solution. What would she have done were she the mommy? She asked me to give her three warnings to help her prepare for the end of the play date. Out of the heat of battle, she was able to process her feelings and come up with a path for positive behavior.

It's in ways like this that the parenting journey holds the potential to be a spiritually regenerative experience for both parent and child, where every moment is a meeting of spirits, and both parent and child appreciate that each dances on a spiritual path that's unique, holding hands and yet alone.

AFTERWORD

UNDERSTANDING OUR
SHARED UNCONSCIOUSNESS

The only way to effect authentic, enduring change is to gain a thorough grasp of what it is that *really* needs to change.

When we undertake the task of becoming conscious, we realize that unconsciousness is the result of a variety of interlocking factors. Each of us has inherited themes of unconsciousness from generations past—and not just from our own ancestors, but also from the cultural collective.

In other words, society—including our peer groups—plays an equal role in conditioning us as do our parents. Indeed, as we embark on an investigation of our unconsciousness, we discover how interdependent we are with all who have gone before us and all who come in contact with us. We awaken to the fact that our unconsciousness is a function of the unconsciousness of everyone around us.

To be a conscious parent requires us to learn to respond to reality in a conscious manner rather than from blind impulse, using reason instead of reacting, and employing our active will in preference to coming from passive conditioning. It helps to realize that children, by their inherent nature, desire deep, lasting, authentic connection with us. If, then, our children have turned against or away from us, it means we haven't met their emotional needs or taught them how to meet their own needs.

WE'RE ALL IN THIS TOGETHER

Becoming a conscious parent requires us to recognize how our unconsciousness, bequeathed to us by the collective unconsciousness, cripples our children. For instance:

> It is we who teach our children how to be greedy by
> giving them diamonds instead of sticks and stones

> It is we who teach our children how to fear adventure
> by rewarding their successes and reprimanding
> their failures

> It is we who teach our children how to lie to us by
> getting angry with them when they tell us the truth

> It we who teach our children how to be mean and
> violent to others by disregarding their emotions
> and denying them unconditional acceptance

> It is we who teach our children to lose their
> motivation and zeal by pressuring them to excel
> and "be something"

> It is we who teach our children to dishonor us by
> pushing them to be who they are not

> It is we who teach our children to be bullies by
> dominating their spirit and silencing their voice

> It is we who teach our children to be confused and
> overwhelmed by giving them all things external,
> but few tools to look internally

It is we who teach our children to be inattentive and
distracted by inundating their lives with busy
activities, leaving no space for stillness

It is we who teach our children to live their life looking
outward by spending our time and energy on our
own looks and acquisitions

It is we who teach our children to disrespect us by not
stopping them the first time they are disrespectful
and every time after

It is we who teach our children to be defiant by not
knowing how to lay down the rules and mean
business when we do

It is we who teach our children to know shame by
shaming their spirits and judging them constantly

It is we who teach our children to become anxious by
denying the celebration of our own present as we
constantly focus on tomorrow

It is we who teach our children not to like themselves
by constantly categorizing their emotions as those
we approve of and those we don't

It is we who teach our children not to trust the world by
betraying them every time we don't see who they
are in their essence

It is we who teach our children how to love or
not love by the extent to which we love or
don't love ourselves.

We all feel the pull to act in familiar, predictable ways. To detach from
this habit and respond in an authentic, spontaneous way isn't easy, though
it's precisely what's required if we are to parent effectively. Challenged by

raising a spirit that's individualistic and idiosyncratic, we simply can't impose our habitual ways on our children or they will suffer a loss of authenticity. Instead of forcing our children to contour their spirit to our inauthenticity, to be a conscious parent is to match our more-jaded, cynical, resentful, bitter approach to their authenticity.

How fulfilling our children's lives will be is so very much affected by their relationship with us. If their relationship with us fails to foster their internal connection with themselves, their parched souls will seek to restore this connection through other means. They will look outward to the boutique, the corporate corner office, the emerald, the casino, the bottle, the needle, or spouse number one, two, or three. But if their relationship with us encourages them to engage in a meaningful dialogue with their inner being, they will be at peace within themselves, which is the key to a life that's resplendent with meaning.

BECOMING A PARENT WHO IS PRESENT

While a parent is called upon to provide their child with emotional guidance, stability, acceptance, and safety, the child is invited into the parent's life to teach something only a child can: how to engage life with the presence, authenticity, and joyful spontaneity that adults have lost as a result of their own unconscious upbringing.

Parenting requires moment-by-moment presence with our children, brought to bear in a zillion incidents of engagement or non-engagement. This is why we can't simply master an ingenious strategy here or a clever technique there. The conscious approach is a living, breathing, organic, every-moment approach through which our children soak in *our* relationship to life and thereby learn to follow their own spirit, thus impressing their own unique imprint on their life. Hence the manner in which we are connected to our own inner self and live out our own purpose ultimately impacts our children more than anything else.

For this reason, it behooves us to monitor how present we truly are by getting in the habit of asking ourselves the following types of questions:

Am I able to quiet my mind and sit in stillness?

Am I able to stop my thoughts and smell, hear, and taste my every moment?

Am I able to laugh uncontrollably even when life isn't working according to "the plan?"

Am I able to show empathy for another even when I'm hurting?

Do I honor my body?

Do I live my passions?

Do I love my imperfect life?

Am I able to be one with myself, while being nothing in particular and doing nothing?

Am I able to access my deepest emotions without fear of judgment or shame?

Do I orient my entire world from an internal axis?

When we can be present in these ways, our children learn the same—not from our words, but from our ability to be present with ourselves; not from what we buy them, or the college we send them to, but from our *awakened* awareness.

The reality is that few of us know how to *experience our experiences* without interference from our mind, just being present with them. Without our realizing, we get stuck in polarities: this or that, either-or, good-bad, pleasure-pain, me-you, past-future—and yes, parent-child. The minute our mind engages in this kind of polarized thinking, it creates a separation between ourselves and our world. We don't realize we are creating such a separation, yet we actually do it much of the time. We meet someone new and we instantly judge them. We observe our children and immediately say to ourselves, "He is good," "She is bad," or, "Why is he behaving like that?" We constantly feel the need to impose our judgment on reality.

To engage with our reality in its *as is* form is simply foreign to us. To be fully present to our reality, *as it is*, and not as we *wish it to be*, requires us to silence our mind and detach from our preoccupation with the past and the future. It requires us to center ourselves in the here and now. Instead of seeing everything through the veil of polarizing thought, we enter into *a state of pure experience*.

It's when we aren't present in our own life that we find it difficult to embrace our children in their *as is* form. Instead, we seek to impose upon them ideals that are plucked from our past conditioning. Because our children are "ours," we believe we have an unbridled right to do this. So it is that we raise our children in a manner that squelches their essential being. We add to the pool of unconsciousness in society instead of lessening it.

Your unconsciousness isn't your children's to inherit; it is yours to excavate. Being a conscious parent means you are increasingly aware of the force and prevalence of your unconsciousness as it arises in everyday situations.

Children who are raised by parents who are conscious, and therefore both at peace with themselves and connected to their inner joy, discover the abundance of the universe and learn how to tap into this ever-flowing source. Viewing life as their partner, such children respond to life's challenges with curiosity, excitement, and a sense of reverent engagement. Brought up to be inwardly peaceful and to know their inherent joy, they in turn teach their children to live in a state of joyful abundance.

Such joy is able to infuse the soul with a sense of empowerment. Mind-heavy games of power and control have no place, replaced by an experience of oneness with everything, so that life flows with healing power for generations to come.

The Consciousness Compass
Questions to Ask Ourselves

What is my life's mission? How do I manifest my purpose in my life?

> Have I arrived at a place in which I am able to connect to a deeper life purpose?
>
> Do I feel fulfilled within myself?
>
> How do I make my every day meaningful?

What are my core ego attachments?

> Am I attached to success in a material form?
>
> Am I attached to my image and the roles I play in my life, such as parent, spouse, careerist?
>
> Do I find myself in constant want or need?
>
> Do I experience myself as lacking, or as having abundance?
>
> Why am I in such a state?
>
> What am I holding onto in my life right now that I feel I can't let go of? What if I was to let go of whatever this may be?

What are my deep fears?

> Have I sat with myself in deep solitude and truly seen myself in the mirror and confronted my fears?

> Am I able to ease into these fears and begin to own them rather than manically soothe them through outward manifestations of control and power?

> Am I able to simply sit with my core fears, understand them, befriend them, and release them?

What life-script am I living by?

> Have I examined my past and seen how I am playing out a particular life-script based on my family of origin?

> Am I able to see the themes upon which I have been structuring my life?

> Am I able to see my recurrent patterns by observing how my relationships with others unfold?

What is my emotional inheritance?

> When life doesn't work out in accordance with my vision, what emotional response do I typically have?

> How do I approach life on a day-to-day basis?

> Am I able to detach from my emotional imprints and become conscious of them?

> Am I aware of how I project my emotions onto my children and spouse?

What are my emotional triggers?

> When do I find myself overwhelmed with emotion?

> What are my primary emotional triggers?

> How do I process my emotions when I'm triggered?

How do I process negative events in my life?

> When I am angry or depressed, do I tend to anchor these feelings on a source outside of myself, or do I anchor them within?

> Do I allow myself to sit with my emotions and watch them as opposed to react to them?

> Am I able to let go of negative emotions?

> Can I see myself when I am projecting my emotions onto another?

Am I able to live in a state of consciousness?

> Am I able to live in a place of trust and insight, or am I clouded by fear, anxiety, and resentment?

> Am I in touch with my essence?

Am I more of a "doer," or am I able to "be?"

> How do I engage in my own life? Does all my doing flow from being?

> Do I feel pressure to constantly fill my every day with activity after activity, or am I able to sit with myself at least once every day and get in touch with my inner stillness?

> Do I engage in acts that foster my inner connection with myself, or have I become so busy that I have lost this inner connection?

> Do I constantly feel the need to judge and be in the space of mental "doing?" Or am I able to simply and fully experience my experiences with a state of neutral but awakened being?

What have I based the pillars of my parenting on?

Have I unconsciously based the pillars of my child's success on their ability to "do," produce, and succeed?

Am I able to allow my child's spirit to first flow naturally before "doing" sets in?

How much pressure do I put on my child to become the person I want them to be, versus who they naturally are?

Do I view my child with a sense of lack or abundance?

Do I look at my child and constantly see them for all they yet need to become, or am I able to sit with my child in the wonder of all they already are?

How do I teach my child to have inner connection?

How do I engage with my child?

How do I listen to my child—passively, or actively with engaged presence?

Am I able to see my child for all that they truly are?

How do I help foster my child's connection with their inner self?

How do I model my own inner connection with myself?

How do I view life? Is it benevolent or evil? Does the answer depend on the circumstance I find myself in?

Some Highlights from
The Conscious Parent

Each of us imagines we are being the best parent we can be, and most of us are indeed good people who feel great love for our children. It certainly isn't out of a lack of love that we impose our will on our children. Rather, it stems from a lack of consciousness. The reality is that most of us are unaware of the dynamics that exist in the relationship we have with our children.

It isn't our children who are the problem, but our own unconsciousness.

Our unconsciousness is not our children's to inherit, but ours to excavate.

Love and truth are simple. Parenting is not that complicated or difficult once we become conscious because a conscious person is naturally loving and authentic.

We teach more by example than in any other way. Children see and imitate everything. They also see through hidden agendas and malicious intent.

Children are too egotistical to be thinking of us when they are acting out; they are only thinking of themselves. So don't take it personally. Inappropriate behavior is a cry from the heart: "Please help me."

The root of a child's acting out is an emotion that was unable to be expressed.

Correction of a child's acting out always needs to occur in the present moment.

If our children are teens, the time when they are going to seek our permission has passed.

When we relate to our children by honoring who they are at any given moment, we teach them to honor themselves. If we seek to shift them from their present state, altering their behavior to meet our approval, we convey the message that their authentic being is inadequate. Our children then begin to adopt a persona, which takes them away from who they really are.

Matching our emotional energy to that of our children is far more effective than asking them to match their energy to ours.

To be triggered into emotional reactivity is to be in resistance.

Behavioral shaping uses all conflict as a laboratory for learning. For this reason, shaping occurs continuously on a moment-by-moment basis instead of being squeezed into punitive time slots. The signature of this shaping is positive reinforcement, which is a more effective tool than punishment.

Our task is to befriend our child's essence.

We fear we'll feel isolated and lonely if we really claim our uniqueness.

Your child's spirit is infinitely wise.

Conscious parents trust implicitly their child's intuition concerning its destiny.